Breaking, not Broken

There are few gifts as precious as being invited to understand from another's experience, and this book is just such a gift. As you read Tim Goode's honest and thoughtful words, you will smile and weep and wonder and repent and grow, and maybe the church of Christ will engage just a bit better with all our sisters and brothers. This is a gift to be treasured which helps each of us treasure the other.

The Rt Revd Mark Tanner, Bishop of Chester

Breaking, not Broken issues a strong and at times uncomfortable challenge, shining a light on an important area of our shared life that we should not ignore. Tim Goode is opening up a long overdue conversation and inviting us into deeper understanding. This is a book born of pain but full of hope for the possibility of transformation, not just for disabled people but for the whole church.

The Rt Revd Dr Guli Francis-Dehqani, Bishop of Chelmsford

This is a passionate and beautifully written appeal for us to centre the wounded and risen Christ and to use this reorientation to transform our buildings, our heritage, our reading of the Bible, and our liturgy. Tim Goode lays bare the extent of ableism in the churches and argues for the benefits for all of us in focusing on being a home where all can belong. Making access possible for everyone is not a logistical chore, not an extra, but an expression of our theology.

Helen King, Chair of Together on General Synod and Professor Emerita, Classical Studies at the Open University

I have received so much from Tim Goode's profound theological insights into the 'risen, wounded body of Christ' and its implications for the Church. I am delighted that this book places this prophetic challenge before the whole church and reminds us that ableism 'is a distortion of the image of God'.

The Rt Revd Richard Atkinson, Bishop of Bedford and Chair of the Church of England's Committee for the Ministry of and amongst Deaf and Disabled People (CMDDP)

Tim Goode has written a book which every church leader should read. He challenges us to consider disabled bodies as sacred texts to be read with reverence, and in his own interpretive reading shines a light on false theologies, false understandings of church and false Christologies. This book is beautifully written, full of poetic language with scriptural echoes, like the best sort of liturgy. It is both deeply personal and wide ranging in scope. In particular, writing from a deeply considered theological perspective, Tim invites us to expand our thinking and practice in worship, in liturgy, in the design of our churches, in our attitudes to music. No one who reads this book will emerge unscathed or unchanged, and nor should they.

The Very Revd Dr Mandy Ford, Dean of Bristol Cathedral

Breaking, not Broken

Ableism and the Church after Constantine

Revd Canon Timothy Goode

scm press

© Tim Goode 2026

Published in 2026 by SCM Press

Editorial office
3rd Floor, Invicta House,
110 Golden Lane,
London EC1Y 0TG, UK
www.scmpress.co.uk

SCM Press is an imprint of Hymns Ancient & Modern Ltd
(a registered charity)

Hymns Ancient & Modern® is a registered trademark of
Hymns Ancient & Modern Ltd
13A Hellesdon Park Road, Norwich,
Norfolk NR6 5DR, UK

All rights reserved. No part of this publication may be reproduced,
stored in a retrieval system, or transmitted,
in any form or by any means, electronic, mechanical,
photocopying or otherwise, without the prior permission of
the publisher, SCM Press.

The Author has asserted their right under the Copyright, Designs and
Patents Act 1988 to be identified as the Author of this Work

British Library Cataloguing in Publication data

A catalogue record for this book is available
from the British Library

ISBN: 978-0-334-06316-2

EU GPSR Authorized Representative
LOGOS EUROPE, 9 rue Nicolas Poussin, 17000, LA ROCHELLE, France
E-mail: contact@logoseurope.eu

Scripture quotations are from New Revised Standard Version Bible: Anglicized
Edition, copyright © 1989, 1995 National Council of the Churches of Christ in
the United States of America. Used by permission. All rights reserved worldwide.

No part of this book may be used or reproduced in any manner for the purpose of
training artificial intelligence technologies or systems.

Typeset by Regent Typesetting

Contents

Foreword by Archbishop Steven Cottrell	vii
Acknowledgements	ix
Introduction: Reclaiming the Sacred Image – Ableism, Heritage and the Re-membering of the Church	xi

1	Framing the Argument	1
2	Christianity as Virus: A Theological Metaphor of Contagion and Contestation	9
3	Scripture and the Pursuit of Perfection	23
4	God with a Body Like Mine? Anthropomorphism, Ableism and the Disabled Reader of Scripture	37
5	Theoretical Frameworks: Theology, Ableism and Heritage	47
6	The Legacy of Exclusion: Ableism in Sacred Heritage Spaces	61
7	Sacred Space and Theological Vision: How Theology Shapes the Design and Layout of Our Sacred Buildings	78
8	Power, Priesthood and the Performance of the Ideal: Ableism in the Liturgies of Empire and Ecclesial Authority	93
9	Embodied Heritage: Disabled Bodies as Living Archives	120
10	Breath Disrupted: Pneumatology, Normativity and the Spirit of the Risen Body	144
11	Cracked Chalices, Overflowing Grace: Disability, Sacrament and the Neurodivergent Body of Christ	153
12	Wounds That Remain: Eschatology, Narrative Bodies and the Kingdom of the Risen Flesh	163

13 Heritage as Contestation: Crip Interventions and the
    Reconfiguration of Sacred Memory   176
14 The Disruptive Grace of Disabled Witness   191
15 Toward a Crip Ecclesiology and Heritage Practice   207
16 Re-membering the Body   218

Postscript: Other Wounds, Same Body: Gender, Sexuality,
Race, Identity and Class in the Shadow of Ideal Flesh   223

A Final Blessing: For Those who Would Re-member the Body   234

Index of Bible References   237
Index of Names and Subjects   239

Foreword by Archbishop Stephen Cottrell

'We are the Body of Christ.' We frequently say these words in our celebration of the Holy Eucharist, at the peace, and we accompany them with a greeting to each other, a touch which affirms the physical reality of that image. Yet the force of the bodily metaphor often gets swept away as we move onto other images and other stories. We do not stop to think about the implications of what it means to embody Christ – as individuals and together – and what expectations we have of that embodiment. Tim Goode writes out of his own experience of what bodily expectations he has encountered, and he reflects theologically on the boundaries and areas of exclusion that he has met as a Christian, a parish priest, and a cathedral canon.

Tim demonstrates how the familiar traditions of architecture, liturgy and performance arise from the assumption that clergy and people will be able-bodied and intellectually regulated. Though ableism is rarely articulated, the Graeco-Roman ideals of physical perfection and ordered philosophy infect the Church's practice and undermine the proclamation of Christ crucified. Tim argues that disabled bodies, voices and lives are indispensable to the life and identity of the Church: these bodies are 'fearfully and wonderfully made.'

This is a deeply personal book, arising from Tim Goode's experience, study and reflection. It is a passionate account of the frustration and exclusion he has met, but it is also a powerful and creative demand that the Church should take disability seriously, not as a polite accommodation to differently able people but as an essential aspect of its identity and mission. The crucified and risen Christ showed the marks of his Passion to the Apostles, even inviting them to touch where his body had been wounded. We come to Christ, and we are accepted and loved by Christ, as we are, with all our capacities and limitations. He does not see in us the lack of a physical or intellectual ideal, but the individual, rich beauty and lovableness of each person, as each in their own way reflects the image of the Creator.

If the Church can take Tim's message to heart, then there will be implications for our buildings, our practice of liturgy, and the expression of our life together. We will be the richer for it, but more importantly we will have gone some way to welcoming and including all those who are called to reflect God's truth and life, and we will be becoming more of a Christ-like Church. Tim Goode is here offering to the Church a deep and at times sorrowful account of what it means to be a disabled priest among us, but also his reflections, in the company of other theologians who have engaged with the theology and anthropology of disability. He is offering creative responses which are both practical and theologically expressive. I commend this book in the hope that it will help the Church to level the floors and open its doors wider.

Acknowledgements

This book would not exist without the encouragement, wisdom and theological insight of the Revd Dr Sally Myers, who instilled in me the confidence to write and think theologically with boldness and clarity. This book would also not have been written without the invitation to speak at the FAC (Fabric Advisory Committee) Conference in June 2025. My thanks go to my cousin, Alex Merry (www.alexmerryart.com), whose artistic brilliance has rendered my vision for the front cover of a *kintsugi* Christ into the striking cover image that now embodies it. I am profoundly grateful to all my colleagues, both lay and ordained, at York Minster, whose companionship and commitment to the gospel continues to sustain and inspire me. I am also so thankful for the unwavering support I received during my time as Disability Advisor in the Diocese of Southwark, as a General Synod member for the Southwark Diocese, as a member of the Archbishops' Council and throughout my ministry at St Luke's Whyteleafe, St Peter and St Paul's Chaldon and St Margaret's Lee. My heartfelt appreciation goes to my fellow members of the Disability Task Group and to Bishop Richard Atkinson for his leadership and advocacy in this vital area of the Church's witness. I am also thankful for Fiona MacMillan and all those who have shaped and shared in the Disability Conferences at St Martin-in-the-Fields, where prophetic voices have continually stirred the Church to greater honesty and hope. To my parents, thank you for your love and steadfastness, especially to my mother, who, living also with Hereditary Multiple Exostoses (HME), has been a quiet theologian of the body and a witness to grace. And finally, to Bernie, my constant, my rock and the love of my life, thank you for walking with me through every twist and turn of the last 30 years. Your love has been for me a sacrament of God's presence. Not because you have seen past my wounds, but because you have met me and loved me within them. Your love is not a balm that denies the breaking, it is a faithfulness that utterly transforms it. This book therefore, in so many ways, is yours too.

Introduction

Reclaiming the Sacred Image – Ableism, Heritage and the Re-membering of the Church

This book has taken a considerable time to come together. It is the fruit of nearly 30 years of theological reflection, lived experience and embodied wrestling with one of the most profound and urgent questions in Christian theology: what does it mean to be made in the image and likeness of God? Not as an abstraction. Not as a doctrinal puzzle. But in the flesh-and-bone, wound-and-glory, breath-and-lament reality of life with a disabled body.

This is not theology from the margins, it is theology from the body – my body, a body shaped by surgery and scar tissue, strengthened through interdependence and marked by a complex and dynamic story. A body that has walked, rolled, stumbled, preached, wept and prayed its way through sacred and secular spaces alike; some of which have welcomed me, others where the welcome has been qualified and many which have shut me out. This book is shaped by how I have encountered and imagined God in and through that lived experience. It is about how the Church I love and serve, both in its structures and its sacraments, its doctrines and its doorways, has often failed to honour the divine image when it is borne in disabled flesh.

My own story is woven throughout. Diagnosed at age six with Hereditary Multiple Exostoses (HME), my childhood was punctuated by surgeries and hospital stays, alternating between periods of wellness and seasons of intense disability. These experiences revealed to me, often painfully, how people treated me differently depending on whether I appeared 'able' or 'disabled'. I saw first hand how physical appearance became a theological battleground, a social litmus test and a mirror for how others projected meaning onto my body.

At 26, a cancerous spinal tumour left me permanently disabled. It grew both down into my lungs and up through my neck, in the process wrapping itself around my spinal cord, which in turn led to paralysis from the chest down. After two significant surgeries and a long and painstaking rehabilitation, I regained partial mobility, but not without lasting impact. I walk today with crutches. I use a mobility scooter. I live with lung damage and a left hand that has no sensation. I also live with the aftermath of Post Traumatic Stress Disorder (PTSD) and anxiety. For the past three decades, disability has been my constant companion, sometimes an adversary, often a teacher, but always part of the sacred journey.

At the heart of this book is both a provocation and a promise. The provocation is this: ableism is not a marginal issue, it is a theological heresy, a distortion of the image of God, a misrepresentation of the gospel and a betrayal of the body of Christ. Ableism runs deep, not just in attitudes, but in architecture, liturgy, ecclesiology and heritage. Ableism affects how we imagine God, how we curate memory, how we teach theology and how we organize the Church's life. Ableism is encoded in who we remember and who we forget, in who is honoured in stained glass and who is left outside the sanctuary.

But there is also a promise, a promise that memory can be 're-membered'. It is a promise that the body of Christ, though dismembered by exclusion, can be healed and restored, not by returning to a mythic past, but by moving forward in truth, justice and grace; that we can rebuild, reconceive and reclaim a Church where disabled people are not just present but central, not merely ministered to but fully ministers.

Breaking, not Broken challenges us to imagine what happens when disabled people are not an afterthought in theological reflection, but its starting point. What if our cathedrals had been designed for bodies that limp, roll, flinch or tremble? What if our liturgies had been written in the rhythms of pain and protest? What if our heritage had included not just the pristine relics of saints, but the lived archives of those whose holiness lies in survival?

So, this is not a book simply about disability, nor is it about legal compliance or access audits, it is a book about identity – your identity and my identity. It is about memory. It is about power. It draws from disability theology, liberation theology and critical heritage studies to interrogate how ableism has shaped not only our theology but our physical and cultural landscapes. I believe, with all my heart, that disabled people are not guests in God's house; we are co-builders of the kingdom. We carry the *imago Dei*. We belong.

Chapter by chapter, I will be building a theological framework for understanding how ableism distorts not just practice, but doctrine. I will explore how church architecture, liturgy and heritage have memorial-

INTRODUCTION

ized exclusion and forgotten flesh. I will offer stories and examples drawn from sacred sites that reveal both harm and hope. And I dream, dream of a Church where disabled lives are not added to the story as footnotes but recognized as chapters without which the gospel itself is incomplete.

To live as a disabled person in the Church is to live in profound tension; between welcome and rejection, between visibility and invisibility, between being held and being held at arm's length and – I say this with sorrow, but also with honesty – I have never experienced more discrimination than I have since being ordained. The very institution that both chose and ordained me to proclaim the resurrection, and to preside at the Eucharist, has often felt like the tomb from which I have had to fight to emerge.

This book is a response to that pain, but it is also a hymn of praise; a theology born in bruises but lit by the Eucharist. I have written it both in grief and in gratitude. It is a protest, and it is a proclamation that things can be different; that the Church might yet be re-membered; that the body of Christ, fractured by prejudice, might still be made whole.

This book is a work of memory and imagination. It is rooted in a conviction that Christian heritage – our buildings, liturgies, doctrines, aesthetics and traditions – is contested ground; that the Church holds within it both treasures and toxins. Too often, it has been shaped by an unspoken normativity, one that is male, white, able-bodied, triumphant. But the gospel actually begins with a wounded God, and the Church's true inheritance is the body of Christ, still breaking, still risen, still bearing the open wounds.

Through this book I expose the legacy of ableism which runs through the deep stones of Christian tradition; not only in what is said, but in what is built, preserved, celebrated and erased. Disabled people, past and present, are not merely recipients of ministry or subjects of pity; we are prophets, theologians, architects and curators of a new ecclesiology. This is not a book about inclusion. It is a book about transformation.

Most importantly, this book is written with hope, hope that through the lens of disability we might reflect more clearly on what it means to be the body of Christ in a world that still too often worships wholeness, while crucifying the broken.

So, what I have written here is both personal and ecclesial. It is theological protest and liturgical hope. At its heart is a promise, the same one spoken at baptism: 'In Christ we have a new dignity and God calls us to fullness of life.' For all are worthy of dignity and all are called to fullness of life. This God-given dignity is not earned, it is not conditional, and it is not lost through suffering. It is gift; pure, enduring, sacred gift.

What I offer here is a reflection on what the Church could have been, should have been and could still become if only it would abandon the idolatry of the idealized norm and embrace the risen, wounded body of Christ as its sacred anthropology. That is the aim of this book. It may sound simple, but if it is fully realized, I believe that it has the potential to shake the foundations of the Church.

And finally, I have not travelled this road alone. I have been sustained by companions whose presence was nothing short of sacred; my family, friends, colleagues, congregants, carers and the cloud of witnesses who walk with me still.

And so, this book ends where it begins: with the cry of a disabled priest, the prayer of one held in love and a vision for a Church that is not yet but might still become. For seated at the right hand of the Father is a disabled person, scarred, radiant, whole. If we recognize Christ as Christ is, we might yet recognize ourselves. And if we recognize ourselves, we might yet re-member the Church.

I

Framing the Argument

There is one verse from Scripture that has been my daily companion for the past 30 years; a verse that has grounded me more than any other, acting as a kind of barometer for how my mental health is: 'I praise you, for I am fearfully and wonderfully made' (Ps. 139.14).

Throughout my childhood and into early adulthood, I had lived with the consequences of a hereditary bone condition known as Hereditary Multiple Exostoses (HME). In simple terms, as I was growing up, my body had a tendency to also produce bony spurs on multiple joints. As a child, the solution was straightforward enough: remove the spurs through surgery. Yet, as each spur was excised, it would return, a protracted cycle that meant I spent far too many days, over many years, in hospital waiting rooms, wards and operating theatres.

Then, at the age of 27, when that cycle of repeated operations had all but come to an end, life took an even more dramatic turn. In July 1996, doctors discovered that a bony spur on my upper rib had become cancerous. But that was not all; the cancerous spur had evolved into what is known clinically as a dumbbell tumour: a single source that split into two distinct growths. One reached down toward my lungs and the other extended through my neck into my spine. The removal of the tumour from my spine resulted in paralysis from the chest down, and when they removed the tumour from my neck and lungs, I suffered double pneumonia. For a time, I was caught in a liminal space between hope and despair, unsure whether I would survive this ordeal.

One memory from those days remains etched in my mind with searing clarity. During a spell in intensive care, through much of which I was unconscious, my parents came to visit me. They were understandably anxious. They'd even brought a CD player, hoping that familiar music might break through my unconsciousness, but when they tried to play the music they couldn't get the CD player to work and an argument ensued, more fuelled by anxiety and frustration than anything else. Always speak to people who are unconscious or in a coma, for in that moment I experienced something indescribably profound. I experienced myself being at the bottom of a very deep circular well. Although I was unconscious, in my unconscious state I was aware, very aware that I was at the bottom of the well, naked, vulnerable and utterly isolated. I struggled to comprehend how I had come to be in such a place, so removed from any comfort, so completely unable to reach out to, or communicate with, my parents. I cannot come close to describing the overwhelming sensation of lethargy I felt, aware but utterly unable to reach out to tell my parents I could hear them. It was deeply traumatic. Even now, that memory of isolation and terror takes me back to that place where my humanity was at its most fragile.

In that dark, suspended hour, I thought, 'This is death. I am dying, and I am utterly abandoned.' I was utterly alone. I felt completely abandoned. No sense at all of the presence of God. No sense of a life beyond. Just an experience of deep, traumatic, fear-filled lament: 'My God, my God, why have you forsaken me?'[1]

After I finally regained consciousness my parents corroborated that experience, confirming that their argument was not one I had imagined. And the long journey back to health began; not just physical health but spiritual health as well, for it was from that valley of the shadow of death that my journey back to life began; a journey not only toward physical recovery (or acceptance) but, more importantly, toward a deep, sometimes arduous, other times uncomfortable, spiritual renewal. For the Christian faith I had grown up with proved not fit for purpose. It could not withstand this experience of the well. Where was God in my illness? Where was God in the well? If the Christian faith could not speak into this experience then was it worth the paper Scripture inhabits?

And yet into that experience of trauma, loss and abandonment, I encountered a moment of grace that would alter the course of my life, one that offered me a road map, as it were, back into faith. Shortly after I regained consciousness in the intensive care ward, a monk from the Benedictine Community at Worth Abbey came to visit. He had married me and Bernie not long before and, with patient, compassionate care and deep wisdom and humility, he listened to my every fear, every complaint and every ounce of desolation as I wailed, sharing with him the very depths of my anger and despair. He sat by my bedside, listening intently, in absolute silence, a constant, unswerving presence, never once looking for a moment to interrupt, to justify or offer answers. Rather he honoured and held my lament as sacred. He finally broke the silence by gently rising to his feet as if to leave. But before he departed, he gently took my hand, gave me God's blessing and offered me a piece of advice that has echoed in my heart ever since: he urged me to begin each and every day by saying out loud, or in the silence of my heart, the words of Psalm 139.14: 'I praise you, for I am fearfully and wonderfully made.'

No matter the state of my feelings, whether buoyed by hope or weighed down by deep-seated anguish, I was to repeat these words as I began each new day. And then he left me.

I have begun each and every morning saying that verse since that very encounter at my bedside in intensive care. This verse now acts as a kind of barometer, words that catch in my throat if I'm laid low in pain and exhaustion, informing me whether I need to take some time to be attentive to my physical and mental health.

In the early days of recovery this verse was simply words without meaning, mere sounds said to fulfil a daily ritual and promise. There were countless mornings when I recited the verse without really believing the meaning it carried, and yet, gently and imperceptibly, a slight glimmer of hope and grace seeped in, hope and grace which gradually developed until there were days when the verse's truth resonated so deeply that I felt embraced by the notion that I had been crafted with purpose and profound love by a Creator who cared deeply for me.

The more I have recited this psalm, the more its meaning has grown into something I could own. It has become less about others telling me I was enough and more about my own conscious reclamation of my identity. Every day, regardless of the physical pain or emotional weight I carried, I have learned to affirm: 'I praise you, for I am fearfully and wonderfully made. Wonderful are your works; that I know very well.'

This simple but no less transformative affirmation has started a ripple in my heart, which in turn has guided me to a deeper theological insight; for when, exactly, are we fearfully and wonderfully made? Is there a specific time in our lives when that verse most fully resonates? For example, are we fearfully and wonderfully made at conception? At birth? Are we only fearfully and wonderfully made when we are strong, productive, healthy, able-bodied and pain-free? Or is it, could it possibly be, that we are also fearfully and wonderfully made when we are dying, when we are wounded, when we are laid low, fragile, utterly dependent and afraid?

I have come to believe, and I now live within the conviction, that we are fearfully and wonderfully made in God's image at all times and in all places. Which means that we are fearfully and wonderfully made in the womb, when we are most dependent. We are fearfully and wonderfully made when we are just born and profoundly disabled. We are fearfully and wonderfully made as we navigate the peaks of health and wealth and the valleys of weakness and fragility. We are fearfully and wonderfully made when we have cancer, dementia or a terminal diagnosis. I was fearfully and wonderfully made even as I was slumped at the bottom of that well as I lay unconscious in intensive care. Through the mystery of the Incarnation, the eternal Word become flesh affirms that our identity does not waver with our condition. We are made in that sacred image from our very beginning, continuously and unchangingly. Our God-given image and identity are constant and unwavering right from our conception, through our journey of life and right to our very last breath.

This is profoundly good news, for in and through all our wondrous diversity and through every moment of our life in Christ Jesus, we are each fearfully and wonderfully made.

I have learned, but now I know, that at every point of my life, when I am at my most mobile and at my least mobile, when I'm up and when I'm down, when life seems deceptively easy and when life feels brutal and bleak, when my faith in God is as strong as a rock and when my faith in God feels as fragile as the foam on the sands, each and every morning I can open my heart in prayer and confidently say, 'I praise you, for I am fearfully and wonderfully made. Wonderful are your works; that I know very well.'

Since that day my Christian faith has evolved to become a steadfast companion, both challenging and consoling, always present and constant, offering guidance even as I slide into self-pity. It has been both a loving critic and an empathetic comforter, a force that has healed through gradually transforming how I integrate my suffering into the whole story of my life thus far, making it a testimony of resilience, hope and grace.

This daily ritual has afforded me a profound insight, one which has deeply informed my own sense of identity and image, that God understands us as story; that God's anthropology, God's theology of the body is not one that is static, impersonal and excluding but rather is one revealed as profound narrative. God's anthropology is storied, one which utterly invests in our story from the very moment of our conception to the final resurrection when Christ returns.

To affirm that we are fearfully and wonderfully made then is to firmly reject the idol of bodily perfection. It is to unmask the static, unstoried Graeco-Roman ideal of the symmetrical, rational, self-sufficient man as a false anthropology. The Christian story begins not with Apollo but with Jesus, not with a chisel but with a cradle, a cross and an empty tomb. Christian anthropology is not about flawless form; it is about the mystery of grace incarnate. We are made holy not because we are strong or beautiful, we are made holy because our God-infused identity is storied, forever shifting, profoundly relational and alive and alert to the Spirit.

Our Christian heritage, in its highest calling, is to be, as it were, a reflection of the risen body of Jesus Christ, itself the ultimate storied body, telling and retelling our stories of both the past and present; with each fresh telling drawing us further toward our future hope. All of our stories live and breathe. All shape our doctrine, fuel our worship and anchor our ecclesial identity. Whether we are talking about grand architecture, ancient liturgies, treasured theological texts or inherited patterns of communal memory, Christian heritage holds profound formative weight. Our heritage tells us who we are, where we have been and what we are called to become. Our sacred buildings are not simply containers of worship; they are catechisms in stone, teaching, shaping, disciplining bodies through space, light, elevation and access. Every arch, every stair, every axis carries theological freight.

But what happens when that very heritage, however beautiful, storied and sacred, is also marked by exclusion? What happens when the spaces and stories we preserve and pass down leave some people out, especially those whose bodies or minds do not align with the unspoken 'norm'? Is it time to critique whether our sacred heritage is actually mirroring the storied risen body of Jesus Christ? That is the theological and ecclesiological heart of this book.

I will be contending that ableism, that is, the structural privileging of able-bodied and neurotypical forms of life, is not just present in Christian heritage; it is built into its very fabric. Ableism is what is primarily being reflected back to us. Ableism is inscribed into the Church's stones, canonized in its saints, curated in its collective memory and assimilated into its imagination. It underpins and informs our theologies of the Holy Spirit, creation, sacrament and eschatology, as well as our theologies of identity, image and healing, and it is disabled people who are calling this out. It is proving to be more than just critique, for disabled people are bringing their reparative and imaginative resources to the table. We are not simply being critics, we are being prophets, pastors and theologians. We are bearers of sacred memory. We are offering the Church not a demand for inclusion at the margins, but a call to conversion at the centre, that our heritage may once more reflect the glorious risen body of Jesus Christ.

I will be exploring how ableism, in this context, is not therefore merely a pastoral or even an ethical concern; it is a profoundly theological one, for the normative body has become, for Christianity, the performance of theological virtue. This is not a neutral association. It is a dangerous conflation of sanctity with symmetry, virtue with visibility and holiness with health. It does not merely shape what we believe, it structures our liturgies, our spatial design, our aesthetics and our theological anthropology. When ancient cathedrals are reached only by narrow steps, or when liturgies are offered without sign language, or when disabled saints are airbrushed from history or remembered only through the lens of healing, we are not just dealing with architectural oversight, we are confronting theologically loaded omissions. They tell us who is holy and who is not, who is welcomed and who is ignored or not acknowledged.

And heritage? Heritage is never neutral. It is not just a collection of things; it is a cultural process that actively engages with acts of remembering which help us to better understand and engage with the present. Understood through this lens, heritage becomes performative. It tells stories. It authorizes some voices and silences others. In churches as in museums, heritage performs identity, values and theological imagination. In sacred spaces, heritage has too often reinforced dominant ideals, of order, purity, symmetry and transcendence, ideals which have historically been weaponized against disabled bodies.

Each of our bodies, understood as fearfully and wonderfully made in the image and likeness of God, become profound texts upon which cultural meanings are inscribed and articulated. In Christian contexts, these inscriptions often take the form of pity, inspiration, burden or miracle and they are rarely questioned. They show up in our icons, our hymnody, our preaching and our policies. The result is a heritage that speaks eloquently of divine transcendence but often stumbles and becomes stuck when asked to speak of embodied vulnerability.

Disability theology, then, is not a theological add-on or an accessibility project, it is a reformation of how we understand God, the human, time, salvation and history itself. Nancy Eiesland's *The Disabled God* is the theological landmark that first articulated for us a vision of the risen Christ who bears the marks of impairment, not just in crucifixion, but in resurrection.[2] Her assertion that disabled people do not lack the *imago Dei* but fully manifest it reorients our vision of theological anthropology. If the Church is the body of Christ, then it stands to reason that our physical spaces, our ecclesial memory and our liturgical practices must be judged by how they receive and honour disabled members. It is not enough to welcome us; we must all be recognized as bearers of Christ's own image.

Part of my aim in this book is to build bridges between disability theology and heritage studies, two fields that have rarely been in direct conversation. One key framework I will use therefore to assist in this conversation is 'crip time', articulated provocatively and beautifully by Alison Kafer.[3] I will explore it further in a later chapter, but *crip time* challenges the assumption that time is linear, uniform or progressive. Traditional heritage often focuses on preserving a stable, idealized past. But for many disabled people, time is recursive, nonlinear, entangled with trauma and embodiment. Our past is not behind us; it is carried in our bodies. This reframes key questions: what kind of past is being preserved? Whose story is being told? And who has access, not just physically, but spiritually, narratively, theologically?

These are not abstract or theoretical concerns. Churches and cathedrals across the UK, and globally, are actively rethinking heritage practices in light of equity, diversity and inclusion. Accessibility improvements like ramps, hearing loops or signage are vital, but when these are implemented without theological reflection, they risk becoming mere optics, for real inclusion is not about adding people into an existing table, it is about reconfiguring the table itself. If heritage is to be faithful, it must not only be accessible: it must also be accountable, accountable to the lived realities, historical exclusions and theological insights of disabled people.

I am so grateful to theologians such as Nancy Eiesland, Amos Yong, John Hull, Deborah Creamer, John Swinton and Jennie Weiss, who have informed my own theological thinking over many years. Activists like Eli Clare and heritage scholars including Rodney Harrison, Laurajane Smith and Sharon Macdonald have helped frame my own thinking around the politics of memory, representation and curation.[4] For those who wish to deepen their engagement in this field of theology I commend their writings to you.

But this is primarily a book rooted in my own experience: 30 years of living with a permanent disability, decades of engagement with disability theology and the past two years serving as a Residentiary Canon at York Minster. That role has given me a front-row seat to the challenges and possibilities of heritage. York Minster is a place of spiritual and cultural power, but like many sacred spaces, its stones carry the weight of exclusion alongside the possibility of transformation.

Each chapter contains reflections structured around a primary theme. These reflections are designed to stand alone, and as such, there will be some repetition of key insights. I make no apology for that. Ableism is insidious. It is pervasive. It has woven itself into the DNA of the Church's theology, memory and space. It must be named at every turn.

So, what is the purpose of this book? It is nothing less than a theological reclamation. To reclaim disabled voices, mine included, not as guests in someone else's house, but as custodians, interpreters and bearers of sacred history. It is to say, with firm conviction, that disabled lives *are* part of the gospel. Not because we are inspirational, but because we are incarnational. We are theologies in motion. We are embodied stories of pain and praise, loss and resurrection. We are fearfully and wonderfully made.

My hope is that this book will expose hidden biases, disrupt complacency, inspire repentance and help birth a more faithful vision of the Church, a Church where no one is disposable, where all bodies are sacred and where the presence of disabled people is recognized not as anomaly but as theological necessity.

For us to better understand how ableism has taken root in Christian thought, we must first understand how Christianity itself took root, how it spread, what it adopted and what it sanctified along the way. For ableism did not enter Christian theology accidentally. It came embedded in the very systems Christianity learned to survive within: Graeco-Roman ideals of bodily perfection, colonial hierarchies of power and intelligence, Enlightenment rationalism and capitalist metrics of worth.

What follows is a theological anatomy of this viral faith, a series of case studies that trace Christianity's spread through five cultural and historical contexts: but these contexts are not merely historical, they are diagnostic. They will prepare the ground for the deeper theological work to come when I seek to unmask how ableism is not peripheral but has become central to the way Christianity has historically understood God, Scripture, the body and the Church.

Only by tracing these paths of assimilation can we begin the work of disentangling the gospel from what it has come to bless. Only by naming the virus can we begin to imagine how to heal its effects.

Notes

1 Psalm 22.1.

2 Nancy L. Eiesland, *The Disabled God: Toward a Liberatory Theology of Disability* (Nashville, TN: Abingdon Press, 1994).

3 Alison Kafer, *Feminist, Queer, Crip* (Bloomington, IN: Indiana University Press, 2013).

4 See also Eli Clare, *Brilliant Imperfection: Grappling with Cure* (Durham, NC: Duke University Press, 2017); Rodney Harrison, *Heritage: Critical Approaches* (Abingdon: Routledge, 2013); Sharon Macdonald, *Memorylands: Heritage and Identity in Europe Today* (Abingdon: Routledge, 2013).

2

Christianity as Virus: A Theological Metaphor of Contagion and Contestation

The metaphor of Christianity as a virus is jarring and provocative, and intentionally so. It unsettles the conventional imagery of evangelism as mere transmission of truth or peaceful conversion. Instead, it calls attention to the unsettling ways Christianity has often spread; rapidly, adaptively and not infrequently through coercive or traumatic contact. Like a virus, Christianity enters a host culture not to simply coexist or replace, but to replicate, embedding itself in local languages, philosophies, symbols and structures. In doing so, it transforms the host and is, in turn, transformed. Theological content is carried along vectors of empire, migration, trade and violence, reshaping cultures even as it is reshaped.

This metaphor need not imply that Christianity is inherently toxic, but it refuses to romanticize the history of mission and expansion. Christianity has always been a travelling religion, but its travel has rarely been innocent. The spread of the gospel has often been entangled with colonization, conquest and the subjugation of bodies, lands and knowledges. In this sense, Christianity's viral quality is not only descriptive but diagnostic: it helps us see how the faith embeds itself through both proclamation and appropriation, both incarnation and infection.

At its best, Christianity's viral spread reflects its incarnational genius, its ability to speak in every tongue, to take root in every soil, to be made flesh in every culture. This is the view of Andrew Walls, who famously described Christianity as a 'serially translated religion', one that survives through constant cross-cultural transmission.[1] The Word becomes flesh again and again, within Jewish, Hellenistic, African, Asian and Indigenous frames, without being reducible to any one expression. Christianity survives, Walls argues, by dying to its previous cultural form and being reborn in a new one.

But this viral metaphor also names the danger of assimilation without discernment, for Christianity did not merely spread; it commandeered. It seized imaginations, languages and lands, often replacing Indigenous ways of knowing with a theologically authorized mimicry of the European self. Here, the virus becomes parasitic, appropriating the host not to coexist or co-create, but to dominate. The gospel, in this mode, is rendered complicit in colonial hegemony.

Understanding how Christianity spreads is not merely a historical or missiological concern, it is essential to understanding the development of Christian anthropology in the West and how it became wedded to a false ideal: the *normate body*. As Christianity mutated within imperial and colonial contexts, it did not simply transmit the gospel of the risen, wounded Christ; it often began to sanctify culturally dominant ideals of perfection, beauty, symmetry and strength. The risen body of Christ, marked by wounds and trauma, was eclipsed by a theology of the unbroken, the orderly, the pure. The viral logic of assimilation produced not only cultural conversions, but anthropological distortions.

This shift, as we shall discover, has left a deep imprint on Christian theology and sacred architecture. In embracing a classical, Graeco-Roman ideal of bodily perfection, Western Christianity reimagined the *imago Dei* in the shape of the able-bodied, rational, male elite. The Church, in this model, became a space of aesthetic and theological exclusion, echoing ideals not of the crucified Christ but of classical statuary, and in doing so it has bred ableism deep into its DNA.

This normate anthropology was built into stone. The wounds of Christ were spiritualized. The broken body became a symbol of sin to be overcome, rather than the revelation of God's love, resulting in this disruptive presence becoming systematically sanitized and embedded in the theology and practice of the Western church.

To speak of Christianity as a virus, then, is to speak not only of cultural transmission but of theological mutation, how the faith, in adapting to empire and normativity, often turned against the very bodies it was meant to honour. The virus replicates, but the replication is not neutral. When Christianity entered the bloodstream of empire, it began to prefer the polished body over the pierced one, the architectural sublime over the embodied prophetic.

I wish therefore to share five case studies – colonial Latin America, sub-Saharan Africa, East Asia, the United States and finally imperial Rome – each demonstrating the diverse nature of Christianity's chameleonic, sometimes coercive, always complex modes of spread. Each illustrates a radically different example of the viral nature of the faith: its capacity to inhabit, adapt and transform a host culture, while risking compromise, distortion and the loss of the cruciform centre. If we are going to name, engage with and ultimately eradicate ableism from our theologies and liturgies, we must first understand better the diverse ways Christianity assimilates itself into differing local languages, cultures, philosophies, symbols and structures and what happens when that assimilation takes on a parasitic nature and supersedes the gospel it purports to share.

1 Colonial transmission: syncretism in Latin America

The Christianization of Latin America is one of the most profound and painful examples of how Christianity spread through entanglement with empire. Catholic missionaries did not arrive as neutral bearers of the gospel but on the ships of conquistadors, agents of empire whose 'evangelization' was inextricable from genocide, land theft and cultural devastation. Christianity was used not only to baptize souls but to legitimize conquest. Entire peoples were declared 'barbarous' if they did not accept European forms of faith, and missionary activity often accompanied the violent destruction of Indigenous religions, social structures and languages. This was not evangelization in the spirit of Christ, but in the name of empire.

Yet, within this traumatic context, something extraordinary occurred. Despite, and perhaps because of, the violence of its arrival, Christianity did not remain a European religion in Latin America. It was taken up, transformed and hybridized by Indigenous peoples who reinterpreted Christian symbols through the lenses of their own cosmologies. Saints were identified with local deities, processions incorporated native rhythms and religious festivals blended Catholic and Indigenous traditions. Nowhere is this more potent than in the figure of the Virgin of Guadalupe, who appeared in 1531 to an Indigenous peasant, Juan Diego, on the hill of Tepeyac, a site sacred to the Aztec goddess Coatlaxopeuh. Guadalupe's mestiza features and her use of Nahuatl language signified a radical reconfiguration of the Marian image, fusing Catholic devotion with Indigenous identity. She became not only a religious icon but a symbol of survival, resistance and liberation, embodying a faith that could no longer be claimed by the colonizer alone.

This process of syncretism, however, raises deep theological questions. Was this a genuine inculturation of the gospel, a contextual embodiment of the Word incarnate in Indigenous flesh or was it merely infection, a coping mechanism within a contaminated faith? Liberation theologians have long wrestled with this tension. Gustavo Gutiérrez, the Peruvian theologian widely regarded as the father of liberation theology, has insisted that the gospel must be reclaimed 'from below', from the perspective of the oppressed, not the colonizer.[2] This radical option for the poor is not an ideological addition to Christianity but a retrieval of its original, cruciform centre; that it is God who walks with the poor in history.[3]

Yet the ambiguity remains. The viral spread of Christianity in Latin America created spaces of profound resilience and creativity. Indigenous peoples did not passively receive the faith; they resisted, repurposed and rewrote it. But the trauma of colonization was never truly healed, only partially veiled. Underneath the Marian blue of Guadalupe is the red of conquest. Her comforting presence conceals centuries of dispossession. The same image that nurtured faith is also the image that bore the mark of empire.

Thus, the legacy of colonial Christianity in Latin America remains both wounded and wondrous. It testifies to the enduring power of Indigenous theological agency to reimagine Christ in a conquered land, but it also reminds us of how easily the gospel can be co-opted as a weapon of empire. Like a virus, Christianity infected the cultural body of Latin America. But this infection, while born of violence, also became a site of subversive regeneration, where faith was not simply transmitted but transfigured.

2 Viral resistance: African Independent Churches

The spread of Christianity across the African continent cannot be disentangled from the deep wounds of colonialism. Missionary Christianity often arrived not as a message of liberation, but as an adjunct to imperial expansion, embedded in the structures of colonial schooling, commerce and governance. Christian mission societies functioned in tandem with European empires, bringing with them not only Bibles and sacraments but also European languages, norms and hierarchies. Conversion was often accompanied by the suppression of Indigenous religions, the attempted erasure of ancestral knowledge and with it the denigration of African cultures. Missionaries planted a foreign God on African soil, and with that God came a cultural and political order that often displaced African cosmologies.

Yet even as missionary Christianity functioned as a parasitic presence, feeding off the body of empire, it also became the seedbed for extraordinary spiritual resistance and reinvention. African communities did not receive the gospel as passive recipients, but as active interpreters. They reimagined the Christian message through the prism of their own cosmologies, kinship systems, healing rituals and spiritual ecologies. Out of this process emerged what are now known as African Independent Churches (AICs), movements that broke away from European ecclesial control and articulated a thoroughly indigenized faith. I saw this at first hand during a visit to the village of Buikwe in Uganda with the charity International Needs back in 2017.

There and in communities across Uganda, the gospel was not preached in the colonial tongue alone, but in the cadence of Indigenous languages and the rhythms of local life. Prophets, visionaries and spiritual healers had become central figures in church leadership. Worship included drumming, dance, dreams and ecstatic prayer. Healing was both physical and communal, a sign of divine presence embedded in the reality of everyday suffering. I was fascinated to discover churches interpreting Christ not as a remote European figure but as an ancestral presence. Christ had become their greatest ancestor – a liberator who walked with the people, who suffered with them in colonization and who offered spiritual power outside of missionary control. I discovered a Christianity that is not a pale imitation of a European religion but a living fire that has jumped cultural boundaries and claimed new sacred ground.

This flowering of African ecclesial life exposed the theological tension at the heart of colonial Christianity. For centuries, missionary theology had treated African religions as superstition and African cultures as inferior. But the rise of independent churches revealed the falsity of this paternalism. These churches challenged not only the theological assumptions of the missionaries but the very structures of colonial domination. They spoke of a Christ who healed the sick, challenged oppression and danced in the dust of African soil. In doing so, they reclaimed the gospel as their own.

Yet the legacy remains ambiguous. The initial spread of Christianity was parasitic on colonial power: it arrived through imperial systems, mission schools and violent suppression. The roots of the faith in African soil were planted under the shadow of domination. And even as African communities transformed the gospel, they could not always escape the deep imprint of colonial theology, its hierarchies, gender norms and imported moral frameworks. The very structures they resisted had already shaped the terrain on which they stood.

Nevertheless, the story of African Independent Churches is one of viral resistance. Christianity, once an imposed religion of empire, became a site of empowerment, innovation and spiritual vitality. The gospel was not merely transmitted but transfigured, claimed by those who had once been deemed unworthy of interpreting it. The Christ of colonial mission became the Christ of African liberation: not clothed in European vestments, but adorned in local fabrics, speaking with the voice of the ancestors and dancing with the joy of a people who had made the faith their own.

3 Inculturation and immunity: East Asia

When Christianity first encountered the ancient cultures of China, Korea and Japan, it did not enter a spiritual vacuum but a world already thick with meaning, cultures shaped for millennia by Confucian ethics, Daoist cosmologies and Buddhist soteriologies. Unlike the relatively young societies of the New World or the violently disrupted systems of colonized Africa, East Asia presented a formidable immune system: deeply integrated traditions that could not be easily displaced or supplanted. Christianity, if it was to survive in this context, had to mutate. It could not merely assert itself as universal truth; it had to speak in the philosophical and religious dialects of the host. It had to become something simultaneously familiar and strange, a faith that did not demand wholesale cultural amnesia but engaged in delicate acts of translation and adaptation.

The most famous example of this theological mutation occurred in the hands of Jesuit missionaries, particularly Matteo Ricci, who entered China in the late sixteenth century with the conviction that the gospel must be clothed in the garments of Confucian wisdom. Ricci learned Classical Chinese, dressed as a Confucian scholar and sought to translate Christian theology into the moral vocabulary of *li* (ritual), *ren* (benevolence) and *tian* (heaven). God was described as *Shangdi* or *Tianzhu*, terms with deep resonance in Chinese cosmology. This was not syncretism in the pejorative sense, but a deliberate strategy of inculturation, aimed at honouring the cultural genius of the host while planting seeds of Christian thought within it.[4]

Similarly, in modern Korea, *minjung* theology emerged not from colonial mission schools but from the blood and fire of political oppression. *Minjung*, meaning 'the people' or, more specifically, 'the suffering masses', became the locus of theological reflection. Christianity here did not simply arrive from abroad; it was born again in the ashes of national trauma and peasant revolt.

But this process of cultural translation raises profound theological tensions. Can Christianity maintain its essence while adopting the DNA of the host culture? When the gospel is reframed in Confucian terms, or aligned with *minjung* political struggles, does it retain its cruciform centre, or does it become something else entirely? Inculturation is a double-edged theological act: it allows the faith to survive, even thrive, in new soils, but it risks mutation so complete that it becomes unrecognizable to its source.

This is the crux of the ambiguity: the virus adapts or dies. Christianity, if it remains rigid, is rejected; if it adapts too fully, it dissolves. It walks a theological tightrope. The reason for Christianity's longevity is that Christianity is always 'translatable', but its translatability is not infinite; for it to flourish it ultimately must remain anchored in the person of Christ. Yet that anchoring must not become cultural imperialism. It is precisely the risk of transformation into a new organism that makes Christianity's spread in East Asia so revealing. It teaches us that survival may depend not on purity, but on the capacity to undergo death and rebirth, again and again.

In China today, churches flourish despite surveillance and repression. In Japan, where Christianity remains a minority faith, Christian aesthetics often blend seamlessly with Buddhist symbols. In South Korea, Christianity has exploded, but its theological forms reflect both Calvinist orthodoxy and nationalist energy. These East Asian contexts remind us that Christianity is neither a single system nor a static creed. It is a living, viral faith; adaptable, unstable and always at risk of either dilution or discovery.

4 Commodified contagion: American civil religion

Nowhere is the metaphor of Christianity as a virus more apt, or more theologically charged, than in the present context of the United States, where the faith has not only spread but fused, at a molecular level, with capitalism, nationalism and celebrity culture. American Christianity, particularly in its dominant evangelical and charismatic expressions, has mutated into something far removed from the radical call to discipleship found in the Gospels. Here, the viral spread of the gospel has instead followed the logic of the market and not the margins. What has become the most significant competitor to Christianity in the West today is not another religion but rather the global economic order, with which Christianity has become entangled to its peril.

This fusion is most visible in the rise of the megachurch; ecclesial empires shaped less by sacramental theology or communal liturgy than by consumer metrics, branding strategies and platform personalities. Pastors become CEOs; congregants become target demographics. Church growth is tracked like corporate expansion. Worship becomes a spectacle of lights, music and motivational rhetoric. The cross, once a symbol of state execution and divine protest, becomes a logo, a lifestyle accessory, a marketing tool. Jesus is reframed as a personal saviour, therapist or self-help guru, offering blessing, emotional uplift and financial prosperity to the faithful. 'He died for your sins' is subtly replaced by 'He wants you to thrive.'

This assimilation of Christianity to capitalist and nationalist logic gives rise to a profound theological tension. Who is being worshipped in these spaces, Christ or Caesar in disguise? When churches display the national flag in the sanctuary, when sermons quote presidents more than prophets, when wealth is treated as a sign of divine favour, has the crucified and risen Lord been replaced by an American idol? The American civil religion has flourished through siphoning off the theological energy of Christianity into the service of the nation-state, creating a faith that has become internalized, baptizing militarism, economic inequality and consumer desire.

Nowhere is this more starkly seen than in the prosperity gospel, a theological framework that preaches health, wealth and personal success as signs of divine blessing. Here, the cruciform nature of Christian discipleship is all but abandoned, replaced by a prosperity theology that, through sacralizing the logic of neoliberal capitalism, is anointed by it. In such a theology, suffering is understood as failure, poverty as sin, and Jesus becomes the guarantor of upward mobility. The God of the Beatitudes, who blesses the poor and calls the meek inheritors of the earth, is replaced by the god of Wall Street.

The ambiguity of this viral spread is deeply unsettling. The gospel does infect culture, but in the American context it often domesticates it. Instead of critiquing unjust structures, it baptizes them. Instead of unsettling the comfortable, it comforts the entitled. Christianity becomes the host's servant rather than its judge, a chaplain to empire rather than a witness against it, so the faith that began with a homeless man executed by the state has morphed into becoming the ideological backbone of suburban security, corporate ambition and military pride.

And yet, within this contagion, there still remain antibodies of resistance. Communities of faith that practise radical hospitality, that critique economic injustice, that reclaim the suffering Christ, still persist. The viral metaphor reminds us that mutation is not always degeneration. It can also open the door to unexpected forms of faithfulness. But for that to happen, American Christianity must confront its own complicity in systems of oppression. It must ask: what has been lost in translation, and can the radical, crucified, risen Jesus be recovered from the ruins of the brand?

5 Imperial contagion: Christianity and the Roman Empire

And so, we finally come to the transformation of Christianity, where, from its roots as a marginal, persecuted sect to becoming the religion of empire, is one of the most astonishing and ambivalent developments in the history of all religion. For us to better understand both the theological and architectural ableism we now inhabit, we must return to the seismic moment: the early fourth century, when Christianity became not just a tolerated religion but the faith of an empire.

The irony is not lost on me that I presently serve at the very place where Constantine was proclaimed ruler of the Roman Empire in AD 306 immediately outside what is now the south door of York Minster, after the death of his father Constantius Chlorus. And yet before Constantine, Christian anthropology was shaped by weakness and marginality. The fledgling Christian communities described in the New Testament were diverse in embodiment and status: the paralytic let down through the roof, the woman with the haemorrhage, the man blind from birth, the enslaved, the poor. These were not mere recipients of charity; they were the fledgling Church's disciples, apostles and leaders.

In 1 Corinthians 12, Paul's radical ecclesiology declares, 'the members of the body that seem to be weaker are indispensable' (v. 22). This was no metaphor. It was an embodied ecclesiology rooted in mutual dependence and divine inversion. The early Church knew the crucified and resurrected Christ not as a concept but as a communal reality, a fellowship of the breaking, the persecuted and the poor.

But after Constantine's Edict of Milan in AD 313, Christianity began its transformation from persecuted sect to imperial religion and with state support came stability, resources and the slow but inevitable seduction of classical aesthetics and anthropological norms.

Graeco-Roman culture revered symmetry, athleticism, proportion and harmony as signs of divine order. The ideal male form – athletic, able, whole – came to symbolize not just civic virtue but cosmic truth. As Christianity rose in status, it increasingly adopted these ideals.

What began as a radical, counter-imperial movement among Galilean peasants, followers of a crucified Jew who proclaimed a kingdom not of this world, became, within four centuries, the spiritual backbone of the Roman Empire.

The transition from persecuted to preferred, from subversive to state-sanctioned that Constantine instigated, did not occur without deep theological and ethical consequence. To become truly embedded, Christianity learned to live with empire by learning to speak its language, think its thoughts and assimilate itself into its social and political structures.

This process of assimilation involved more than institutional acceptance; it demanded a complete philosophical translation. Early Christian thinkers, seeking legitimacy and intelligibility in the Graeco-Roman world, adopted prevailing philosophical frameworks to express theological truths. Platonism, with its dualistic metaphysics, and Stoicism, with its emphasis on divine order and reason, became tools in the hands of theologians like Origen, Clement of Alexandria and later Augustine. Thus, the Christianization of the Roman world was as much a transformation of Christian theology as it was a conversion of Roman society. The apocalyptic fervour of Jesus and the early Church, expecting the imminent return of the Messiah and the collapse of worldly powers, was gradually reshaped into a universal metaphysical system. The kingdom of God, once anticipated as near and disruptive, became interpreted as spiritual, inward and eternal.

Origen's *On First Principles* represents one of the earliest systematic efforts to reconcile Christian doctrine with Platonic cosmology. He spiritualized the resurrection, interpreted Genesis allegorically and conceptualized salvation as the soul's return to divine unity.[5] Augustine, writing in the wake of the sack of Rome, reimagined Christian eschatology through the lens of Neoplatonism, distinguishing sharply between the 'City of God' and the 'Earthly City', while also legitimizing Christian authority within the earthly realm.[6] This philosophical turn enabled Christianity to enter the imperial bloodstream, no longer as an outsider faith but as a coherent, universal worldview.

The liberation theologian Leonardo Boff observes that the Church's process of assimilation unfolded through a deliberate courting of those who held influence over the levers of modernity, especially the scientific, technological and political elites. In its eagerness to remain relevant within shifting cultural paradigms, the Church adopted the structures and sensibilities of the age, streamlining its institutional forms, aligning more closely with bureaucratic norms and reshaping its liturgical practices. This adaptation, far from neutral, involved a secularization of its symbols and a softening of its prophetic edge. As Boff suggests, such accommodation risked blunting the Church's capacity to critique dominant power structures, even as it gained a seat at their table.[7]

It should not surprise us therefore that this assimilation came at a theological cost. The Christ who had identified with the dispossessed, the breaking body on the margins, was now enthroned in basilicas, flanked by emperors and surrounded by wealth. The cruciform heart of the gospel, the radical solidarity of God with the oppressed, risked being obscured by its institutional triumph.

Theologically, this moment introduced a deep and enduring tension. On one hand, the imperial Church facilitated unprecedented theological development. Councils such as Nicaea (325) and Chalcedon (451) formalized orthodoxy, articulated the doctrine of the Trinity and preserved the apostolic faith. Canon law was developed. The Bible was copied, protected and standardized. Monasticism flourished. At the same time, the Church became entangled in empire's logic of control, hierarchy and violence. The tragedy of Imperial Christianity is that once Christians had achieved political power, they began to wield it much as their predecessors had done, often against one another.

The resulting ambiguity is not easily resolved. Christianity's imperial contagion has given it institutional permanence and global reach, but it has also left it vulnerable to the seductions of power. Thus, the infection runs deep, not simply as a moment in history but as a persistent temptation in ecclesiology, the recurring temptation to exchange prophetic witness for political utility, exchange kenosis for control.

Christianity's encounter with empire is thus the viral parable. It spread by adapting to the host, embedding itself in the cultural, philosophical and political life of Rome. In doing so, it survived, and thrived, but not without mutation. The gospel retained its power, but its shape was forever altered. The body of Christ was no longer fashioned on the storied risen body of the resurrection. The body of Christ mutated into the static, implacable, unyielding, able body of Imperial Rome.

A faith that infects, and is infected

The viral metaphor, purposely provocative and unsettling, has guided our exploration of how Christianity spreads: not as a neutral or antiseptic gospel, but as a living, mutating presence that replicates within host cultures, sometimes healing, sometimes harming. We have traced its movement through the corridors of empire and colonization, through cultural resistance and reinvention, through syncretic survival and commodified betrayal. From the flag-draped altars of American civil religion to Latin America's Marian shrines, from African prophetic churches to Korean liberation theology and finally to Rome's basilicas, Christianity has never existed apart from the bodies, powers and stories into which it embeds itself.

But this viral character, this capacity to adapt and assimilate, has come at a theological cost. What Christianity has inhabited, it has also often mirrored, and what it has mirrored, it may also have come to bless. In each of these historical moments, we have seen how the gospel has risked losing its cruciform identity, exchanging the radical solidarity of the incarnate God for the logic of empire, patriarchy, market or state. Christianity's ability to survive has also become its greatest danger, that its capacity to accommodate injustice comes under its very guise of faithfulness.

Few examples illustrate this more starkly than the Church's long and largely unrepentant history of ableism. Ableism is not an exception to the story of viral Christianity, it is a central chapter, a vivid example of how the faith has embedded itself in cultural ideals of strength, productivity and control, thus rendering the disabled body, like the colonized culture or the economically excluded, theologically suspect.

If Christianity were ever to be healed of its viral compromises, it must first turn away from purity and return once more to incarnation, to the Christ who entered the world as a vulnerable infant, who touched the untouchable and who let his own body be vulnerable. It must first reclaim the risen body not as flawless, but as wounded and glorified, for this is the body that judges our idols and heals our theologies. This is the Christ who unmasks the viral infection of ableism, not with condemnation, but with disruptive grace.

From viral faith to scriptural frames: naming the pursuit of perfection

Through these preceding reflections I have traced Christianity's viral expansion across empires, continents and cultures, showing how the Christian faith has not simply travelled, but mutated, taking on the logics of empire, capital, conquest and control. In every context examined, Latin America, sub-Saharan Africa, East Asia, the United States and Rome, I have sought to illustrate how Christianity has adapted to survive, often assimilating itself to dominant ideals of strength, success, purity and normalcy. These ideals did not remain on the surface; they sank deep into the theological bloodstream of each of the traditions, and among the most enduring and insidious of these assimilations has been the pursuit of ableist perfection, a pursuit that has been devastatingly exclusionary to disabled people.

The virus, in other words, did not stop at architecture or empire: it has infected our biblical imagination. This has to be named and owned and understood by each generation, at all the times and in all the places where Christianity has taken root.

This is now where I wish for the story to turn inwards. If Christianity has taken on the DNA of its host cultures, then we must ask how this has shaped the way we read Scripture itself. How have ancient texts, interpreted through the lenses of empire and normativity, come to sanctify able-bodiedness, marginalize difference and portray disability as sin, punishment or lack? How has the pursuit of moral and physical perfection become a theological default, upheld by biblical readings that prioritize healing as erasure, purity as exclusion and wholeness as conformity to an unexamined norm?

In the chapters that follow I will examine in detail how ableism has assimilated itself into the bloodstream of Christianity, not only through historical mission and cultural translation, but within the very heart of our biblical interpretations, our theological doctrines, our ecclesial architecture and our understanding of what it means to be human. I will trace how the normate ideal has distorted our reading of Scripture, shaped our built environments, informed our liturgical practices, defined our theological anthropology and distorted how we have understood the actions of the Holy Spirit and our eschatology. And I will ask, again and again: what might the Church look like if it were formed not by the fantasy of an idealized norm, but by the memory of Christ's wounded resurrection?

But this is not merely a critique. It is an invitation; an invitation for us all to reimagine the Church not as a shrine to ability, but as a home for breaking bodies, gathered by grace, held together by wounds and animated by the Spirit of the Risen One who still bears his scars.

Notes

1 Andrew F. Walls, *The Missionary Movement in Christian History: Studies in the Transmission of Faith* (Maryknoll, NY: Orbis Books, 1996), pp. 17–25.
2 Gustavo Gutiérrez, *A Theology of Liberation: History, Politics, and Salvation*,

trans. Sister Caridad Inda and John Eagleson (Maryknoll, NY: Orbis Books, 1988), pp. 162–73.

3 Gustavo Gutiérrez, *We Drink from Our Own Wells: The Spiritual Journey of a People*, trans. Matthew J. O'Connell (Maryknoll, NY: Orbis Books, 2003), pp. 122–7.

4 Matteo Ricci, *The True Meaning of the Lord of Heaven (Tianzhu Shiyi)*, trans. Douglas Lancashire and Peter Hu Kuo-chen (St Louis, MO: Institute of Jesuit Sources, 1985), pp. 65–98.

5 Origen, *On First Principles*, trans. G.W. Butterworth (New York: Harper & Row, 1966), especially Book II, ch. 10.

6 Augustine, *The City of God*, trans. Henry Bettenson (London: Penguin, 2003), Books XIV and XIX.

7 Leonardo Boff, *Church: Charism and Power; Liberation Theology and the Institutional Church*, trans. John W. Diercksmeier (New York: Crossroad, 1985), pp. 47–88.

3

Scripture and the Pursuit of Perfection

The Bible is a living text, breathed into being by communities shaped by struggle, longing and encounter with the divine. Yet too often, the Church has read this living Word with rigid lenses, flattening its poetry into prescription, and its stories of flesh and fracture into demands for purity, healing and conformity. Nowhere is this more apparent than in the Church's treatment of disability, where ableist assumptions have been sacralized through selective readings, exclusionary theologies and a failure to recognize the complex embodiment of God's people.

This chapter begins with a bold claim: ableism in the Church is not a modern contamination but is deeply entwined with how sacred Scripture has been interpreted, preached and applied. The problem is not the Bible itself, but the hermeneutics that have too often framed disability as deficit, healing as erasure and wholeness as return to a presumed norm. These interpretive habits did not emerge in a vacuum; they were shaped by ancient purity codes, Graeco-Roman ideals of bodily perfection, and later, theological frameworks that prized strength, autonomy and visual coherence over weakness, interdependence and hidden grace.

When Jesus heals, why is it always a restoration to an idealized form? When Paul speaks of a thorn in the flesh, is he inviting shame or solidarity? When Levitical laws restrict access to the sanctuary, are they describing divine exclusion or human fear? This chapter will interrogate the dominant narratives, ask uncomfortable questions and retrieve neglected voices, especially those of disabled readers and theologians who have long lived at the margins of scriptural engagement.

The Word made flat: Scripture, interpretation and the seeds of ableism

Sacred Scripture notably lacks a distinct social category for disabled individuals. Unlike contemporary disability studies, which examine disability systemically, the biblical world tended to frame it through visible conditions, often interpreting them in individualistic, moralistic or ritualistic ways. This absence is significant. Nancy Eiesland observes that while disabled people do appear in Scripture, they are primarily depicted as subjects of healing, judgement or pity rather than as active contributors to theological meaning.[1]

This scriptural silence on systemic disability must be understood in light of ancient social and medical realities. High infant mortality rates meant that many children born with severe impairments often simply did not survive and when they did, their participation in society was shaped by economic roles tied to physical labour, military service or domestic duties. Without institutions of education or care, those with impairments may have lived in familial dependence and been kept from public view.

Furthermore, ancient Israelite religion, like many religious traditions of the ancient Near East, linked wholeness with holiness. The priesthood in particular was governed by strict purity codes, such as Leviticus 21.17–23, which excluded men with 'a blemish' from offering the bread of God. The logic was not necessarily that such individuals were sinful, but that the symbolic order of the sanctuary required an unblemished offering and an unblemished priest. Physical impairments were not excluded from the Temple in Jerusalem for any particular moral reasons, rather because they interrupted the ideal of physical perfection that symbolized the wholeness of divine holiness. This anthropomorphic understanding embedded itself deeply within the post-Constantinian imperial faith and it persists to this day within the conscious and unconscious bias of the Church. My priestly orders have been questioned on many occasions over the last 16 years on the back of this deeply unhealthy bias.

Impairment as metaphor

Further compounding this exclusion is Scripture's extensive use of disability as metaphor. Impairments – especially people with visual impairments, people who are deaf/Deaf, people who are non-verbal or who have speech impairments, people who are neurodivergent and people who are physically impaired – are routinely used as symbols of spiritual failure or moral rebellion. For example:

- **Blindness** is repeatedly invoked as a metaphor for spiritual ignorance or resistance to God. Isaiah declares, 'Israel's sentinels are blind, they are all without knowledge' (Isa. 56.10). Jesus, in rebuking the Pharisees, calls them 'blind guides' (Matt. 23.24).

- **Deafness** is similarly spiritualized: 'They have ears, but do not hear' (Ps. 115.6), suggesting stubbornness and moral decay.
- **Lameness** and **paralysis** are used to symbolize moral and communal dysfunction. In 2 Samuel 4.4, Mephibosheth's lameness, though physical, is narratively connected to political failure and dynastic vulnerability.
- **Epilepsy** as a clinical diagnosis is not explicitly named in Scripture, as ancient cultures lacked modern medical categories. However, several passages describe symptoms consistent with what we now understand as epilepsy, especially seizure activity, falling, foaming at the mouth and loss of control, often interpreted in the biblical context as signs of spiritual affliction or demonic possession. The most widely cited biblical account that resembles epilepsy is found in Matthew 17.14–18 (cf. Mark 9.14–29; Luke 9.37–43): 'Lord, have mercy on my son, for he is an epileptic and he suffers terribly. He often falls into the fire and often into the water' (Matt. 17.15). The Greek term used here is *selēniazetai*, literally 'moonstruck' or 'lunatic', reflecting a common ancient belief that seizures were linked to lunar cycles. The boy's symptoms (sudden falling, convulsions, danger of harm) closely resemble epilepsy. In Mark's version, the father says: 'He has a spirit that makes him unable to speak; and whenever it seizes him, it dashes him down; and he foams and grinds his teeth and becomes rigid' (Mark 9.17–18).

Such metaphors have been shown to have enduring power, but they carry theological risk, for the pervasive metaphorical use of disability in biblical texts often renders invisible the lived experience of disabled people; for when impairments are used exclusively as symbols for sin or ignorance, they obscure the real lives of disabled people, who, in both ancient and contemporary contexts, are full moral agents and not stand-ins for theological defects.

Shaping the ideal: wholeness and perfection

In light of these metaphors, it is only too easy to see how Christian tradition began to associate bodily wholeness with divine favour and perfection. This is especially evident in early Christian eschatology. Even Paul's vision in 1 Corinthians 15 of a 'glorified body' that is 'imperishable' has often been interpreted – though it is important to stress not necessarily by St Paul himself – as implying a healed, perfected body, free of weakness or impairment.

In the medieval period, Thomas Aquinas taught that in the resurrection, the body would be restored 'to its optimal state', a pejorative statement if ever there was one, meaning not only the removal of disease and decay, but also the erasure of what he termed 'defects' of nature, such as blindness or deformity.[2] This theological vision, though perhaps hopeful in intent, casts disability as something that must be left behind in the perfection of heaven. Such views remain influential today in churches that equate divine blessing with healing and health, and that understand salvation in terms of bodily restoration to a normative ideal.

Yet this idea of perfection is increasingly contested. Modern theologians such as Stanley Hauerwas and John Swinton have challenged the presumption that health or ability is a prerequisite for holiness. Instead, they argue that perfection in Scripture ought to be interpreted not in terms of physical form but of faithful relationship.[3] As Jesus says in the Sermon on the Mount: 'Be perfect, therefore, as your heavenly Father is perfect' (Matt. 5.48). The important thing to note is that the Greek word *teleios* here connotes completeness or maturity, not flawlessness or bodily integrity.

Thus, the biblical call to perfection may be less about erasing disability and more about deepening love, justice and relational fidelity. We will be returning to this theme in later chapters as this reframing is a clear invitation for the Church to resist ableist assumptions and to reimagine perfection through the lens of community, vulnerability and divine embrace.

Disability as punishment and exclusion

The earliest explicit connection between disability and divine action in the Bible appears in Genesis 19.11, where the men of Sodom are struck with blindness after attempting to assault the divine visitors in Lot's home. The text reads: 'And they struck with blindness the men who were at the door of the house, both small and great, so that they were unable to find the door.' Blindness here is not explored as a human condition, nor is compassion offered; instead, it functions as a divine weapon, a means of halting violence. The act dehumanizes blindness by stripping it of any personal or embodied context, making it purely punitive.

This theme only further deepens in Exodus 4.11, when Moses objects to his prophetic calling by citing his speech impediment. God responds:

'Who gives speech to mortals? Who makes them mute or deaf, seeing or blind? Is it not I, the LORD?' While this verse affirms divine sovereignty over all bodily states, it also reflects a world in which difference is not neutral, but suspect, where physical or sensory variation is presented as originating from divine design, yet is most visible when it signals human resistance or deficiency.

A further intensification occurs in Deuteronomy 28, part of the blessings and curses discourse tied to Israel's covenantal obedience. Verse 29 states: 'You shall grope about at noon as blind people grope in darkness.' Here the punishment is not merely metaphorical; it reflects a theological worldview in which blindness, madness and confusion of heart (v. 28) are divine responses to unfaithfulness. These are not neutral conditions of human embodiment; they are curses, inflicted conditions that signify distance from divine favour.

This theology of retributive embodiment, where the body bears the marks of covenantal violation, saturates so much of Israel's collective imagination. It is not coincidental that the Hebrew word for impurity (*ṭum'ah*) often overlaps with language used for disease, blemish and exclusion. In this schema, the disabled body is not merely marked; it is marked off, pushed to the periphery of the sacred community.

The Book of Psalms, frequently used liturgically to express repentance and divine supplication, reinforces this connection between sin and physical affliction. Psalm 38.3–5 laments: 'There is no soundness in my flesh because of your indignation; there is no health in my bones because of my sin. For my iniquities have gone over my head ... My wounds grow foul and fester because of my foolishness.' Here, the body is a moral register. Physical suffering is read as a sign of divine displeasure and moral failing.

This dynamic is codified most explicitly in the Holiness Code of Leviticus. Leviticus 21.16–23 outlines strict requirements for priests, declaring that no man with a 'blemish' may offer the bread of God: 'He shall not come near to offer the food of his God. He may eat the food of his God, of the most holy as well as of the holy. But he shall not come near the curtain or approach the altar.' Blemishes listed include lameness, blindness, disfigurement and crushed testicles. The exclusion is not personal, it is theological, based on the symbolic order of sacred space. Priests, as representative of divine wholeness, must themselves be whole.

While this passage may appear merely ritualistic, its implications are far-reaching. The logic is not that disabled people are sinful, but that their bodies symbolize brokenness in a system obsessed with purity, order and perfection.

Even Leviticus 19.14, often cited as a protective text, 'You shall not revile the deaf or put a stumbling-block before the blind', does not actually affirm the personhood of disabled individuals. Rather, its emphasis lies in warning the able-bodied observer not to offend God's justice. The blind person remains passive, their dignity inferred only indirectly. The Levitical law in this context becomes less about inclusion and more about restraint, looking to protect rather than to necessarily empower.

The cumulative effect of these texts is the construction of disability not merely as a condition but as a sign of failure, of curse and of divine wrath. The disabled person becomes a theologically fraught figure, their body inscribed with meanings that have more to do with covenantal drama than with lived experience.

These portrayals were not just confined to ancient Israel. As the early Church engaged these texts, they inherited their symbolic grammar. Inherited too was a deep ambiguity; whether disability was consequence of sin or a mystery of divine providence, whether it was barrier to sacred participation or a vehicle for divine revelation. Directly responding to this ambiguity, as we will discover, is central to any theological attempt to reclaim disability from the margins of Scripture.

Disability and lineage: the case of Meribbaal

Among the few explicitly named disabled figures in the Hebrew Bible is Meribbaal, more commonly known by the redacted name Mephibosheth, the son of Jonathan and grandson of King Saul. His story, scattered across 2 Samuel, provides one of the most striking illustrations of how disability intersects with lineage, political vulnerability and theological marginalization in the biblical narrative.

According to 2 Samuel 4.4, Meribbaal became disabled when his nurse fled with him following the news of Saul and Jonathan's deaths at Mount Gilboa: 'His nurse picked him up and fled; and, in her haste to flee, it happened that he fell and became lame.' The text is stark. His disability is not congenital but acquired, the result of trauma, both personal and political. His impairment marks the end of an era, a dynastic rupture and the vulnerability of Saul's household in the face of David's rise.

In 2 Samuel 9, David seeks to show *ḥesed*, understood as covenant loyalty or steadfast love, for the sake of his deceased friend Jonathan. Upon discovering that a descendant still lives, David restores to Meribbaal the lands of Saul and invites him to dine regularly at the royal table.

The text reads: 'Mephibosheth lived in Jerusalem, for he always ate at the king's table. Now he was lame in both his feet' (2 Samuel 9.13). Despite this act of restoration, the final sentence still draws attention again to his disability. It is not forgotten, nor is it incidental. Its effect is still *othering*.

The politics of naming

Names in the Hebrew Bible are deeply symbolic, often reflecting identity, theology or divine intention. The original name Meribbaal combines *merib* (possibly meaning 'advocate' or 'contender') with *Baal*, the name of a Canaanite storm god. This name would have carried political-religious overtones during the monarchy, as Baal worship was a persistent issue in Israelite religion. By the time of the Deuteronomistic historians, writing centuries later in the exilic or post-exilic period, references to Baal were systematically removed or altered in the biblical text. Thus, Meribbaal becomes Mephibosheth, with *bosheth* meaning 'shame' or 'disgrace'.

This renaming is theologically charged. The suppression of Baal's name was part of Israel's effort to assert monotheism and purify its historical memory. But in this instance, it also transfers shame to the person of Meribbaal, who is already marked by bodily impairment and dynastic failure, for the change of name from Meribbaal to Mephibosheth ends up performing a double function, namely religious correction and personal diminishment.

Lo-Debar: the geography of marginalization

Meribbaal is introduced as living in Lo-Debar, a location whose name means 'no pasture' or 'no word'. Both translations are symbolically resonant. 'No pasture' suggests barrenness, a place of scarcity and exile, far from the abundance and status of Jerusalem. 'No word' on the other hand implies silence, absence of revelation or relationship. In either case, Lo-Debar becomes a place of marginalization, fitting for a character whose body, lineage and name have been relegated to the theological and political sidelines.

David's act of welcoming Meribbaal to his table might seem redemptive, but it is deeply ambiguous. Meribbaal is treated with kindness but also infantilized. He is not given a voice in the narrative; he is spoken about, not with. His presence at the table is framed less as a restoration of agency than as a fulfilment of David's oath. Some scholars, like Walter Brueggemann, have suggested that this 'hospitality' may also serve to neutralize a potential political threat.[4] The royal table becomes both a site of honour and a tool of surveillance.

Disability, dependence and dignity

Throughout these texts, Meribbaal's disability is not simply physical, it is narrative. It functions as a marker of political impotence, dynastic failure and theological ambiguity. Though he receives David's protection, he remains dependent, vulnerable and, most crucially, *unrepaired*. Unlike the many healed figures in the Gospels, Meribbaal is never cured. His disability remains part of his identity, an unresolved tension in a narrative that otherwise privileges strength, lineage and divine favour.

His story invites us to consider the complex ways in which disability is framed in Scripture, not merely as personal tragedy, but as a symbol of historical transition, political uncertainty and theological marginality. It also compels us to interrogate the assumptions that link bodily difference with shame, passivity and dependence, for disability disrupts both the illusion of self-sufficiency and the myth of independence, reminding us that all bodies, both disabled and enabled, are vulnerable.

Meribbaal's life, then, is not only a testimony to survival but a theological challenge; that we recognize the dignity in dependence, the agency in silence, and sacredness of the disabled body never as a site of shame but as a vessel of covenantal memory.

Disability as spiritual deficiency

The prophet Isaiah frequently uses the language of disability to critique Israel's religious failures. In Isaiah 6.9–10, God commands the prophet to declare: 'Keep listening, but do not comprehend; keep looking, but do not understand. Make the mind of this people dull, and stop their ears, and shut their eyes.' Here, spiritual blindness and deafness are cast as divinely imposed judgements, rendering the people impervious to repentance and renewal. Disability becomes the medium through which divine alienation is expressed.

This metaphorical pattern recurs in Jeremiah 5.21, where the prophet rebukes the people: 'Hear this, O foolish and senseless people, who have eyes, but do not see, who have ears, but do not hear.' In these texts, physical impairments are not conditions to be lived with, but symptoms of theological blindness, ethical confusion and hardened hearts.

The hope of reversal and its problems

The prophets do not stop at diagnosis; they also imagine a future of divine healing and renewal. One of the most cited passages is Isaiah 35.5–6:

> Then the eyes of the blind shall be opened,
>   and the ears of the deaf unstopped;
>   then the lame shall leap like a deer,
> and the tongue of the speechless sing for joy.

This vision's purpose is to articulate a profound eschatological hope, a return to wholeness, joy and embodied freedom. Yet this very hope raises troubling theological questions. If the marks of salvation are expressed through the undoing of blindness, deafness and lameness, then disabled bodies are implicitly rendered incompatible with God's restored order and I am left wondering what it says about God if God's kingdom turns out to be an ableist kingdom where bodies such as mine are continually undone or rejected.

In Isaiah 42.6–7, the Servant of the Lord is appointed 'as a covenant to the people, a light to the nations, to open the eyes that are blind, to bring out the prisoners from the dungeon, and from the prison those who sit in darkness.' While this passage has often been read as a mission of justice and liberation, it once again roots divine activity in the eradication of disabled conditions, blindness as captivity, sightedness as freedom.

These images resonate powerfully in Christian theology, especially when Jesus appropriates this Isaianic mission in Luke 4.18–19:

> The Spirit of the Lord is upon me,
> because he has anointed me
> to bring good news to the poor.
> He has sent me to proclaim release to the captives
> and recovery of sight to the blind ...

Jesus' self-identification with this mission underscores the continuity between prophetic and messianic expectations, but it also risks further reaffirming an ableist vision of salvation, one where impairment is something to be undone, not dignified.

The Suffering Servant and theological scapegoating

Nowhere is the metaphorical weight of disability more theologically intense than in Isaiah 52.13—53.12, the fourth of the so-called Servant Songs. The Servant is described as 'despised and rejected by others; a man of suffering and acquainted with infirmity; ... one from whom others hide their faces' (Isa. 53.3). He has 'no form or majesty that we should look at him, nothing in his appearance that we should desire him' (v. 2). These are not merely poetic flourishes; they are embodied descriptions of disfigurement, estrangement and humiliation.

The Servant is, to all appearances, disabled. He is 'wounded for our transgressions, crushed for our iniquities' (v. 5). His suffering is not accidental but vicarious: 'upon him was the punishment that made us whole.' As such, he becomes the theological scapegoat, absorbing into his body the punishment meant for others. It did not require a huge leap of the imagination for early Christians to appropriate this image and interpret onto it the suffering and death of Jesus. This in turn became the foundation for theories of *substitutionary atonement*: the belief that Christ bore the punishment for humanity's sins in his suffering body.

In patristic and medieval theology, this suffering was not abstract; it was vividly embodied. As Athanasius wrote, Christ 'became what we are, that he might make us what he is.'[5] The emphasis on physical disfigurement and humiliation, his torn flesh, wounded hands, pierced side, became symbols of divine love. Yet this model also created a theological template in which bodily suffering, especially visible suffering, was valorized not in its own right but because it pointed beyond itself to glory. Suffering was holy because it was temporary and transformed.

For disabled people, this logic is double-edged. On the one hand, the suffering Christ affirms that God enters into bodily weakness. But on the other, the disabled body is only theologically meaningful if it mirrors Christ's suffering on the way to being healed, perfected or transcended. Nancy Eiesland, in her seminal book *The Disabled God*, draws attention to the inherent problems that surface when this framework casts disabled people as the recipients of charity or the objects of moral lessons, rather than full participants in the life of faith.[6] Disability, in this framework, becomes a metaphor, often for sin, sometimes for sanctity, but rarely for sacred presence in its own right.

Christian interpreters, particularly in patristic and medieval theology, have identified this Servant with Christ. While this has profound Christological significance, it has also had unintended consequences for disability theology. The disabled, disfigured body is rendered salvific, but only because it is ultimately transcended. The suffering body is a necessary intermediary, not an enduring reality. Deborah Creamer, in her book *Disability and Christian Theology: Embodied Limits and Constructive Possibilities*, critiques theological frameworks that all too easily valorize suffering as the central or only lens through which disability can be understood. Rather, she argues for alternative approaches that recognize the fullness and complexity of disabled lives, apart from suffering or redemptive pain. She does not have a problem identifying Christ with disability; what she questions is the theological logic that sees suffering as the only way disability can be said to be of consequence.[7]

When the prophetic imagination uses disability to signify spiritual failure or eschatological reversal, it risks reinforcing a theological binary, that only the healed are holy and the impaired are not yet redeemed. The metaphors may not target disabled individuals, but they nonetheless shape perceptions, casting disabled embodiment as lack, loss or limit.

This theological marginalization is further exacerbated because, unlike other oppressed groups (the poor, widows, orphans and strangers), disabled people in the prophetic tradition are not consistently defended or centred. They appear as tropes rather than as subjects. The prophetic vision of renewal, therefore, becomes double-edged: it promises liberation, but all too often at the cost of disabled identity.

The persistent association between disability and divine judgement in Scripture did not remain a static theological idea; it evolved into a deep structural feature of Christian tradition. This association, inherited from the prophetic imagination and the purity codes of Leviticus, profoundly shaped how the Church interpreted suffering, salvation, embodiment and perfection.

Healing and the messianic identity of Jesus

The Gospels reinforce this pattern by positioning Jesus' miracles of healing as signs of his messianic identity. In Matthew 11.4–5, Jesus responds to John the Baptist's disciples: 'Go and tell John what you hear and see:

the blind receive their sight, the lame walk, the lepers are cleansed, the deaf hear, the dead are raised, and the poor have good news brought to them.'

In this catalogue of miracles we hear clear echoes of Isaiah's eschatological vision (Isa. 35), linking Jesus explicitly to the fulfilment of prophetic hopes. Healing becomes, in this context, not merely an act of compassion; it becomes a theological declaration that the kingdom of God is arriving, and it is arriving through the erasure of physical and sensory impairments.

In narrative after narrative, the pattern holds: the blind man in John 9, the paralytic lowered through the roof in Mark 2, the woman with a haemorrhage in Luke 8, the deaf man in Mark 7. In each case, the moment of healing is not private or incidental; it is public, performative and symbolic. The healing confirms Jesus' power and divine authority. Thus the healing narratives in the Gospels are Christological first and foremost and not anthropological, for though they reveal who Jesus is, they are not so interested in who the disabled person is.

While these stories affirm God's concern for the suffering, they often do so in a way that marginalizes the lived experience of disabled people. The person's body is made acceptable through transformation; the community is reassured that difference is only temporary. This framing raises a difficult theological question: if perfection is defined by the removal of impairment, what then is the spiritual status of unhealed bodies?

The theological problem of perfection

This question strikes at the heart of Christian anthropology. If bodily wholeness is equated with spiritual wholeness, then disability becomes a problem to be fixed. The Church, in such a framework, becomes the agent of cure, whether through prayer, sacrament or charity, rather than the community of belonging where diverse bodies are already bearers of the divine image.

Such a view flattens the complexity of disabled life into a binary; broken or healed, cursed or blessed, fixed or failed. It leaves little room for those whose impairments are chronic, non-healable or integral to their identity. The problem therefore does not belong with the disabled body but rather with a social and ecclesial imagination that cannot make room for such a body. Such a view therefore becomes a complete failure of theological imagination.

The consequence of this failure of theological imagination is that disabled people are often positioned as objects of divine intervention rather than subjects of divine presence. Our bodies are talked about, prayed over or used as sermon illustrations, but not often received as loci of revelation, theological depth or sanctity in their own right. This has directly influenced our theology of sacred heritage over the intervening centuries. I will be exploring this in greater focus in the fifth chapter.

The erasure of flesh, the distortion of blame

Throughout this chapter I have sought to uncover how disability, within much of Christian thought and practice, has been systematically stripped of agency and burdened with projections. Rather than being understood as a lived and diverse experience of embodiment, disability has too often been reduced to metaphor, symbol or spiritual lesson, rarely granted the dignity of personhood, let alone accountability or theological voice. We are spoken about, rarely with; blamed without being believed; pitied without being empowered. Our bodies and minds become canvases onto which the Church paints its fears, fantasies and failures.

In this process, agency is not only denied, it is displaced. We are either rendered passive recipients of charity or warnings of divine judgement, while simultaneously being excluded from moral or theological complexity. Even sin, suffering and sanctity are differently apportioned: the disabled figure is somehow always either too responsible (for their condition) or not responsible enough (for their voice to count). This theological double-bind sustains an ableist imagination in which disability is either a problem to be solved or a spectacle to be endured, never a vocation to be lived or a perspective to be honoured.

Yet such distortions do not emerge in a vacuum. They are nurtured by the images and assumptions that shape the Church's understanding of God. And here we must ask harder questions still: what kind of God is reflected in these narratives? What vision of divinity undergirds the refusal to see disabled bodies as sacred, complex and capable? What happens when the God we imagine looks only like the powerful, the whole, the unmarked?

The next chapter turns to these very questions, beginning with the anthropomorphic portrayals of God in Scripture, especially in the Hebrew Bible, and asking how these representations have been used to enshrine able-bodiedness, aesthetic dominance and cognitive control as divine attributes. We will explore how such portrayals have shaped an exclusionary theological anthropology and consider how re-reading these texts through a disability lens might reveal a very different God: one whose image is not marred by disability but revealed through it.

Notes

1 Nancy L. Eiesland, *The Disabled God: Toward a Liberatory Theology of Disability* (Nashville, TN: Abingdon, 1994), pp. 31–48.

2 Thomas Aquinas, *Summa Theologica, Supplementum*, Q. 85, Art. 1.

3 Stanley Hauerwas and John Swinton both challenge the assumption that perfection in Scripture aligns with health or normative ability. See Stanley Hauerwas, *Suffering Presence: Theological Reflections on Medicine, the Mentally Handicapped, and the Church* (Notre Dame, IN: University of Notre Dame Press, 1986); Brian Brock and John Swinton, *Disability in the Christian Tradition: A Reader* (Grand Rapids, MI: Eerdmans, 2012); and John Swinton, *Becoming Friends of Time: Disability, Timefullness, and Gentle Discipleship* (Waco, TX: Baylor University Press, 2016).

4 Walter Brueggemann, *First and Second Samuel* (Louisville, KY: John Knox Press, 1990), pp. 265–94.

5 Athanasius, *On the Incarnation*, trans. John Behr (Yonkers, NY: St Vladimir's Seminary Press, 2011), §54.

6 Eiesland, *The Disabled God*, pp. 49–68.

7 Deborah Beth Creamer, *Disability and Christian Theology: Embodied Limits and Constructive Possibilities* (Oxford: Oxford University Press, 2009), pp. 75–92.

4

God with a Body Like Mine? Anthropomorphism, Ableism and the Disabled Reader of Scripture

The Scriptures are rich in metaphor, and among the most persistent is the anthropomorphizing of God. From the Garden of Eden to the Psalms of David, God is depicted as walking, seeing, smelling, hearing, touching, writing, sitting, breathing and even laughing. These bodily images are not literal, but they shape the theological imagination profoundly. They give the ineffable a face, the transcendent a hand, the eternal a voice. Such imagery anchors divine activity in human experience, rendering the mysteries of God relationally and narratively intelligible.

As theologian Terence Fretheim observes, the Old Testament exhibits a theology of divine embodiment, wherein God's presence is rendered in profoundly physical terms, communicating nearness and relationality. This embodiment is not incidental; it is integral to how Israel understands God's engagement with the world. God is not merely transcendent, aloof or disembodied, but intimately involved in creation and history through embodied acts of justice, mercy and covenant.[1] Thus Israel's testimony manifests God as a real character with real bodily capacities, who acts decisively in time and space. These depictions serve as rhetorical devices through which the community's faith experience is articulated and remembered, giving voice to divine action in the syntax of human embodiment.

Anthropomorphism is not only literary convenience; it is theological conviction. The God who speaks, walks, listens and smells sacrifices is a God who is profoundly invested in the material world. The Old Testament therefore consistently portrays a God whose relational fidelity is expressed through concrete action rather than abstract metaphysics, so that the bodily depictions of God serve not to define God's form but to narrate God's involvement with human suffering, liberation and covenantal belonging.

This covenantal belonging indicates a regular, almost domestic intimacy between Creator and creation and offers a theologically rich insight because it emphasizes several profound aspects of God's relationship to the world.

In many ancient Near Eastern religious traditions, gods were distant, capricious or hostile. By contrast, the image of God walking in the garden suggests divine immanence; God is not only transcendent and sovereign but also present, relational and near. This presence is habitual, not episodic: God's description, for example, as one who walks, implies a routine, perhaps even a divine delight in creation.

God is therefore not presented as a detached observer but as an engaged partner in covenantal relationship. John Goldingay emphasizes that the biblical motif of God 'walking' in the garden is not just a picture of divine movement but also intimates a closeness, warmth and familiarity akin to the domestic sphere. In other words, God's walking is not a distant or abstract activity; it underscores an intimate, everyday engagement with creation similar to the intimacy found in family or household life.[2] Thus God's proximity is revealed not as intimidating but familiar, suggesting that communion between the divine and human was always God's original intention.

Walking is a bodily, physical act. When God is imagined walking, the metaphor invites us to think of divine–human interaction in tangible, bodily terms. It aligns with the Old Testament's consistent use of the body to signify real, enacted relationships, not abstract theology.

So if God walks in the same space as humanity, it affirms the dignity of the created world and the human body. The garden is not a playground for divine manipulation but a shared space of encounter. This portrays creation as hospitable to divine presence, not in need of escape or denial.

Importantly, the walking of God in Genesis 3.8 is followed by God's question, 'Where are you?' The intimacy is disrupted. Thus, this act becomes a symbol of divine faithfulness in the face of human failure, and it inaugurates the long biblical theme of God seeking out humanity despite estrangement.

Goldingay's insight draws attention to the core biblical conviction that God desires relational nearness, embodied presence and routine intimacy with creation, not power over it, but companionship within it. But the metaphor is not without serious issues.

For disabled readers, these images, when not interpreted carefully, can also seriously wound. When God is repeatedly imagined in able-bodied terms, walking upright, speaking with fluency, seeing with clarity, reaching with strength, divine embodiment risks becoming exclusionary. The body of God, as imagined in Scripture, all too easily can then reflect normative assumptions that may alienate those whose bodies do not conform to those ideals. In a world where divine agency is consistently described through normative sensory and motor functions, the absence of alternative bodily representations has contributed to theologies that risk sanctifying able-bodiedness as divine.

Claus Westermann draws attention to the persistence of anthropomorphic imagery in the Hebrew Bible not as a primitive relic but as a theological strategy; that the God of Israel is imagined with human attributes in order to express divine involvement, agency and relationality.[3] This perspective helps illuminate how bodily metaphors communicate proximity and divine action but also opens up critical questions about which human bodies are being invoked, and which are left out. If divine walking, touching and seeing are always performed through able-bodied frames, then those outside those norms may come to view themselves as less proximate to the divine image. If we are said to be made in the image and likeness of God and yet all the anthropomorphic descriptions of God are those expressed through a normative perspective, then such an image is going to exclude as well as include.

Rolf Jacobson helpfully cautions us against the uncritical perpetuation of such metaphors, noting that they often mirror human ideals more than divine mystery. That is, our theological anthropomorphism can subtly shift from metaphor to model, from poetic device to doctrinal standard. The risk is that the God who walks might inadvertently become the God who only walks, and thus, not the God who crawls, limps, rolls or is carried.[4]

Thus, when engaging with the anthropomorphic tradition in Scripture, while meaningful, we must be alert to the risk that our projections become a vehicle of ableism rather than revelation when left uncritiqued. The metaphors that once bridged the gap between God and humanity may come to inscribe new forms of theological exclusion, rendering some bodies, in this case, disabled bodies spiritually peripheral.

I am therefore seeking to draw attention to the theological and hermeneutical challenges posed by the able-bodied anthropomorphism of God in the Old Testament and how disabled readers engage with these metaphors, how such portrayals can marginalize non-normative embodiments and how the Church might reclaim a more expansive, inclusive vision of the divine body.

A theology attentive to the complexity of embodiment invites the Church to a more nuanced reading of Scripture's anthropomorphisms. As John Goldingay suggests, the Old Testament is not embarrassed by the physicality of God, but neither does it limit God to a single human form.[5] This theological range must now be expanded further, not in contradiction to Scripture, but in continuity with its deeper impulse, the witness to a God who is present, who responds and who moves not in perfection but in faithfulness.

A theology of divine embodiment, attentive to the implications of ableism, calls us to confront the normative power of Scripture's anthropomorphisms and to discern within them both the promise and peril of how God is imagined and who is included in that imagining.

God described in ableist form

We have ascertained that across the Hebrew Scriptures God is presented in vivid anthropomorphic terms and that these metaphors render divine action intelligible in human terms, grounding theology in the lived experience of embodiment. But I have also warned of the risk of reinforcing a normative bodily ideal when read uncritically. Let me offer some specific examples so that we can examine these images a little more closely.

1 *Walking*

In Genesis 3.8, God is heard 'walking in the garden at the time of the evening breeze'. Here we are presented with an image which portrays God as mobile, moving through creation in a rhythm familiar to able-bodied human beings. The image of the walking God evokes divine presence and relational nearness. Yet portraying God as walking may also have the knock-on effect of subtly elevating one mode of movement as normative, thus excluding those whose bodies do not walk but roll, limp, crawl or remain still. This could then assimilate itself into an unconscious bias as we further engage with characters in the Bible who are presented as lame.

2 *Seeing and hearing*

Psalm 34.15 proclaims, 'The eyes of the LORD are on the righteous, and his ears are open to their cry.' Likewise, in 2 Chronicles 7.15, God declares, 'Now my eyes will be open and my ears attentive to the prayer that is made in this place.' The purpose of these metaphors surely is to convey to the reader the God of attentiveness, responsiveness and divine justice, that God *sees* the suffering of his people and *hears* their cry, and through this *seeing* and *hearing* begins the history of salvation. Yet because divine sensory engagement is described through human experience of sight and hearing, which are the predominant senses in cultures shaped by able-bodied experience, they have the potential to marginalize or ignore completely alternative modes of perception. It also risks the projected perception that those who are visually impaired also lack attentiveness and responsiveness, that they are sensorily lacking.

3 Speaking and breathing

Genesis 1.3 narrates, 'Then God said, "Let there be light,"' inaugurating creation through speech. In Genesis 2.7, God breathes the breath of life into the human, animating dust into being. These acts depict divine agency through voice and breath, acts of utterance and respiration that are profoundly embodied. As I will discuss in greater depth in a later chapter, God's divine breath is not merely symbolic but represents for us God's life-giving and sustaining presence. However, these images can also all too easily imply a theological idealization of fluent speech and independent respiration, subtly excluding those who communicate differently or who breathe with assistance.

4 Hands and arms

In Exodus 6.6 and Deuteronomy 4.34, God acts with a 'mighty hand' and 'outstretched arm'. These are images of power, protection and deliverance. They communicate the strength of God to liberate, particularly in the context of Israel's exodus from oppression. Walter Brueggemann interprets the outstretched arm as 'an idiom of covenantal fidelity manifest in historical rescue.'[6] Yet the persistent use of arm and hand imagery may reinforce a narrow standard of bodily agency and physical capability.

5 Sitting and writing

Isaiah 6.1 envisions God 'sitting on a throne, high and lofty', while Exodus 31.18 and Daniel 5.5 describe God writing with a finger. The enthroned God evokes sovereignty and order; the writing God communicates clarity, authority and record. These images present God as both judge and scribe. Christoph Levin, in his book *Re-reading the*

Scriptures, draws our attention to the fact that God who is described as one who writes equates with the God who communicates covenant and commands with precision and permanence.[7] But once again, it is all too easy for these metaphors which valorize modes of bodily control – sitting upright, writing legibly – to become aligned with ableist assumptions of dignity and intellect.

6 Smelling, touching and feeling

In Genesis 8.21, God 'smelt the pleasing odour' of Noah's sacrifice. In Genesis 6.6, God is 'grieved ... to his heart,' and in Hosea 11.8, God cries, 'My heart recoils within me.' Psalm 2.4 presents God as laughing. These metaphors display divine emotion, sensory engagement and affective capacity. They portray God not as impassible but responsive, vulnerable and moved, a God who is deeply affected by human suffering. Still, such images often assume normative bodily faculties and emotional legibility, framing divine relationality through able-bodied and neurotypical forms of response.

Summary

Each of these metaphors is not inherently harmful. They can evoke intimacy, agency and care. Indeed, they reflect a deep theology of divine relationality, grounded in Israel's embodied experience of covenant. However, their cumulative effect often betrays and defaults to an able-bodied norm, that of the God who walks upright, sees clearly, speaks eloquently and moves with power. The embodied divine is consistently represented through modes of capacity and sensory engagement that align with dominant bodily expectations. Disability, by contrast, is rarely integrated into divine representation and is more often linked with brokenness, punishment or the need for healing. The result is a theological imagination that, while rich in embodied metaphor, risks excluding many human bodies from recognition within the *imago Dei*.

The theological cost of bodily normativity

For disabled readers, for those whose own bodies may not walk, speak, see or move in these conventional ways, this imagery can alienate. God is not just other; God is normatively other. The divine body, as imagined in Scripture, implicitly reinforces ideals of strength, symmetry and functionality.

This creates several theological tensions:

- ***Imago Dei* dissonance.** If God is repeatedly figured in able-bodied form, does that imply disabled bodies reflect the divine image less clearly?
- **Access to God.** When divine presence is imagined through senses and movements that some people do not possess or experience in typical ways, is access to God mediated through an ableist lens?
- **Exclusion from theological agency.** If God's authority is expressed through physical might, visual perception or speech, what happens to those whose power, perception or communication do not conform to these norms?

The ambiguity of metaphor and the need for hermeneutical expansion

It is crucial as we journey through this book to remember that these anthropomorphisms are metaphors. They are not meant to describe God's essence, but to evoke God's action and presence in human terms. However, metaphor does not occur in a vacuum. Metaphors form and deform theology. When repeated without critique, they solidify norms and marginalize difference.

Disabled theologians have consistently called for a hermeneutic of suspicion toward Scripture's bodily assumptions and a hermeneutic of reclamation that finds resonance in overlooked or ambiguous images. This invitation opens up new readings of Old Testament anthropomorphism:

- The God who smells 'the pleasing odour' (Gen. 8.21) can be interpreted as the God who is sensorially engaged in non-visual ways.
- The God whose 'heart recoils' (Hos. 11.8) becomes the God who is emotionally vulnerable.

- The God who appears not in earthquake or fire but in 'a sound of sheer silence' (1 Kings 19.12) becomes the God who defies the sensory hierarchy of volume and visibility.
- God's breath (Gen. 2.7) is now interpreted through the lens of assisted breathing, ventilatory dependence or respiratory precarity.
- God's outstretched arm evokes not just strength, but the extended hand of interdependence.
- The walking God is imagined not striding, but rolling, limping or pausing.
- Divine speech now includes AAC (augmentative and alternative communication), silence or echolalia.

Such readings are not whimsical. They are theological acts of survival and subversion. They expand the metaphoric range of Scripture to affirm disabled lives as fully within the *imago Dei*.

Moreover, some anthropomorphic portrayals, particularly the wounded God of Isaiah 53, disrupt ableist patterns. The 'Suffering Servant' is described in terms of rejection, disfigurement and pain. While this passage has historically been interpreted Christologically, it offers space for imagining divine solidarity with bodily divergence.

Toward a breaking hermeneutic of divine embodiment

I am therefore calling on the Church to adopt a hermeneutic of divine embodiment, to not merely reinterpret old texts but to interrogate the assumptions beneath them and to ask the questions: what bodies are imagined when God is described? What bodies are excluded, implicitly or explicitly, from those images? How might the multiplicity of human embodiments illuminate rather than distort our understanding of God?

This hermeneutic sets out to resist the idolatry of the normate God. It insists that divine mystery exceed ableist constructions. And it honours the truth that God is encountered in disabled lives, not as pity or test, but as presence.

The challenge of divine anthropomorphism is not its human language, but its uncritical attachment to normative embodiment. Disabled people have the theological right, and responsibility, to claim God with a body like ours: limited, vulnerable, glorious.

In doing so, we are reclaiming Scripture not as a closed canon of perfection, but as an open space for radical divine–human encounter. The God who walks in the garden also rolls through hospital corridors.

The God who breathes life also breathes through a tracheostomy. The God who sees and hears is encountered in ways that transcend any one sensorium. Such a God is not less divine. Such a God is more real. A God who moves differently. A God whose body, like ours, reveals grace.

Unmasking the idol of the perfect God

Throughout this chapter, I have traced how anthropomorphic representations of God, fashioned in the image of strength, wholeness, beauty and sovereign control, have subtly and persistently underwritten ableist theologies. When God is imagined exclusively as omnipotent, physically unblemished and emotionally unassailable, we inherit not the God revealed in Christ crucified, but an idol shaped by the projections of the dominant and the non-disabled. The consequences are not abstract. They form the bedrock of ecclesial assumptions that cast disability as a problem to be overcome, a deviation to be corrected or a symbol of spiritual deficiency.

Such theological constructions do not simply distort our view of God; they distort our view of what it means to be human. By severing divine image-bearing from woundedness, dependence or neurodivergence, the Church has too often silenced those whose very bodies and minds reveal a different kind of sacred truth. But when we begin to dismantle the idol of the flawless God, we encounter a richer theological anthropology: one in which vulnerability is not the enemy of divinity, but its echo; one in which disabled lives are not theological puzzles, but theological witnesses.

This unmasking is essential if we are to confront the next frontier of ableism: how these theologies have shaped not only our doctrines, but our cultural and physical inheritance. In the next chapter, we turn to Christian heritage, its sacred spaces, relics, rituals and commemorations, to ask how the same ableist logic that shaped our image of God has been inscribed into the very stones, stories and systems of the Church. How has the pursuit of bodily and architectural perfection excluded disabled people from belonging? And what might it mean to reclaim heritage not as static tradition, but as a living archive where disabled memory, resistance and presence speak with prophetic force?

The journey ahead demands courage, imagination and the willingness to listen again, this time, to the voices the Church has too often left outside the frame.

Notes

1 Terence E. Fretheim, *The Suffering of God: An Old Testament Perspective* (Philadelphia, PA: Fortress Press, 1984), pp. 79–106.

2 John Goldingay, *Old Testament Theology*, vol. 1, *Israel's Gospel* (Downers Grove, IL: IVP Academic, 2003), pp. 131–92.

3 Claus Westermann, *Elements of Old Testament Theology* (Atlanta, GA: John Knox Press, 1982), pp. 9–34.

4 Rolf A. Jacobson, introduction in *The Book of Psalms*, ed. Nancy deClaissé-Walford, Rolf A. Jacobson, and Beth LaNeel Tanner, New International Commentary on the Old Testament (Grand Rapids, MI: Eerdmans, 2014), pp. 1–45.

5 Goldingay, *Old Testament Theology*.

6 Walter Brueggemann, *Exodus: Commentary* (Nashville, TN: Abingdon Press, 1994), p. 88.

7 Christoph Levin, *Re-reading the Scriptures: Essays on the Literary History of the Old Testament*, Forschungen zum Alten Testament 87 (Tübingen: Mohr Siebeck, 2013), pp. 245–60.

5

Theoretical Frameworks: Theology, Ableism and Heritage

When we begin to explore the intersection of ableism and heritage through a theological lens, we enter a terrain shaped not only by history, but by what the exclusion's history has failed to name. These exclusions are often embedded in what appears benign: the aesthetics of a stained-glass window, the architectural grandeur of a church nave, the rhythm of a liturgy. The question is not simply whether disabled people have been included in church history or heritage institutions. It is whether our theological constructs, ecclesial spaces and cultural traditions have been formed by the systematic sidelining of disabled bodies and minds.

To address this, we need a framework that is interdisciplinary and disruptive, one that fuses theology, critical disability studies and heritage theory into a lens capable of exposing not only what has been left out, but the assumptions that rendered that exclusion possible. This chapter proposes three such strands: rethinking the body in theology, unmasking ableism as a system and reimagining heritage as contested memory.

Rethinking the body in theology

Christian theology has long borne the influence of Graeco-Roman ideals that exalt symmetry, strength and perfection. These ideals have subtly shaped ecclesial life, casting the 'fit' body as a symbol of divine order and reducing disability to affliction. The Pauline metaphor of the body of Christ, too often flattened into a symbol of institutional functionality, has obscured a deeper call to radical inclusion.

Nancy Eiesland's *The Disabled God* disrupts this pattern: 'Our bodies participate in the imago Dei, not in spite of our impairments and contingencies, but through them.'[1] For Eiesland, this is not a call for inclusion alone, but a theological reorientation. Her depiction of a disabled God, wounded yet glorified, calls on the Church to see disabled bodies not as problems but as sites of divine disclosure.

This reorientation is deepened by disability theologians such as John Swinton, Thomas Reynolds and Sharon V. Betcher, who insist that theology must emerge from lived, embodied experience, for disability is not a lack or a defect, but a mode of being that unveils for us the relational nature of all humanity. Community, then, is not built on a shared strength but our mutual vulnerability, for Christ did not come as a reflection of the idealized norm, but as the one who was wounded. If our icons and liturgies exclude the broken and dependent, our worship becomes malformed.

Liberation theology furthers this critique by aligning theology with the margins. Gustavo Gutiérrez's 'preferential option for the poor'[2] challenges us to centre those whose bodies challenge norms of productivity and independence. Lisa D. Powell extends this, arguing that justice must include 'the corporeally excluded'.[3] Inclusion is not enough; the theological centre must be redrawn.

Both of these insights expose a theological fault line. If holiness has been conflated with perfection, and agency with autonomy, then the gospel calls us to reconfigure both. Theology must not merely accommodate disabled people; it must be remade in the image of the disabled God.

Unmasking ableism as a system

Ableism is more than personal bias, it shapes perception itself; it informs us who is real, who is visible and who is grievable. In ecclesial life, ableism is expressed through inaccessible buildings, liturgies that privilege speech and cognition, and theological norms that render some bodies as spiritually lesser.

It is a system that rewards self-sufficiency, marginalizes dependence and treats non-normative expression as pathology. The result is a Church that often unconsciously replicates the world's exclusions, despite professing the hospitality of Christ.

Amos Yong warns us that we all need to attend to the ways in which the 'normal' has been baptized in our theologies and the 'abnormal' demonized.[4] Theology itself is implicated in constructing exclusionary norms. To serve liberation, it must unlearn habits of ableist reasoning and listen to voices it has too often silenced.

Accessibility is not charity but justice, for disability brings into view what is true for us all: that to be human is to be limited, and to need one another. A theology that ignores this truth risks idolizing invulnerability and misrepresenting grace. To speak of justice rather than accommodation is to call the Church not merely to include, but to repent and reform.

God is encountered not within the temple's flawless structure but in the lamentations of those whom the temple has pushed aside. This is not a marginal claim but a reorientation of theological vision. Christ is encountered not at the inaccessible altar, but in the one kept from reaching it.

Rethinking heritage: what gets remembered, and who decides?

Heritage is not merely an inert repository of the past; rather it is an active cultural process that validates some historical narratives while marginalizing or silencing others. In ecclesial contexts, heritage often defaults to the monumental and pristine, stained glass unbroken, relics revered; but whose stories are missing from these narratives?

Mitchell and Snyder's concept of 'narrative prosthesis' reveals how disability often appears only as something to be corrected, healed or erased.[5] Disabled people are rarely represented as full participants in sacred memory. The question is not whether they appear, but how they are portrayed and what their marginalization signifies.

The architectural inaccessibility of churches, the sanitized sainthood of hagiography, and the absence of disabled voices in ecclesial storytelling all testify to a heritage shaped through an ableist lens. Remembering properly involves acknowledging the wounds of the past. A memory that redeems does not worship what has been but rather faces its omissions in order to create an opportunity for healing and genuine understanding. A heritage that forgets disabled lives is not only incomplete, but also theologically deficient. It forgets the wounds of Christ and the resurrection that did not erase his scars.

What emerges from these three strands is not an inclusion checklist, but a theological transformation. The body is no longer idealized but inhabited. Ableism is unmasked as a structuring power, not a minor prejudice. Heritage is revealed as a contested space, not a neutral record.

This is not about fitting disabled people into existing ecclesial forms, it is about reimagining those forms from their perspective. To achieve this, we need to rethink our understanding of boundaries. Instead of perceiving them as obstacles, we need to view them as potential gateways to grace. From this perspective, limitations then serve as valuable theological insights rather than mere shortcomings that demand fixing, and the disabled body becomes not merely an object of theology but a source of theological insight. Heritage must become a witness not to permanence, but to grace manifest in fragility.

To remember the body of Christ rightly is to remember the glorious and the wounded, the silenced and the re-membered. It is to affirm, with St Paul, that 'the members of the body that seem to be weaker are indispensable' (1 Cor. 12.22). It is to make of our theology, our heritage and our churches a home for all flesh.

Ableism as theological heresy

Let me name it plainly: ableism is not just a social or cultural problem; it is a theological one. And more than that, it is a heresy. It distorts our understanding of who God is, who we are and what it means to be saved. It preaches a false gospel: one that equates bodily perfection with divine favour, that mistakes independence for holiness and that sees vulnerability as failure. When this logic infiltrates our theology, our worship and our imaginations, it does more than marginalize disabled people, it misrepresents the very heart of the gospel.

Ableism imposes a distorted hierarchy upon bodies and minds, equating strength, productivity and coherence with the *imago Dei*. Within this framework, God is envisioned as an idealized abstraction, omnipotent, untouched and inherently able-bodied. Sharon V. Betcher cautions that such a conception does not reflect the Christ revealed in the Gospels but rather an idol shaped by societal norms, reinforcing autonomy and economic utility as theological virtues. This vision prioritizes control over incarnation, distancing divinity from the embodied vulnerability that Christ himself embraced.[6]

Such distortions lead to a salvific vision where healing becomes the prerequisite for belonging, and heaven is imagined as a place scrubbed clean of any bodily difference. What sounds comforting to some becomes, for many disabled people, an existential erasure. Nancy Eiesland named this clearly as 'soteriological eugenics', where salvation functions as the annihilation of disabled identity rather than its redemption.[7] The gospel, if it is to be good news for all, must not promise escape from disability but the recognition of grace within it.

This is why the resurrected Christ matters so deeply. His risen body bears wounds that are not signs of defeat but marks of glory. They are not obstacles to resurrection; they are integral to it. Deborah Creamer's theological insights are so helpful here as they emphasize that human limitations are not merely obstacles to be surpassed but sacred spaces where divine grace is encountered and theological reflection takes root. The crucified and risen Christ embodies this truth, revealing that vulnerability is not opposed to divinity but is, in fact, its very expression.[8]

Neglecting this reality has implications that extend well beyond theological discourse. The pervasive influence of able-bodied norms has not only shaped ecclesial practices but has also informed the very architecture and sensory expectations of worship. John Hull, in his book *In the Beginning There Was Darkness: A Blind Person's Conversations with the Bible*, highlights how Christianity has been moulded into a tradition that prioritizes visual experience, thus reinforcing an implicit hierarchy of perception.[9] The visual reigns supreme: stained glass, printed texts, elevated pulpits, illuminated sanctuaries. Theological metaphors privilege sight – vision as insight, light as truth – while non-visual ways of knowing are neglected. Those who engage with the world through different sensory modes are often unintentionally excluded because theology and liturgy have been calibrated for the dominant gaze.

Lisa D. Powell describes a theological framework in which salvation is closely tied to bodily and cognitive idealism, a perspective that carries profound pastoral and doctrinal implications. For individuals with chronic or degenerative conditions, this emphasis on perfectionism does not extend hope but instead reinforces feelings of inadequacy. It suggests, whether overtly or subtly, that their bodies require correction to be deemed acceptable in the presence of God, distorting the true nature of divine grace and inclusion.[10]

Yet Scripture tells another story. Moses stammered. Jacob limped. Paul's 'thorn in the flesh' was never removed. These biblical witnesses are not perfected icons; they are testimonies to divine power made manifest in human limitation. Their witness contradicts a heritage that glorifies idealized bodies and sanitized saints. Our cathedrals and iconography rarely reflect this truth. Crutches appear only in pre-healing scenes. Aids like hearing devices or white canes are absent. Disability is shown only to be overcome, never to be revered.

Such exclusions communicate more than aesthetic choices; they communicate a theological lie. If holiness is always symmetrical, unblemished and powerful, then there is no room for the real, embodied lives of many faithful people. If our sacred art and stories render disability invisible, we risk building churches that no longer resemble the incarnate Christ.

The call, then, is not to retrofit accessibility into an otherwise complete theology. It is to confess that our theology has been incomplete all along. The disabled body is not a disruption to the Church's holiness; it is its witness. The needs, adaptations and resistances of disabled people are not burdens to be managed but theological gifts that challenge and renew the Church.

To centre disability is not a concession to inclusion, it is a demand for truth. A Church shaped by the crucified and risen Christ must be a Church where wounds are not hidden, where limits are not pathologized, and where all bodies, not just the idealized norm, are understood as a site of divine presence.

Disability theology: the broken body as theological revelation

Disability theology emerged not as an abstract academic development but as a necessary response to the historical failures of Christian thought and practice. In the aftermath of two world wars, the silence surrounding disability in mainstream theology became too conspicuous to ignore. The Church had long spoken of human dignity while misrepresenting or ignoring disabled experience. When it did engage, it often did so in theologically narrow and harmful ways – casting disability as sin's punishment, a metaphor for spiritual brokenness or a prop for miraculous healing. These readings did not merely misrepresent disabled lives; they underwrote cultural exclusion and ecclesial marginalization.

At the heart of these frameworks lay a theological error: the assumption that disability was incompatible with the image of God. This rendered disabled bodies as theological problems to be solved, not as bearers of divine wisdom. The Church's failure to interrogate this assumption did not merely result in pastoral neglect – it distorted core doctrines of creation, incarnation and salvation.

Disability theology arose first as a critique of this distortion and then as a bold reconstruction. It asked disruptive and generative questions: what if disability is not a departure from the *imago Dei*, but a dimension of it? What if our notions of healing and wholeness have been shaped by normative ideals rather than by the gospel? What if God's self-revelation occurs precisely through bodies the world deems broken?

Nancy Eiesland's *The Disabled God* continues to be a crucial work in this field. She presents a vision of the risen Christ – who still bears the scars of crucifixion – that reinterprets divine power from the perspective of disabled embodiment. She writes that in the resurrected Christ, disability is not a mark of sin or merely something to be healed, but rather a defining aspect of identity.[11] Christ's glorified but wounded body becomes the theological site where disabled people can recognize themselves not as objects of pity or healing, but as full participants in the divine image. Eiesland's work radically shifts theological anthropology: God is not distant from disabled flesh, but dwells within it.

This Christological vision has direct ecclesiological implications. If the Church is the body of Christ, then its shape is not normative or perfect, but scarred, interdependent and diverse. Disabled people are not merely to be included, they are indispensable to revealing what the Church *is*. In this body, vulnerability and mutual dependence are not deficits, but signs of grace. The disabled presence is not a challenge to ecclesial identity, but its fulfilment.

Such insights demand a re-examination of Christian heritage. Our sacred memory, expressed in art, architecture, hagiography and tradition, has often reinforced ideals of perfection and strength. Saints are sanitized, sacred spaces are made inaccessible, and fragility is edited out of ecclesial narrative. Eiesland's theology invites a different memory: one that honours fragility, adaptation and the theological richness found in bodily variance. To remember Christ rightly is to remember the disabled body as central to that memory.

Amos Yong develops this perspective through his Pentecostal-informed disability theology. In *Theology and Down Syndrome*, he challenges the notion that salvation amounts merely to a cure, suggesting instead that it involves the restoration of relationships and the cultivation of belonging. He argues that God's work of redemption validates differences rather than erasing them. For Yong, pneumatology reveals that the Spirit is not limited to conventional expressions but also emerges in the quiet, repetitive and hesitant aspects of neurodivergent and cognitively disabled lives. In his view, the divine is visible throughout the entire range of embodied experience.[12]

Thomas Reynolds adds another valuable critical strand by dismantling the theological valorization of autonomy. In *Vulnerable Communion*, he critiques the elevation of independence and rational control as ultimate virtues, a stance he argues is a significant theological error. This valorization of so-called normalcy not only sidelines disabled individuals but also warps the Christian understanding of human nature. According to Reynolds, disability exposes the misplaced emphasis on self-reliance and invites a return to a truer recognition of our interconnected, relational existence. In his vision, the Church is not called to overcome vulnerability, but to embody it as a communal grace.[13]

This has profound implications for how we understand Christian heritage. Reynolds prompts us to examine how theological and material traditions, our buildings, icons, rituals, have been shaped by ideals of coherence and wholeness. The polished stone, the heroic saint, the inaccessible sanctuary: all communicate a silent norm. The result is a heritage that excludes not by accident but by design.

Disability theology exposes this exclusion and proclaims a richer truth: disabled lives are not marginal to the sacred story; they are central to it. The wounded Christ does not erase his scars; he bears them in glory. Likewise, the Church is not called to erase disability, but to learn from it and be reshaped by it. This is not about making space for the disabled as guests, it is about recognizing them as hosts of theological meaning.

In this way, disability theology performs a double movement: it deconstructs distorted assumptions in Christian tradition, and it offers a constructive vision in which disability is not a deviation from holiness, but one of its clearest expressions. It does not accommodate disability at the edge; it centres it as a site of divine disclosure, theological renewal and ecclesial healing.

Liberation theology and the preferential option for the disabled

Liberation theology emerges from a fundamental inquiry: whose suffering remains unseen, and how must faith respond? Developed in Latin America amid systemic injustice, it redefined theology as an act of resistance, grounded in lived experience. Gustavo Gutiérrez articulated the preferential option for the poor as a core theological principle; an affirmation of God's nearness to the oppressed and a call for the Church to embody that solidarity in action.[14]

But that same theological lens compels us to ask: what if the Church's preferential option must also include the disabled, those rendered invisible not only through economic systems, but through inaccessible theology, architecture and ecclesial memory? What if ableism functions as a structural oppression, no less theological than material poverty?

Disability liberation theology engages these questions, not through sentimentality, but through a prophetic reimagining of justice. It challenges the notion of disability as an individual misfortune and instead unveils the systemic forces – social, political and ecclesial – that actively disable. Sharon V. Betcher emphasizes that disability is not merely a personal limitation, but a status imposed by unjust structures. These injustices manifest both physically and theologically: in the absence of ramps where access should be guaranteed, in doctrines that proclaim wholeness yet erase difference, and in liturgies that extend verbal welcome but fail to embody true inclusion.[15]

Rooted in the principles of liberation theology, disability theologians emphasize that justice is not an act of charity, nor is inclusion a gesture of benevolence. Gutiérrez underscores that the realities of poverty demand justice rather than generosity, a conviction that applies equally to the presence of disabled people within the Church. Their participation is not a difficulty to be accommodated but a summons to repentance and transformation. True theological hospitality therefore does not seek assimilation but calls for a radical reimagining of ecclesial life, one that prioritizes interdependence and the sacredness of embodied difference.[16]

This reframing reshapes not only ethics and accessibility but how we think about theology itself. Disabled lives become theological texts, sites of divine meaning and witness. Their ways of praying, moving, communicating and resisting do not interrupt the sacred; they reveal it. In this sense, the hermeneutics of liberation theology deepen; theology must not only be read from the margins but composed from them.

This vision compels a radical rethinking of heritage. So much of ecclesial memory has centred the powerful, the heroic and the healed. The stories told in stained glass and marble are curated through a lens that privileges coherence, strength and triumph. But a liberative approach to heritage demands that we ask: whose memories were never preserved? Whose holiness was never canonized?

Throughout history, disabled individuals have demonstrated profound faithfulness, persevering through exclusion, enduring segregation and passing down wisdom within communities that often failed to acknowledge their contributions. Hans Reinders emphasizes that their lives are not peripheral to the Church but are essential to its very identity. The absence of these narratives from ecclesial records is not merely an oversight, it reflects a deeper theological erasure that must be confronted and remedied.[17]

Here, the liturgical concept of anamnesis becomes crucial. In the Eucharist, anamnesis is not mere recollection but re-presentation: a sacramental remembering that makes the past present and redemptive. Applied to the Church's heritage, it becomes a call to remember not just what happened, but what was ignored. To remember Christ rightly is to remember the broken and discarded, the forgotten and the resilient, not only as a gesture of justice, but as a theological imperative.

James H. Cone, drawing from Black liberation theology, warns against the tendency to domesticate the radical significance of the cross. Rather than a symbol of dominance, it serves as a revelation of God's solidarity with those who suffer. Through this lens, the crucified Christ is not merely a redeemer of disabled people but a profound witness to their central place within the gospel. This perspective is not an ancillary interpretation; it is a necessary correction to ecclesiologies that obscure the full breadth of divine justice and inclusion.[18]

What emerges then is the call for a *disabled heritage*, not a side project or a one-off exhibition, but a continuous, embodied memory that reshapes how the Church remembers itself. This means liturgies that tell stories of exclusion and adaptation, spaces that bear witness to interdependence, and icons that reflect the breadth of human variation. Our disabled heritage belongs in the pulpit, in the sacrament and in the canon of memory.

Disabled people are not late additions to the Church's story. They are part of its foundation. Their testimonies of persistence, resistance and sacred creativity are not exceptions to be honoured; they are the logic of the gospel itself, a gospel that refuses to equate sanctity with symmetry or salvation with perfection.

If the Church is to remember Christ truthfully, it must also re-member itself – broken, diverse, interdependent – and do so not out of pity, but in pursuit of truth and justice.

Heritage as ideological performance

So with all that I have shared so far, let me engage with heritage, not as a sentimental word or a museum label, but as something that is understood as powerful, political and profoundly theological. Heritage, as I have stated, is not merely the conservation of objects or the upkeep of buildings; it is the active production of memory, identity and belonging. It is not passive. It is both profoundly communicative and performative.

Popular imagination may frame heritage as a collection of sacred treasures: stained glass windows, ancient texts, inherited rituals and architectural beauty. But critical heritage scholars remind us that heritage is not simply what is preserved; it is what is *chosen*. It is a selective process, shaped by priorities and power, constructing a story of the past that justifies the present. And more than that, it is ideological.

Laurajane Smith describes heritage as an active cultural process that shapes how people remember and engage with the present. It is not merely a reflection on the past but a forward-looking act that constructs identity, reinforces values and asserts power. Within the Church, heritage functions as a theological performance, influencing its beliefs, determining inclusion and shaping its understanding of God.[19]

Christian heritage takes tangible form in churches, cathedrals, shrines and sacred spaces, places that are far from neutral. These sites function as curated liturgies of memory, shaping theological narratives through their material presence in stone, wood, glass and silence. Willie James Jennings observes that the architecture of the Church itself serves as a theological argument, revealing what communities cherish, preserve and commemorate.[20] What we build, preserve and elevate tells a story about what we value and who we remember.

Within these spaces, patterns emerge. Plaques honour donors and clergy. Chapels commemorate monarchs and martyrs. Saints are depicted with poised serenity, physical symmetry and heroic posture. These choices are not accidental. They are embedded in inherited frameworks shaped by class, colonialism, whiteness, patriarchy and, crucially, ableism. The result is a theological narrative that often forgets the wounded, the fragile and the non-normative.

Heritage, then, is not a mirror of the past; it is a construction of it. And that construction tells a theological story about who counts, who belongs and who is left out. Heritage is a form of future-making. What we choose to remember, or forget, shapes the kind of Church we imagine ourselves becoming.

The absence of disabled bodies therefore in ecclesial heritage is not merely an oversight but a deep theological concern. It conveys an understanding of holiness rooted in able-bodiedness, cognitive sharpness and aesthetic precision. Heritage inherently signals belonging, meaning that the exclusion of disabled bodies suggests they are not recognized as part of the sacred community's lineage. This omission ultimately skews the narrative of salvation, constructing a tradition that remains both theologically and historically incomplete.

Ableism, in this context, functions as a curatorial principle. It determines whose stories are preserved, whose bodies are depicted, and who is physically welcomed into sacred space. A stair without a ramp is not just an architectural failure: it is a theological boundary. Every decision about space and story reveals what we believe about humanity, holiness and God.

The heritage embodied in our churches often communicates a theology of control and coherence, a God of order, symmetry and strength. But heritage that reflects the messiness of lived faith and the truth of marginalized experience must move beyond preservation toward prophetic remembering. This kind of heritage resists the tendency to sanitize the past and instead embraces the complexity of lives lived in tension, exclusion and grace.

This process would require confronting difficult realities – the exclusion of disabled individuals from sacraments, the theological implications of inaccessible architecture and the neglect of those who worshipped from the margins. Jennie Weiss Block refers to this as sacramental remembering, a practice that acknowledges disabled lives not as mere footnotes in church history but as essential witnesses to grace and theological insight.[21]

It would also mean seeing accessibility as integral to the Church's sacramental life. A ramp is not a convenience; it is an embodied declaration of welcome. A signed liturgy is not a service add-on; it is an expression of the Spirit speaking in many tongues. A heritage trail that includes disabled saints and witnesses is not a niche initiative; it is a confession of the Church's wholeness.

This is the work of ecclesial re-membering, not simply recalling the past, but liturgically, architecturally and narratively piecing the body of Christ back together. Not with symmetry, but with scars. Not with nostalgia, but with justice.

A Church committed to this kind of heritage is not curating a static archive; it is enacting a living theology. It is building a memory that is not ornamental but eucharistic. It does not preserve for prestige but remembers for transformation.

Such heritage is not static. It is disruptive, dynamic and deeply theological. It refuses to forget. And in refusing to forget, it tells the truth. But what happens when the ideology of heritage is not only taught but built, not only inherited but carved into the stones of our sacred spaces?

The performance of heritage does not stop at language, ritual or narrative. It materializes. It becomes spatial. It is rendered in architectural grammar and liturgical geography. The exclusionary scripts of ecclesial history are not only spoken in sermons or embedded in stained glass; they are concretized in steps that separate sanctuaries from naves, in narrow doorways and inaccessible pulpits, in acoustics that privilege one kind of hearing, and in seating that assumes a normative body. In other words, ideology becomes masonry.

And it is here, at the intersection of memory and material, that ableism most persistently hides. Not only in overt acts of discrimination, but in the unspoken norms assumed by our built environments. These norms are not accidental. They are theological. They express, however implicitly, a vision of the 'ideal' human: mobile, upright, neurotypical, visually and aurally unimpeded. And this vision is reinforced by centuries of theological anthropology shaped more by classical symmetry than by the wounds of the risen Christ.

As we move forward, we turn our gaze to the physical fabric of our churches, cathedrals and so-called sacred heritage sites. What bodies do these spaces welcome? What bodies do they resist? How has ableism been inscribed not just in our ideas, but in our walls, thresholds and sacred elevations? And what would it mean to design, or to remember, otherwise?

This is the contest we now enter: the contest over space, presence and theologies of embodiment. For the question of heritage is no longer merely what we remember, but where, and for whom.

Notes

1 Nancy L. Eiesland, *The Disabled God: Toward a Liberatory Theology of Disability* (Nashville, TN: Abingdon Press, 1994), p. 101.

2 Gustavo Gutiérrez, *A Theology of Liberation: History, Politics, and Salvation*, trans. Sister Caridad Inda and John Eagleson (Maryknoll, NY: Orbis Books, 1988), pp. 162–73.

3 Lisa D. Powell, 'Liberation Theology and Disability: Unlikely Allies', *Journal of Disability & Religion* 16, no. 2 (2012).

4 Amos Yong, *The Bible, Disability, and the Church: A New Vision of the People of God* (Grand Rapids, MI: Eerdmans, 2011), pp. 145–8.

5 David T. Mitchell and Sharon L. Snyder, *Narrative Prosthesis: Disability and the Dependencies of Discourse* (Ann Arbor, MI: University of Michigan Press, 2000), pp. 47–64.

6 Sharon V. Betcher, *Spirit and the Politics of Disablement* (Minneapolis, MN: Fortress Press, 2007), pp. 48–67.

7 Eiesland, *The Disabled God*, pp. 98–9.

8 Deborah Beth Creamer, *Disability and Christian Theology: Embodied Limits and Constructive Possibilities* (Oxford: Oxford University Press, 2009), pp. 93–114.

9 John M. Hull, *In the Beginning There Was Darkness: A Blind Person's Conversations with the Bible* (London: SCM Press, 2001), pp. 67–75.

10 Lisa D. Powell, 'Disability and Resurrection: Eschatological Bodies, Identity, and Continuity', *Journal of the Society of Christian Ethics*, 41, no. 1 (2021), pp. 89–106.

11 Eiesland, *The Disabled God*.

12 Amos Yong, *Theology and Down Syndrome: Reimagining Disability in Late Modernity* (Waco, TX: Baylor University Press, 2007), pp. 227–58.

13 Thomas E. Reynolds, *Vulnerable Communion: A Theology of Disability and Hospitality* (Grand Rapids, MI: Brazos Press, 2008), pp. 73–101.

14 Gutiérrez, *A Theology of Liberation*.

15 Betcher, *Spirit and the Politics of Disablement*.

16 Gutiérrez, *A Theology of Liberation*.

17 Hans S. Reinders, *Receiving the Gift of Friendship: Profound Disability,*

Theological Anthropology, and Ethics (Grand Rapids, MI: Eerdmans, 2008), pp. 194–7.

18 James H. Cone, *The Cross and the Lynching Tree* (Maryknoll, NY: Orbis Books, 2011), pp. 1–29.

19 Laurajane Smith, *Uses of Heritage* (London: Routledge, 2006), pp. 44–84.

20 Willie James Jennings, *The Christian Imagination: Theology and the Origins of Race* (New Haven, CT: Yale University Press, 2010), pp. 207–49.

21 Jennie Weiss Block, *Copious Hosting: A Theology of Access for People with Disabilities* (New York: Continuum, 2002), pp. 101–28.

6

The Legacy of Exclusion: Ableism in Sacred Heritage Spaces

Sacred space is never neutral. It is not merely functional or decorative, it is theological. Every font, altar rail, pulpit or stained-glass window does more than guide movement or adorn worship. These elements enact a material theology. They shape how we imagine God, how we gather as a community and how we hold time and memory. Sacred space is not simply where theology is spoken; it is where theology is seen, touched and lived.

This is especially clear in Christian heritage architecture: the cathedrals, cloisters, shrines and parish churches that stretch across centuries and continents. These spaces do not just contain belief, they perform it. We do not only think theology here: we inhabit it. Our bodies move through its claims, kneeling, processing, looking up, pausing to smell incense or hear echoes across stone. Architecture shapes not only our gaze, but our imagination. The Church's built environment becomes doctrine rendered in stone.

And yes, these spaces can be breathtaking. Their scale and beauty inspire reverence. Their continuity connects us to centuries of faith. But beauty, as critical heritage scholars remind us, is never innocent. And heritage, especially ecclesial heritage, is never simply a neutral preservation of the past.

In this chapter, we confront the ableist legacy embedded in our sacred built environment, asking how ecclesial heritage has reflected, reinforced and, at times, resisted the marginalization of disabled people in the very spaces where the body of Christ gathers. Historically, churches have been shaped by a narrow model of the human body, what disability theorist Rosemarie Garland Thomson calls the 'normate body'.[1] These are the bodies presumed by liturgy, accommodated by architecture and dignified in art: able-bodied, neurotypical, mobile, symmetrical and orderly. The sacred was cast in their image. Others, especially disabled people, were often excluded, not just practically but theologically.

Cathedrals, parish churches, chapels and monasteries stand as stone testimonies to the faith, artistry and liturgical imagination of centuries past. They are revered as vessels of holiness, bearers of memory and touchstones of ecclesial identity. Yet these very spaces, so often described as timeless and inclusive, have also been constructed through the selective vision of normate bodies, designed for those who walk upright, climb steps, hear without aid, and see without obstruction. The theological architecture of sacred space has rarely accounted for disabled presence, let alone welcomed it as integral. Indeed, these structures too often inscribe exclusion into stone and wood, sanctifying able-bodied access as the default and rendering disabled bodies as architectural intrusions or logistical inconveniences.

Laurajane Smith writes of heritage as a dynamic cultural process that shapes and authorizes identity narratives. In religious contexts, this process takes on a theological dimension, where decisions about what is preserved, emphasized or restored reflect deeper values about significance and belonging. Sacred architecture and curated spaces reveal not only liturgical priorities but also underlying anthropological frameworks. In this regard, ableism is not a mere oversight – it is embedded within the very structures of ecclesial heritage.[2]

Consider the built environment. A flight of steps to the altar communicates more than inaccessibility, it encodes hierarchy. Pulpits without ramps, sanctuaries without room for wheelchairs, chapels designed around visual veneration, these do not merely reflect oversight; they perform exclusion. They say, 'You were not imagined here.' This is not just a design issue. It is a theological one.

This exclusion is compounded by doctrinal history. Patristic thinkers like Augustine and Aquinas, despite their foundational contributions, internalized classical ideals that prized rationality, symmetry and form.[3] Disability, under these frameworks, was often interpreted as a disruption of divine order, something to be pitied, cured or transcended. These ideas became embedded in theological anthropology, subtly informing the design of ecclesial spaces and the expectations of worship.

When worship becomes calibrated around assumed capacities – standing, speaking, seeing, processing without assistance – it ceases to be universal. Participation is no longer a shared invitation but a selective performance. For disabled people, the message becomes clear: your presence is a problem to be accommodated, not a gift to be welcomed. Ableism in sacred space is not metaphorical. It is literal. It is carved into stone, structured into liturgy and sanctified by tradition. Its presence distorts the theology it claims to uphold. It renders the body of Christ incomplete while performing wholeness. It confuses aesthetic coherence with divine favour. And if left unchallenged, it perpetuates a vision of the Church that is not gospel but gatekeeping.

Yet this chapter is not only a critique. It is also a testimony to change. Disabled people are not only entering sacred spaces; we are reshaping them. Not as guests, but as leaders. Not as anomalies, but as bearers of theological insight. The work of access is no longer framed as concession, but as transformation. The presence of disabled people is not a disruption to tradition: it is a return to the radical hospitality of the gospel.

This transformation is not about retrofitting old structures to meet minimal compliance. It is a theological reimagining. It refuses to separate beauty from justice, or heritage from truth. It insists that sacred space is not sacred because it is preserved, but because it is shared. And the measure of its sanctity is not in grandeur, but in generosity.

This is not rebellion against the tradition. It is fidelity to its core. It returns to the One who made space at tables, welcomed interruption and revealed glory through wounds. Sacred space becomes truly holy when it is opened to all bodies, when it reflects not idealized humanity but beloved community.

To reshape sacred space in this way is not simply a practical task, it is sacramental. It is a reorientation of the Church's self-understanding. It is a liturgy of justice. It is the architectural expression of a deeper truth: that the body of Christ has room for every member, and that no one is whole until all are welcomed in.

Sacred architecture and the theology of space

Church buildings are not just functional shelters for worship. They are sermons in stone. They preach, whether we intend them to or not. They encode and extend theology. Their arches, thresholds, steps, aisles and altars are not neutral elements; they are theological artefacts. These architectural decisions materialize ideas about God, humanity, holiness and belonging.

Sacred architecture mirrors the values and priorities of the communities that built them, including assumptions about which bodies belong within their walls. In this way, church buildings are not only reflections of inherited belief; they are instruments that form belief. They teach us how to move, who may lead and what kind of presence is imagined as welcome.

Many historic churches manifest an architecture of separation and spectacle. Elevated sanctuaries, narrow staircases to pulpits, long axial naves, these are more than aesthetic or acoustic choices. They represent theological commitments. They privilege a spirituality of ascent, hierarchy and visual centrality, rooted not in the radical openness of Christ's ministry but in centuries of inherited metaphysics that conflate holiness with elevation and perfection with symmetry.

These design choices are often accepted as sacred norms rather than questioned as theological statements. The result is that sacred spaces frequently function as gatekeepers. They quietly proclaim who may draw near to the holy, and who must remain at the margins.

The most visible expression of this exclusion is physical. Steep stairs, uneven floors and inaccessible chancels signal an unspoken assumption about the 'normal' worshipper: mobile, sighted, hearing, neurotypical and verbally fluent. Others are positioned as exceptions, accommodated, if necessary, but rarely centred. Even when access features are added, they are often installed with reluctance, reinforcing the idea that access is a concession to modernity rather than an expression of gospel welcome.

This exclusion is not merely logistical; it is theological. Architecture shapes participation. When sacredness is marked by height and distance, it implicitly aligns divine proximity with physical capability. This vertical theology owes more to Neoplatonic cosmology than to the incarnational, grounded ministry of Jesus, whose way was always downward, toward the lowly, the excluded and the vulnerable.

As John Hull observes in his critique of visual-centric church design, such spaces often embed a spirituality of transcendence that marginalizes those who cannot see, walk or climb.[4] This aesthetic reinforces a false anthropology – one in which wholeness is equated with the capacity to move, to see, to access without adaptation. A chancel reached only by steps says more than we think. It whispers that grace is elevated, that God is up there, and that some bodies are simply too far down.

This distortion carries particular weight in the sacramental economy of space. When fonts, pulpits and altars are inaccessible, the very means of grace are placed beyond reach. The Eucharist becomes a spectacle rather than a shared meal. Baptismal fonts become ornamental rather than communal. The architecture does not just exclude, it withholds.

Compounding this exclusion is a longstanding theological tradition that idealized the rational, symmetrical and self-contained body. From classical philosophy through Scholasticism, these ideals became woven into Christian doctrines of sanctity, order and purity. Disability was frequently cast as deficiency, sin or anomaly, an interpretation reflected not only in theology but in the built environment. These spaces were not designed with disabled bodies in mind because they were not imagined as part of the body at all.

Yet even as churches attempt to address this legacy, the response is often shallow. Ramps are added to side doors, lifts hidden behind locked cupboards, access discussed as a problem of logistics rather than as an expression of theology. The very language of accommodation suggests that inclusion is optional, even regrettable, a compromise with modern expectations rather than a manifestation of ancient hospitality.

This is a liturgy of exclusion in stone. And it is doctrinally incoherent. A Church that names itself as the body of Christ cannot simultaneously design its spaces in ways that dismember that body. It cannot claim universal grace while restricting who may access the altar. The contradiction is not just ethical, it is ecclesiological.

This exclusion is often perpetuated by an appeal to 'historical integrity' or 'aesthetic preservation'. But we must ask: what is the theology behind these values? What vision of God is being preserved when we prioritize stone over presence, or symmetry over welcome? When did access become an affront to beauty? These are not architectural questions alone; they are theological ones.

What is needed is not the demolition of heritage, but its theological reinterpretation. Sacred architecture must be read anew, not only as an artefact of the past but as a site for contemporary ecclesial imagination. What do these spaces reveal about what we have believed? And what might they become if reconfigured in light of the God who meets us not at the summit, but on the road?

Sacred space becomes truly sacred not because it preserves an ideal form, but because it opens itself to grace in the present. It becomes holy not through elevation, but through embrace. When space is reconfigured to welcome all bodies, not as guests but as members, then the architecture begins to align with the gospel it proclaims.

The false binary of beauty and belonging: aesthetic resistance and theological misrecognition

In heritage churches and cathedrals, the conversation often begins politely. A suggestion is made, to add a ramp, to install a lift, to introduce tactile or audio signage. And then comes the quiet resistance: concern about 'aesthetic integrity'. The implication is clear, if rarely spoken aloud, that access threatens beauty. That making space for disabled bodies might somehow desecrate the architectural or historical sanctity of the church building.

Bodies like Historic England have at times reinforced this caution, emphasizing 'minimal intervention' as a guiding principle in the stewardship of listed buildings.[5] While preservation has value, it can also conceal a deeper problem: the idea that a sacred building's worth is tied to its visual and material continuity, that its holiness is compromised by change, especially change demanded by bodies long excluded.

But this is not simply a dispute about design. It is a theological crisis. When the aesthetics of a building are prioritized over the accessibility of its worship, the Church makes more than a stylistic choice. It enacts a theological misrecognition: it treats stone as sacred and bodies as conditional.

At its core, this is not merely about heritage conservation. It is about which bodies are seen as worthy of accommodation, and which are expected to remain invisible for the sake of architectural purity. The claim that access 'disrupts' beauty rests on an ableist aesthetic, a visual normativity that idealizes coherence, symmetry and unbroken form. This is not neutral. It has doctrinal implications. It tells a story about who belongs.

What is called beautiful is never free from cultural valuation. In sacred space, this entanglement becomes theological. When disabled access is seen as a blemish, it is not only an aesthetic judgement; it is a moral one. It implies that the disabled body is out of place, not just practically, but spiritually.

This exclusion extends to how we imagine God. A theology that clings to unaltered stone as the measure of sacredness risks misrepresenting the divine as static, distant and flawless. It forgets that holiness is revealed in the disruption of expectations, in the breaking of bread and barriers alike. If a wheelchair ramp is treated as a defilement of a sacred threshold, what does that say about the Church's understanding of incarnation?

These attitudes have roots in the aesthetic theology of the Western tradition. Augustine, deeply shaped by Neoplatonic ideals, interpreted beauty through transcendence, immutability and order.[6] Aquinas systematized this view, defining beauty as 'integrity, proportion and clarity'.[7] These classical ideals became the foundation for ecclesial aesthetics, transposed into architecture, liturgy and theological imagination. But they also constructed an implicit hierarchy: that which conforms to order is closer to the divine; that which disrupts it must be overcome or corrected.

The disabled body, which rarely conforms to classical proportion or functional ideals, was seldom imagined as capable of disclosing beauty. Early theologians like Origen compounded this view by interpreting physical impairments as allegories for spiritual blindness or sin.[8] Chrysostom, though more pastorally attuned, often presented disabled people as passive instruments of divine display rather than as theological subjects.[9] These traditions cast disability not as a locus of grace, but as a canvas for correction, a test, or a lesson for others.

The result has been centuries of theological misrecognition, where disability is spiritualized, aestheticized, or erased, but rarely centred as a theological resource. Beauty, shaped by these frameworks, came to mean wholeness, and wholeness meant bodily conformity. In this schema, access was always a compromise, never a manifestation of grace.

Yet this binary, beauty versus access, is being actively dismantled. Disability aesthetics, a growing field of theological and cultural critique, rejects the assumption that access undermines design. Scholars like Sara Hendren insist that accessible design is not a blemish, but a blessing.[10] Ramps, lifts, tactile signage and hearing loops are not intrusions. They are declarative. They reveal who the space is for. They are architectural sacraments that embody welcome.

Hendren's work reframes access not as accommodation but as design justice. A ramp is not a visual disturbance; it is a material proclamation. It announces that beauty lies not in preservation but in participation. That sacred space is made holy not by its cohesion, but by its capacity to receive the diversity of bodies that form the body of Christ.

When churches resist access in the name of aesthetic integrity, they risk preserving exclusion under the guise of reverence. But when they embrace design as a theological act, they proclaim a different gospel, one that honours adaptation as revelation, and accessibility as grace enfleshed.

The most faithful churches are not those that refuse to change. They are those that let themselves be changed by the presence of those they once excluded. Access, far from diminishing beauty, reveals its truest form. Not symmetry, but hospitality. Not preservation, but transformation. A ramp, in this light, is not a compromise. It is an altar of justice.

The liturgical marginalization of disabled people

While architectural exclusion in churches often draws attention, the liturgy, the rhythm, language and choreography of worship can be just as marginalizing. Their excluding effect often goes unnoticed precisely because it is embedded in the presumed 'shared' life of the worshipping body. Liturgy is intended to express the unity of the Church, the common praise of a gathered people before God. Yet for many disabled people, it becomes a site where exclusion is not only practised but sanctified.

A major form of this exclusion is linguistic. Disability metaphors remain embedded in the liturgical and theological imagination. Phrases such as 'spiritually blind', 'lame in faith', 'deaf to God's call' or 'crippled by sin' are pervasive across hymns, prayers and sermons. These expressions draw from a long tradition that uses physical difference as shorthand for moral or spiritual failure.

The result is deeply problematic. These metaphors not only misrepresent the lives of disabled people but reduce their bodies to rhetorical tools. Disability becomes a spiritual condition to be overcome, rather than a mode of embodied experience through which faith is lived. The metaphoric use of disability reinforces a theology in which certain bodies signify deficiency and thus, by implication, a distance from God.

The issue is especially acute in heritage liturgies; those traditional texts celebrated for their poetic elegance or historical lineage. Because they carry weight and continuity, they are often exempt from scrutiny. But uncritical repetition of these texts risks preserving the prejudices they encode. To treat their language as sacred simply because it is old is to mistake longevity for holiness.

Yet language is only part of the problem. Liturgical structures themselves often presume a normative way of being in the body. Many disabled people are unable to engage in worship in the ways assumed by traditional liturgical choreography: standing, kneeling, processing, speaking aloud, maintaining stillness or silence. The physicality of liturgy, often designed with symbolic richness, can become a barrier when it fails to accommodate varied bodies and neurotypes.

Consider the experience of a wheelchair user who cannot access the altar. A blind congregant given only printed material. A non-verbal worshipper offered no alternative form of confession. An autistic person overwhelmed by unanticipated noise or sensory triggers. These are not isolated incidents. They are symptoms of a liturgical framework that equates uniform participation with proper worship.

This assumption, that worship requires physical and cognitive conformity, is a subtle but potent form of ableism. It constructs an ideal worshipper and renders everyone else a deviation. And when participation becomes a measure of belonging, disabled people are too often treated as disruptions, rather than full members of the worshipping body.

The theologian John Swinton offers vital insight into dementia and ecclesial life, emphasizing that Christian identity is not contingent on memory, rational thought or verbal clarity. He highlights that God's remembrance is steadfast, even when human memory falters. This perspective reshapes understandings of liturgical belonging: if divine hospitality is not bound by cognitive ability, then church communities should reflect the same inclusivity.[11]

This has profound implications for how we understand participation. A liturgy that centres grace must not require fluency, predictability or control. It must learn to embrace unstructured silence, spontaneous sound, non-verbal gestures and alternative rhythms of engagement. These are not deviations from worship. They are worship.

Too often, heritage worship styles prioritize aesthetic consistency – chant, eloquent cadence, choreographed ritual – over adaptability. But we must ask: whom does this serve? If tradition silences the people it claims to gather, then its authority must be questioned. Not rejected, but reshaped. Tradition must become porous, not preserved in place but opened through encounter.

A liberating liturgy does not fear messiness. It finds God not only in eloquent proclamation, but in murmured prayers, in restless bodies, in the sacred stimming of neurodivergent praise, in the quiet presence of those who may not speak but who profoundly belong.

Reimagining liturgy through the lens of disability does not dilute its richness. It deepens it. It offers a fuller vision of the body of Christ, one that is not defined by uniformity but knit together by grace. It reminds us that worship is not a performance for God, but an invitation into communion. And that communion must make room for all bodies, all voices, all modes of presence.

York Minster and the tensions of sacred heritage

York Minster is one of the most magnificent ecclesiastical buildings in Europe, an astonishing masterpiece of Gothic architecture and a cornerstone of English religious heritage. For me, it is also a deeply personal space: it is not only the place where I primarily minister and worship, but it shares, with so many of our historic cathedrals and parish churches, a site that embodies the tensions between beauty and exclusion, tradition and transformation. Its grandeur is unmistakable. The vaulted ceilings, intricate stone tracery, and luminous, medieval stained glass offer a visual theology of transcendence and continuity. The architecture is often described as a sermon in stone, a testament to the ordering of the sacred through form and space. But, as in all our sacred buildings, these forms are not ideologically neutral. As discussed elsewhere, their proportions and hierarchies reflect historical ideals of beauty that assumed a normative human subject, able-bodied, upright, rational and ordered.

For many disabled people, these celebrated features can become obstacles. Until recently, step-free access to core liturgical spaces was limited. Acoustics that amplify choral beauty can disorient worshippers with sensory or auditory processing differences. Provisions for neurodivergent and Deaf worshippers, though improving, remain uneven. The visual harmony of the building does not always translate into an experience of inclusion.

To its credit, the minster has made significant strides. Ramps have been and are being installed. Accessible facilities added. There is a growing realization that independent access for disabled people is needed. Sensory-friendly trails and visual guides have been introduced. These changes reflect the dedication of staff, volunteers and consultants who believe that heritage must serve people, not merely preserve history.

And yet, deeper questions remain. What is the driver of these changes? Are they grounded in a theological understanding of access, or are they primarily responses to compliance, funding, or visitor expectations? When access is added as a functional overlay rather than as a theological imperative, there is the risk that it becomes symbolic rather than transformative.

Inclusion that is not rooted in ecclesiology can easily become aesthetic access, visible, respectable and limited. A ramp becomes an architectural gesture, not a cultural shift. A welcome sign appears without a corresponding redistribution of leadership or power. Without disabled people shaping the liturgical, pastoral and interpretive life of the institution, the underlying structures remain unchanged.

For all our historic cathedrals and parish churches, this is where the challenge becomes not one that is solely architectural, but one that is cultural and theological. Disabled people must be seen not only as recipients of welcome but as authors of ecclesial meaning. Leadership, not just access. Recognition, not just accommodation. The minster, like so many other cathedrals, must ask not only *who* can enter the space, but *whose* voice shapes the space.

This same pattern of omission is visible in the narratives told through heritage interpretation. Tours and exhibitions frequently centre monarchs, bishops, craftsmen and military leaders. The disabled, if mentioned at all, are peripheral. There are few accounts of impaired clergy, no known stories of disabled pilgrims, no plaques commemorating disabled parishioners whose faith endured architectural and cultural exclusion. The theological significance of their lives goes unspoken.

This is not simply a curatorial gap; it is a theological one. The absence of disabled lives from the story told by the minster suggests that disability has little to contribute to the Church's memory. This reinforces centuries of doctrinal habits that spiritualized, pathologized or erased disability rather than recognizing it as integral to the experience of faith.

These omissions are part of a broader phenomenon: heritage as theological curation. York Minster, like many historic cathedrals and parish churches, preserves a canon of stories that elevates symmetry, hierarchy and conquest. Without critical reflection, that heritage risks enshrining a purified vision of the Church, a vision in which the messy, dependent and diverse body of Christ is nowhere to be found. What might a different vision look like?

A theology of heritage grounded in access would begin by shifting the interpretive lens. It would make visible the hidden saints: the blind monk who composed sacred music by memory; the neurodivergent child whose repeated gestures were a form of liturgical joy; the parishioner who returned each week on crutches, moving with reverence through the stone nave. These are not marginal figures. They are witnesses. They are the Church.

York Minster has opportunities to reimagine itself, not only as a monument to Christian art, but as a living institution shaped by the gospel's call to justice, and it is rising to this challenge, recognizing that this will not be achieved by ramps and guides alone, but by inviting disabled voices to shape how the space is understood, narrated and used. It will mean letting heritage be interrupted by lived experience and recognizing those interruptions as revelation.

This is not about discarding tradition. It is about renewing it. Not about erasing the past but about expanding the story. Because the Church is not built of perfect stones, but of people, and no part of the body is dispensable.

Reimagining sacred space: disabled leadership and the future of Christian heritage

Much of Christian heritage has long been shaped by exclusion, architecturally, liturgically and narratively. But today, a different story is beginning to emerge. Across the Church, sacred spaces are being reimagined, not merely renovated or retrofitted, but theologically reconstituted. These are spaces where holiness is no longer equated with symmetry, silence or tradition, but with access, attentiveness and justice.

Crucially, these transformations are not limited to physical adaptations. What marks these spaces as truly sacred is that they do not treat inclusion as a concession or technical fix. Instead, they approach access as an ecclesiological imperative and a theological gift. These are spaces where disabled leadership shapes the liturgy, interprets Scripture, forms theology and embodies the future of Christian community.

St Martin-in-the-Fields in London is one such space. Widely known for its commitment to social justice and public theology, it has also become a leading model of disability inclusion. At St Martin's, access is not an afterthought. It is embedded from the ground up, shaping everything from liturgical form to leadership structure. The annual Disability Conference, organized by and for disabled people, has become a rare and vital ecclesial space where power is shared and where theology is not merely discussed but embodied. Here, disabled people are not invited in to diversify the conversation: we lead it.

My own formation has been profoundly shaped by my years on the planning team for that conference. What made it unique was not only its welcome, but its trust: disabled people were trusted with worship, with structure, with voice. The space became one where creativity and theological depth could flourish precisely because disabled people were not managed or tokenized but trusted as agents of the Church's renewal.

Elsewhere, more contemplative models are emerging. In Tremeirchion, St Beuno's Jesuit Spirituality Centre has quietly nurtured a different kind of spiritual access, one rooted in stillness, sensory accommodation and non-verbal prayer. Rather than adjusting existing worship for inclusion, the Centre reframes the very grammar of encounter. Unbusy spaces, textural prayer practices and neurodivergent-friendly rhythms point to a deeper shift: a move from intellectual mastery to embodied presence. From liturgical performance to sacramental attention.

What connects these examples is not a shared architectural style or doctrinal emphasis, but a common refusal to let inherited norms define what counts as church. These communities are intentionally decentring inherited forms that have historically excluded disabled people, be they visual perfectionism, verbal fluency or spatial coherence, and replacing them with practices of radical welcome.

In doing so, they confront a long theological history that has cast disabled people as symbols, objects or anomalies. The legacy of Origen's spiritualization of physical impairment, or Chrysostom's portrayal of disabled persons as moral metaphors, still lingers in ecclesial memory. What these reimagined spaces offer instead is a vision in which disabled lives are neither sermon illustrations nor theological puzzles. We are the community. We are the ones who remember, pray, build, bless.

More radically, new kinds of sacred spaces are emerging outside traditional church buildings altogether, spaces that do not seek heritage recognition but offer something more profound: lived ecclesiology. These may be temporary, mobile or digital. A collage-based teleconference liturgy. A mutual aid ritual of prayer and protest. A service where no one must speak aloud to be heard. What makes these spaces sacred is not their permanence, but their participation.

The online ministry 'Disability and Jesus' exemplifies this shift. Born from the recognition that many disabled Christians could not access traditional churches, the group has developed an alternative liturgical landscape: online prayer services, digitally accessible Stations of the Cross and social media liturgies that span geography and time.[12] These are not placeholders for 'real' church. They are church. They are acts of sacramental presence in a digital wilderness.

These innovations do not diminish Christian heritage, they deepen it. They show that holiness has never been about elevation or prestige, but about presence. A mobility scooter is not an intrusion on liturgy: it is part of it. A screen-reader-friendly prayerbook is not less sacred than parchment: it may be more so. These spaces reconfigure what counts as altar, sanctuary and church, and in doing so, they extend the tradition rather than break it.

What is emerging is not just a more inclusive architecture, but a more faithful one. Disabled people are not being added into a previously coherent whole. We are helping to recompose it. We are the builders and the bearers of a future Church that remembers not only its saints, but its wounds. Not only its stained glass, but its stuttering prayers. Not only its order, but its openings.

This is the sacred heritage the Church must now embrace. Not a legacy preserved in stone alone, but a living testimony carried in scarred bodies, in altered liturgies, in brave, unfinished prayers. These are the spaces where disabled people are not recipients of inclusion, but the architects of communion. Where we are not remembered as afterthoughts but recognized as prophets of a Church that might still be born.

Reorienting access: from compliance to consecration

What if we stopped treating access as a concession to modernity? What if ramps, hearing loops, subtitles and sensory spaces were not seen as accommodations, but as sacraments, material signs of grace and theological fidelity?

To frame access in this way requires more than practical awareness. It demands a reorientation of our theological imagination. Access must no longer be justified by compliance or courtesy. It must be seen as discipleship. As worship. As fidelity to the God who, in Christ, crossed every boundary to dwell with us, not in abstract form, but in human flesh, with all its vulnerability and need.

Disability theologian Nancy Eiesland makes a decisive claim: access is not separate from reverence but an expression of it. Her understanding of the disabled God challenges the notion that divine presence resides in bodily perfection, instead locating it in adaptation, mutual care and the shared experience of human limitation. From this perspective, a ramp does not intrude upon sacred space but prepares it. A loop system is not merely a technological accommodation: it becomes a vessel for proclaiming the Word. Subtitles are not additions, but embodiments of the gospel made clear.[13] When our churches fail to embody these practices, we are not simply neglecting inclusion; we are misrepresenting the gospel.

Every architectural gesture of access is a liturgical act. To lower a pulpit is to raise another voice. To widen a door is to open the Church to a fuller humanity. The inclusion of disabled bodies and minds is not a dilution of holiness, but a discovery of it in new and necessary form.

This perspective challenges the logic that often undergirds heritage preservation: the notion that sacred authenticity depends on immutability. But Christianity does not proclaim a static God. It proclaims an incarnate God. The Incarnation is the theological rupture that overturns the preservationist impulse. It insists that faithfulness lies not in repetition, but in response.

While ecclesial architecture has often been shaped by ideals of order, balance and formal continuity, drawn from thinkers like Thomas Aquinas, those ideals have been elevated at the expense of bodies that do not conform to them. But the Gospels bear no such anxiety. Jesus consistently reorders the sacred around the needs of those deemed disruptive. He touches, listens, waits and responds.

The question for churches and cathedrals, then, is not whether an intervention 'fits' the original design. The question is whether it reflects the character of Christ. Access is not a stylistic question: it is a Christological one.

This dynamic is particularly evident in heritage spaces, where the formation of ecclesial identity is often guided by architects, curators and conservators. Theologian Luke Bretherton challenges this by asking whose voices genuinely shape the Church's shared life. If participation is limited only to those who are articulate, audible, ambulatory and well-paced, then what has been safeguarded is mere aesthetic continuity rather than the deeper call of the gospel.[14]

True sacredness may come not from the pulpit or the pipe organ, but from a typed prayer, a signed song, a body that rests while others stand. That is not inversion for its own sake – it is fidelity to the gospel's own pattern of reversal. The last are not added in as symbols. They are the starting point of divine order.

To build a ramp is to level a mountain. To add captions is to proclaim the Word with clarity. To offer a quiet space is to echo God's own command to rest. These are not additions. They are consecrations.

They are spatial liturgies. They reorder the Church not just in metaphor, but in brick and breath. They make visible the parts of the body that have long been kept out of sight – and in doing so, they reveal the fuller shape of communion.

This is what access is: not a gesture of compromise, but an act of consecration. It is the Church remembering what it is. And becoming what it is called to be.

Reclaiming the flesh: cracks in the temple, scars in the body

Christianity has long loved stone, glass and ritual. It has inscribed memory into stained-glass windows, carried theology in chant and cloth, and shaped reverence into soaring spires. These artefacts have preserved centuries of faith, grounding the Church in a visual and material continuity that can evoke deep awe. But heritage, no matter how beautiful, is never neutral. Its materials are also marked by the power that shaped them.

Much of what has been called sacred, be it architecture, liturgy or tradition, has too often mirrored dominant ideals: bodily control, sensory coherence, rational fluency. These ideals are not benign. They have created environments where disabled people have been not only overlooked but theologically misconstrued. Our bodies have been used as metaphors, our lives reduced to moral illustrations, our presence cast as disruption.

Behind this exclusion lies an enduring theological bias: the preference for form over flesh. From Platonic idealism to scholastic frameworks of clarity and order, the tradition often rendered the divine in abstract symmetry rather than in embodied encounter. The result has been a Church more attuned to polished surfaces than to the texture of human pain.

But the gospel does not unfold in ideals. It unfolds in incarnation.

The God we meet in Christ does not shimmer with aesthetic coherence. He arrives hungry, dusty, interrupted. His miracles are not displays of perfection but of proximity. His wounds are not concealed in resurrection – they are glorified. In this, the Christian story refuses the premise that holiness means wholeness in any narrow sense. Instead, it reveals that scars, breaks and interruptions are not barriers to grace. They are its very channels.

This is the mistake of aestheticism in theology: the conflation of beauty with conformity, of holiness with control. When worship becomes spectacle and perfection its unspoken requirement, we lose sight of the God who was born in a borrowed room, whose most powerful act was to be broken.

Yet there are cracks in this tradition, literal and theological, where light breaks through. A worn stone where a wheelchair has passed. A silence held in reverence when words fail. A community pausing not to perform perfection but to dwell with one another in vulnerability. These moments are not ruptures in holiness; they are revelations of it. This is not to deny suffering, but to affirm that grace does not depend on transformation into another kind of body. It is discovered in the truth of this one.

If the Church has often forgotten this truth, then the task is not simply critique. It is conversion. A return, not to old forms, but to the radical flesh of the gospel. A faith not carried in polish, but in presence.

Throughout this chapter, we have not only named the problem. We have begun to glimpse the alternative: a Church where disabled people are not merely welcomed but needed. Where liturgy is not diluted by adaptation but made more fully itself. Where memory is not curated through absence but re-membered in flesh.

This is not about sentimentality. It is about fidelity. To the Christ who still bears wounds. To the body that still aches. To the Spirit who still broods over disorder and brings forth new creation.

In the next chapter we will now discover how theology, particularly theological anthropologies of resurrection, participation and memory, is already moulding the design and layout of our sacred buildings, and how some contemporary restorations and reorderings are now beginning to speak a different word: not of perfection, but of transformation.

So let us turn to the spatial expression of theological vision, to churches, cathedrals and public buildings that, in their scarred beauty, invite us to imagine what sacred space might look like if it were formed not by the fear of brokenness, but by the promise of resurrection.

Notes

1 Rosemarie Garland Thomson, *Extraordinary Bodies: Figuring Physical Disability in American Culture and Literature* (New York: Columbia University Press, 1997), pp. 19–54.

2 Laurajane Smith, *Uses of Heritage* (London: Routledge, 2006), pp. 44–83.

3 Augustine, *The City of God*, trans. Henry Bettenson (London: Penguin Classics, 2003); Thomas Aquinas, *Summa Theologiae*, trans. Fathers of the English Dominican Province (London: Blackfriars, 1963–76).

4 John M. Hull, *In the Beginning There Was Darkness: A Blind Person's Conversations with the Bible* (London: SCM Press, 2001), pp. 67–73.

5 Historic England, *Easy Access to Historic Buildings*, 3rd ed. (Swindon: Historic England, 2015).

6 Augustine, *On Order* and *The City of God*, trans. Henry Bettenson (London: Penguin Classics, 2003).

7 Aquinas, *Summa Theologiae*.

8 Origen, *Contra Celsum*, Book III; Commentary on the Gospel of John, Book I.

9 John Chrysostom, *Homilies on the Gospel of John* and *Homilies on the Gospel of Matthew*.

10 Sara Hendren, *What Can a Body Do? How We Meet the Built World* (New York: Riverhead Books, 2020), pp. 65–94.

11 John Swinton, *Dementia: Living in the Memories of God* (London: SCM Press, 2017), pp. 110–34.

12 Disability and Jesus, https://www.facebook.com/DisabilityAndJesus, accessed 13.08.2025.

13 Nancy L. Eiesland, *The Disabled God: Toward a Liberatory Theology of Disability* (Nashville, TN: Abingdon Press, 1994), pp. 107–8.

14 Luke Bretherton, *Christ and the Common Life: Political Theology and the Case for Democracy* (Grand Rapids, MI: Eerdmans, 2019), pp. 258–90.

7

Sacred Space and Theological Vision: How Theology Shapes the Design and Layout of Our Sacred Buildings

One of the central themes of this book is that our foundational Christian theology of the body has profoundly shaped the architecture, liturgy and furniture of our churches and cathedrals. From the placement of altars and pulpits to the orientation of naves and the height of sanctuaries, sacred space has always been designed in light of implicit (and often unspoken) assumptions about what the human body is, should be and must do. This is not surprising. Just in the last 60 years the reforms of the Second Vatican Council in the Roman Catholic Church, for example, brought about a radical rethinking of church architecture, liturgy and furnishing, precisely because theology had shifted. When the Church reimagined itself as the People of God, rather than a clerical hierarchy, the space in which it worshipped had to change too.

As I have already stated, the architecture of sacred space is never neutral. It reflects theology, enacts ecclesiology and silently proclaims who belongs in the body of Christ. Across history, sacred buildings have not simply provided places for worship: they have made theological statements in stone, light and layout. From the towering Gothic cathedrals of medieval Europe to the liturgical reconfigurations of the post-Vatican II era, church architecture has always revealed and then embodied the shared theological and cultural anthropology of a given age: a shared vision of our understanding of the human person, the Church and God.

It is the job of theologians and sociologists to ask for whom our churches have been built at each age of design and construction. What bodies have they welcomed, and what bodies in the process did they exclude or simply not acknowledge? This chapter gives examples of how theology has shaped the design and layout of sacred buildings in our own age, comparing the vertical transcendence of Gothic cathedrals with the participatory and inclusive spatial theologies of Vatican II. Drawing on case studies including Liverpool Metropolitan Cathedral,

Worth Abbey and Clifton Cathedral, we will consider how theology moulds architecture, and how sacred buildings might have looked had our theological anthropology been shaped not by the idealized norm, but by the full diversity of the body of Christ.

The soaring cathedrals of the Gothic era – Chartres, Notre-Dame, Lincoln, York – were built within a theological worldview in which the architecture of space mirrored the order of heaven. Height and hierarchy were core theological principles. Their verticality invited awe, directing the gaze heavenward in a symbolic ascent toward the divine.

We have already ascertained that sacred order was also a social and bodily one. The design of medieval cathedrals presupposed a particular theological anthropology: the idealized male, clerical, upright, able-bodied figure, moving confidently from nave to sanctuary. Spatial divisions mirrored theological and ecclesial hierarchies, sanctuary separated from nave, clergy from laity, men from women, insiders from outsiders. Processions assumed walking. Choirs assumed singing. Pews, where they existed later, assumed sitting. The very fabric of the building assumed a normative body.

But what would our medieval cathedrals have looked like had the predominant anthropology not been the idealized norm? What if the theological imagination had centred not the upright, rational, clerical male, but the full spectrum of human embodiment: the disabled pilgrim, the elderly widow, the neurodivergent child, the traumatized veteran, the blind singer, the limping priest? Surely the very layout of space, the gradients of access, the placements of thresholds, and the focal points of reverence would all have radically shifted. The sanctuary might have been reachable in a wheelchair. The pulpit might have accommodated the seated preacher. The labyrinth might have been navigable with support. The nave might have held less symmetry, and more sanctuary.

The Gothic period embedded its vision of human form within architecture itself, shaping worshippers to align with an ideal, upright, controlled and striving toward transcendence. Gothic cathedrals convey a theology of divine distance and ecclesial mediation, where grace descends from above. In this spatial hierarchy, those unable to ascend with the vertical structure were, by implication, excluded from its theological vision.

So let us explore the architectural impact of the Second Ecumenical Council of the Vatican, commonly known as the Second Vatican Council or Vatican II, which met in St Peter's Basilica in Vatican City in the autumn of each of the four years from 1962 to 1965 and produced one of the most seismic theological shifts in liturgical practice and, as a result, architectural design, of the twentieth century.

Vatican II: participation and the reformation of space

The Second Vatican Council (1962–1965) marked a turning point in ecclesiology and, by extension, in sacred architecture. *Sacrosanctum Concilium*, the Constitution on the Sacred Liturgy, declared that 'all the faithful should be led to that fully conscious and active participation in liturgical celebrations which is demanded by the very nature of the liturgy.'[1] The Church was reimagined as the People of God, not as a stratified clerical hierarchy as before, but as a pilgrim body united by baptism and Eucharist.

This reimagined theology demanded therefore a radical spatial reconfiguration. Altars were brought forward and made freestanding. Priests turned to face the people. Choirs moved into the midst of congregations. Spaces were opened, thresholds lowered, and linear, processional models gave way to circular and semicircular gathering spaces. The very arrangement of furniture and floor plan became an embodiment of ecclesiology.

Rudolf Schwarz asserted that a church must not simply contain the liturgy but embody it architecturally, shaping worship as an active, spatial experience. Vatican II's theology advanced this vision, urging the design of church spaces that moved beyond reinforcing clerical hierarchy or rigid bodily norms. Instead, it called for environments that cultivate shared visibility, relational proximity and communal participation, ensuring that worship is experienced as an inclusive act rather than a segregated performance.[2]

But, as we will discover in the three examples that I critique below, even this renewed ecclesiology retained traces of the normative body. Participation was reimagined, but often still for those who could stand, speak, kneel and hear. The active worshipper remained a physically and cognitively normative figure. The reformation of space had begun, but it was not yet complete.

Liverpool Metropolitan Cathedral: embodied theology in the round

Sir Frederick Gibberd's Liverpool Metropolitan Cathedral (1967) is one of the most iconic architectural responses to Vatican II. Its circular plan positions the altar at the geometric and symbolic centre, encircled by congregational seating, expressing the Church's unity and shared liturgical life. The tent-like form of the structure evokes both pilgrimage and presence, echoes of the Exodus tabernacle and the eschatological dwelling of God with humanity.[3]

Richard Giles articulates an architectural theology in which the church building itself embodies its theological commitments – not as a hierarchical structure but as a space of gathering; not as a fortress but as a family. This vision reverses the traditional verticality of Gothic cathedrals, emphasizing that grace is not solely transcendent but immanent, dwelling among the gathered community. Here, the Eucharist moves from distant ritual to central presence, reinforcing a theology of proximity and shared participation.[4]

Yet even this space, radical in form, sadly still reveals subtle remnants of exclusion. Fixed pews, for example, steps, and assumptions of visual and auditory access still point to the lingering presence of the idealized norm. It is therefore a theology of inclusion striving toward justice, but unfortunately still constrained by the unexamined anthropology of architectural tradition.

Worth Abbey: monastic participation and simplicity

Worth Abbey, also designed by Gibberd and completed eight years later in 1975, manifests the theology of Vatican II this time through a monastic lens. The building is circular, contemplative and quietly radical. The altar stands at the heart of the community, surrounded by monks and guests alike, reflecting a liturgical rhythm that balances silence, Scripture and sacrament.[5]

The paper for the United States Conference of Catholic Bishops 2000 (*Built of Living Stones: Art, Architecture and Worship*) states, 'The church building should be beautiful. The external and internal structure of the church building should be expressive of the dignified beauty of God's holy people who gather there and of the sacred rites they celebrate.' Thus the intentional absence of hierarchical structuring within Worth Abbey's layout fosters an atmosphere of collective prayer, reinforcing a theology of mutual presence and shared spiritual engagement.[6]

This is a church that I know intimately, having stayed in the monastery on retreat on countless occasions and it being the church where Bernie and I were married.

And yet, monastic liturgy, as I have personally observed and like so much of the Church's tradition, relies on coordinated, choreographed and embodied action: genuflection, chant, prostration. These movements assume bodies that conform to the Benedictine norm. Worth Abbey's beauty lies in its physical simplicity, but its inclusivity, especially in how its liturgy is expressed, is still bounded by a bodily ideal.

Clifton Cathedral: clarity, access and participation

Clifton Cathedral, completed in 1973, was designed with Vatican II's ecclesiology at its core. Architect Ronald Weeks conceived a space that was again open, egalitarian and clear in its theological messaging. The altar, once again, is central. The sanctuary is approachable, not elevated. Light floods the space, reducing mystery in favour of communion.[7]

Theologically, this space echoes. That visibility is achieved not just through transparency but through access. Wide aisles, ramped entries and integrated spaces begin to speak the language of justice. It is not a complete reimagining of space, but it is a meaningful gesture toward embodiment beyond the idealized norm.

Rebuilding the body's house

From the soaring Gothic cathedrals to the open sanctuaries of post-Vatican II churches, sacred buildings have always embodied theological commitments. But too often, those commitments have been bounded by the idealized norm, bodies that ascend, sing, process, kneel and conform.

Vatican II marked a shift toward a theology of presence, participation and communion. Buildings like Liverpool Metropolitan Cathedral, Worth Abbey and Clifton Cathedral enact this vision, sometimes fully, often imperfectly. They reveal to us that theology does indeed mould architecture, and that architectural decisions do reveal a Church's anthropology. We should be encouraged by this.

The question though still remains: what would our churches look like if they were built, from the foundation up, for the real body of Christ? For the wheelchair user and the child with autism, for the woman at the font and the disabled priest at the altar? That is the theological imagination our sacred architecture must now serve.

Storied architecture, risen bodies: reordering sacred and civic space as theological witness

In the Christian tradition, the body is not merely a vessel or container; it is sacred, storied, and destined for transfiguration. The risen body of Christ, still wounded, still recognizably human, stands at the heart of a Christian anthropology that resists both perfectionism and erasure. This theology invites us to consider how our built environments might also bear the marks of rupture and resurrection. What if our architecture reflected not only our doctrinal convictions but the scars and graces of our collective ecclesial and civic histories? What if buildings, like bodies, could rise again, retaining their wounds as part of their glory?

I wish now to explore a selection of contemporary buildings and restoration projects that I believe, whether consciously or unconsciously, embody such a *risen body* theology: places where the old is not replaced by the new but is held in generative tension with it. In these spaces – Gray Court in Gloucester, Alexandra Palace in London, All Saints Church in Dulwich, the Alte Pinakothek and Basilika St Bonifaz in Munich, the Kaiser Wilhelm Memorial Church in Berlin, the Kolumba Museum in Cologne and St John's Waterloo in London – we find diverse architectural examples of what might be called *storied design*: spaces, both secular and sacred, that speak honestly of trauma, change, endurance and hope. These are not smooth or perfect spaces. Most importantly, they are places where rupture has not been hidden, and where beauty is reimagined in the broken.

The risen body as architectural anthropology

A theology of the risen body embraces both continuity and transformation. Christ's resurrected form carried the scars of crucifixion – his hands, feet and side still marked, even in glory (John 20.27). The resurrection was not a restoration of Eden nor an escape from embodiment, but a profound transfiguration of memory. As theologian Sarah Coakley observes, the resurrected body does not erase the suffering of the cross but reinterprets it divinely, embodying both history and hope. It is a body that remembers while being made new.[8]

This theological anthropology challenges both nostalgia and utopian idealism. It rejects the romanticization of the past and the demand for an unblemished future, offering instead a vision of redemptive continuity. The risen body embodies both suffering and transformation without erasure or concealment. As Rowan Williams observes, the resurrection does not erase human history but unfolds it into a future where the past is held without constraint. In this framework, brokenness and glory are not opposing forces – rather, they coexist, affirming that grace does not necessitate the erasure of history.[9]

This anthropology has profound architectural implications. In contrast to the *tabula rasa* approaches of much twentieth-century modernism, which often sought to erase the past in the name of rationality or purity, a risen body theology embraces architectural layering. It welcomes imperfection, fracture and reassembly as part of the design language. This is not ruin as spectacle, but the visible witness of the trace of memory that all architecture must carry.

Such buildings do not seek an illusion of completeness; rather, they bear the marks of their history, much like Christ's wounded body, finding integrity in their honesty. Architecture is never detached; it is always rooted in history, place and memory. This approach allows structures to narrate their past, speaking of war and reconciliation, destruction and renewal, brokenness and grace. The design embraces tension, welcoming contradiction, for resurrection does not erase complexity; it holds paradox, allowing glory to coexist with scars and light to dwell alongside shadow.

Resisting the drive to aesthetic purity or nostalgic revivalism, risen-body architecture instead cultivates *dialogue*. It brings together old stones and new steel, preserved ruins and luminous additions, layered flooring and adaptive thresholds. It is inclusive of time, material and person. The 2022 Stirling Prize-winning architect Niall McLaughlin puts it this way: 'A good building is like a well-told story … something remembered, something broken, something surprising, something kind.'[10]

This architecture does not insist on forgetting; rather, it nurtures a theological imagination that embraces pain, transformation and grace together. It functions as a form of public discipleship, teaching communities that healing is not synonymous with returning to what once was. Shelly Rambo, in her theology of trauma and resurrection, reminds us that resurrection must be understood through wounds that persist, recognizing that true redemption must account for what cannot simply be undone. An architecture shaped by this perspective becomes a companion to human bodies, which are likewise restored not through erasure but through meaning. It also prompts essential questions: who remains unseen? Whose presence has been neglected? Whose story has been left out?[11]

To design or restore a building in light of the risen body is to resist the smooth surfaces of triumphalism. It is to ask: what has this place suffered? What has it survived? What grace has emerged here? And how can the very *form* of the space bear witness to that?

In what follows, I will explore six compelling examples of what could be coined *risen body design*: architectural projects where rupture is neither hidden nor glorified, but held within a narrative of dignified, storied renewal. These are not buildings that seek to erase the past or mimic it, but spaces that bear witness to the reality that resurrection does not require perfection. In each case, history is allowed to show through the seams, restoration meets resistance and beauty is found not in smoothness but in truthfulness.

This perspective aligns closely with the vision presented in *Pitching the Tent*, where Richard Giles, the former Anglican Dean of Philadelphia Cathedral, pioneered imaginative and innovative approaches to liturgical space, influencing the design of numerous church interiors, including Newcastle Cathedral. Giles advocates for a reordering of sacred spaces that does not conform to liturgical idealism but reflects the Church's lived reality, marked by both wounds and vitality. In his theology of architecture, churches are not meant to be frozen in aesthetic nostalgia but must remain open to the life surrounding them, bearing the scars of the communities they serve. What *Pitching the Tent* articulates conceptually, these risen body structures embody physically, an ecclesiology shaped by fracture and grace.[12]

These spaces embody a liturgical vision where proximity replaces triumphalism, where thresholds welcome rather than exclude and where light is permitted to settle unevenly, mirroring the complexities of faith and history. Scars of fire, war and loss are not erased but honoured, integrated into the worshipping memory of the place. This is precisely the kind of adaptable, living sacred architecture that Giles envisions – a space where design does not imprison the community's story but instead opens it up for continual unfolding. More than thoughtful liturgical planning, this is resurrection woven into the material world, inscribed in brick, timber, concrete and glass.

These architectural interventions, then, become companions to the theological claim at the heart of this chapter: that the Church, like Christ, is not resurrected into seamlessness, but into *recognizability* – wounded, real and radiant with grace.

Blackfriars Priory, Gloucester: chapel as wounded witness

The hall at Blackfriars Priory, Gloucester, formerly Greyfriars Chapel, offers a striking example of theological restraint and architectural redemption. Restored within the ruins of a thirteenth-century Franciscan friary, the chapel stands as a space that honours absence. It does not attempt to reconstruct the past; instead, it holds space for it.[13]

The rebuilding of the chapel incorporates rough stone, partial walls and open sky. The threshold between ruin and refuge becomes part of the spiritual grammar of the space. The design does not cover its scars, rather it lets them speak. This is *risen body* architecture: not seamless, not symmetrical, but alive with history and hope.

The liturgical implications are profound. Worship in this space cannot pretend that the world is unbroken. And yet, it proclaims a quiet resurrection, a place of presence amid collapse.

All Saints, West Dulwich: liturgical repair and architectural grace

All Saints Church, West Dulwich in south London, ravaged by fire in 2000, was restored not through imitation but through innovation that respected its history. The architectural team retained key Victorian elements, arches, columns and the overall footprint, but introduced contemporary interventions: glass, steel, light-filled additions.[14]

This fusion produces a liturgical space that breathes. Light falls through glass onto scorched stone. Transparency meets weight. The altar stands not as a triumph but as a site of gathering and recovery. The restored church honours both the vulnerability of the community and the resilience of their witness.

All Saints, Dulwich, therefore proclaims a profound theology of continuity, not a return to what was, but a transformation that includes what has been. It is an ecclesiology of memory, in stone.

Alexandra Palace, London: resurrection in the public square

The long-delayed restoration of Alexandra Palace in north London is another powerful example of storied architecture. Badly damaged by fire in the 1980s, the building was not entirely restored until 2018. The restored East Court and theatre deliberately retain charred surfaces, soot-darkened walls and exposed brickwork. The restoration strategy was not to return the palace to some imagined pristine past, but to honour its scars.

Here, resurrection happens in the secular public realm. Alexandra Palace becomes a civic body that remembers its trauma. The aesthetic is not *ruin porn* but *curated honesty*. In the context of a risen body theology, this building models what public institutions might look like when they embrace damage not as failure but as testimony.

Theologically, such a space becomes a kind of civic liturgy: a material participation in the Paschal mystery. Here the built environment performs what theologian Jürgen Moltmann has coined 'the memory of hope'.[15]

Alte Pinakothek and Basilika St Bonifaz, Munich: war, scar and continuity

The post-war restoration of the Alte Pinakothek, one of Europe's oldest public galleries, and the adjacent Basilika St Bonifaz in Munich, exemplifies a particularly German commitment to architectural honesty. Both were severely damaged during World War II. Their restorations refused complete concealment of trauma. At St Bonifaz, the rebuilt nave retains simplicity and sparse ornamentation, contrasting visibly with its richly decorated nineteenth-century choir. The visual rupture between old and new is not smoothed over. It is presented as theological truth: the Church as broken yet enduring, the liturgy as simultaneously mourning and praising.[16]

Similarly, the Alte Pinakothek's reconstructed galleries maintain subtle differences in material and tone, discrepancies that invite the viewer to notice. This is architecture as visual theology, resisting amnesia. In a city marked by complicity and suffering, these buildings refuse to forget, and in so doing, participate in resurrection without denial.

The Kaiser Wilhelm Memorial Church: the hollow tooth and the risen body

The Kaiser Wilhelm Memorial Church in Berlin stands as a striking architectural witness to risen body theology. Instead of concealing the scars of its history, the church holds them in view – preserving the bomb-shattered spire of its 1890s predecessor alongside a luminous modern chapel completed in the 1960s. This intentional pairing – locals call the ruin the 'hollow tooth' – refuses erasure and transforms destruction into declaration. The fractured tower does more than recall the violence of war: it embodies a redemptive insistence on remembrance. This is risen body architecture: wounded yet enduring, marked yet transfigured. In its interplay of ruin and renewal, the church offers a theology where the breaking deepens beauty, and memory becomes the soil from which hope rises.[17]

Kolumba Museum, Cologne: a theology of layering

But there is perhaps no modern building that better expresses risen body theology more fully than Peter Zumthor's Kolumba Museum in Cologne. Built over the ruins of the bombed-out Gothic Church of St Kolumba, the museum enfolds archaeological remains, a 1950s chapel by Gottfried Böhm and a contemporary gallery space into a seamless-yet-fractured whole.[18]

Zumthor's design does not merely preserve the past; it dialogues with it. Medieval walls remain exposed. Charred beams are displayed alongside contemporary sculpture. Light filters through perforated grey brickwork, casting shadows that shift with time and season. The visitor's journey through the building becomes a quiet pilgrimage through ruin, memory and grace.

The museum reflects what Rowan Williams describes as the ethics of delay, resisting the impulse for immediate resolution and instead fostering a space for contemplation, grief and resurrection. Its design moves through layers of architectural history, embodying a theological vision in which nothing is discarded, nothing is erased and everything is gathered into sacred remembrance.[19]

St John's Waterloo

The recent reordering of St John's Waterloo in south London, in which I was involved as the disability advisor for the Southwark DAC (Diocesan Advisory Committee), is a tangible sign of hope and can be understood as a powerful and generative act of ecclesial imagination, one that aligns profoundly with the theological anthropology of the risen Christ. For this reordering is not merely architectural or aesthetic: it is a reconstitution of space that speaks of inclusion, story, beauty and redemption. In this light, St John's stands as a beacon of what it means to reimagine sacred space through the lens of a risen body theology rather than an idealized or normative anthropology.[20]

The architecture of St John's Waterloo, particularly the decision to retain and integrate damage from the Blitz into the restored sanctuary, functions theologically, articulating the wounds of Christ, not as a sign of failure or shame, but as permanent markers of love, justice and truth-telling. The building thus becomes a witness to trauma that has not been smoothed away or hidden, but incorporated into a story of renewal, proclaiming that resurrection is not perfection but transfiguration: a wounded beauty.

The reordered space embodies an ethic of inclusion that disrupts the spatial hierarchies of many ecclesiastical buildings. The reconfigured sanctuary is accessible, open and welcoming, affirming the God-given dignity and participation of all bodies, including disabled, elderly, neurodivergent and economically marginalized bodies. This speaks directly to the body of Christ that is not composed of sameness but of radical difference united in grace. It is a spatial declaration that the Church is not built around an 'ideal body' but around the body of Christ as crucified and risen, wounded and glorified.

The entrance offers an extravagant welcome, where the agency of a diversity of bodies is affirmed and honoured. Automatic sliding doors and push pads offer autonomy and access for all who enter to freedom of thought, so often denied to disabled people, even in some accessible interventions.

The use of sustainable and locally sourced materials, and the commissioning of contemporary artists and craftspeople, signals a commitment to theological materiality, the conviction that matter matters. A risen body theology affirms that the body is not discarded in resurrection but restored in continuity. In this way, the reordered St John's bears witness to a sacramental theology of place: the past is not overwritten, but gathered up into a living memory, one that includes the Church's long-standing commitment to social justice, the arts and community solidarity. This participatory heritage becomes an embodiment of the memory-bearing body of Christ.

By relocating the altar closer to the people and enabling more fluid gathering, the reordering breaks down clerical and lay divisions that are often enshrined in fixed chancels and elevated sanctuaries. It refigures the Church not as a spectacle but as a shared liturgical body, one animated by mutuality, encounter and the Spirit's improvisation. This resonates deeply with Pauline ecclesiology, in which no one member is dispensable and all contribute to the body's flourishing. It is a vision of the Church not as perfect form, but as risen community.

Artistic interventions, such as the restoration of the Grade II* listed ceiling, the inclusion of new sculpture and iconography and the integration of visual elements from diverse traditions, reflect the diversity of the risen Christ's body. They speak not of uniformity but of plurality held together in love. The risen body is not homogenized; it is differentiated and glorified. The church becomes a canvas of eschatological hope, where beauty arises not from control or conformity, but from faithful attention to difference, history and grace.

St John's Waterloo has not simply undergone a reordering; it has undergone a theological metamorphosis. Through its embrace of woundedness, its dismantling of spatial hierarchies, its honouring of bodily diversity, and its incarnational aesthetic, it points toward a church configured not around the idealized norm, but around the scarred and risen body of Christ. It offers a powerful model of how ecclesial space can be reordered in the image of resurrection, holding past and future together in a sanctified now.

What might be their next steps? Perhaps liturgies that more fully integrate the crypt's communal tables or dance and art installations in the nave that celebrate bodily diversity. How might the solar arrays' hum be woven into prayer rhythms, reminding worshippers of their kinship with the sun-lit world? In this way, the architecture and liturgy continue to dialogue, deepening the church's witness to a resurrection that renews every nook of human and cosmic space.

Resurrection through architecture

Each of these examples – chapels, churches, galleries, palaces – do not simply represent good design – they embody a theological claim: that resurrection is not the denial of brokenness but its transformation. The risen body of Christ, still bearing its wounds, becomes the pattern for a new kind of architecture, one that is storied, scarred, but radiant with grace. This is a design language that honours the integrity of fracture. It is not aestheticized damage, nor the architecture of spectacle, but a deeply theological refusal to conceal what has been lost and lived.

It is in these structures that we discover a resistance to erasure, of history, of pain, of embodied struggle. They honour rupture without idolizing it. They speak of trauma, but also of survival, dignity and future. These are not passive restorations: they are active witnesses to the truth that damage need not mean disqualification. They model what sacred and civic architecture might become when it is shaped by a theology of the risen body: inclusive, honest, beautiful and unfinished. Their very incompleteness becomes an eschatological sign, a pointer toward a future not yet resolved but held open by grace.

Such architecture is a form of public prophecy. It resists the impulse toward sanitized memory or pristine spectacle. It tells the truth in brick and stone, in glass and light. These buildings teach with their wounds. They catechize communities into the ethics of repair, reconciliation, and interdependence. They become places where the very structure calls the body into new postures of worship and witness.

As Christian communities seek to reorder their spaces, architecturally, liturgically and relationally, they would do well to learn from these examples. In a world saturated by polished surfaces and architectural amnesia, such places invite us to imagine churches and cathedrals that not only accommodate difference but proclaim it as integral to the gospel. They are not merely accessible: they are theologically accessible. They do not simply make room; they declare that all bodies, every story, every scar belongs within the sanctuary of memory and meaning.

This vision reaches its most profound and urgent expression through the work of disabled theologians and practitioners, voices and bodies long absent from the Church's theological framework. Their witness is not simply a call for inclusion but a prophetic reshaping of ecclesial identity itself. Nancy Eiesland underscores this transformation by portraying the resurrected Christ as the disabled God, revealing a theological narrative that does not bypass suffering but carries it forward in redemption. Here, theology does not erase the wound – it bears it into new life.[21]

Notes

1 *Sacrosanctum Concilium*, Second Vatican Council, 1963.

2 Rudolf Schwarz, *The Church Incarnate: The Sacred Function of Christian Architecture*, trans. Cyril Edwards (Chicago, IL: University of Chicago Press, 2017), pp. 67–94.

3 https://liverpoolmetrocathedral.org.uk, accessed 28.08.2025.

4 Richard Giles, *Re-pitching the Tent: The Definitive Guide to Reordering Your Church* (Norwich: Canterbury Press, 2004), pp. 161–6.

5 https://worthabbey.net, accessed 28.08.2025.

6 United States Conference of Catholic Bishops, *Built of Living Stones: Art, Architecture and Worship* (Washington DC: USCCB, 2000), paragraph 44.

7 https://cliftoncathedral.org, accessed 28.08.2025.

8 Sarah Coakley, *God, Sexuality and the Self: An Essay 'On the Trinity'* (Cambridge: Cambridge University Press, 2013).

9 Rowan Williams, *The Resurrection: Interpreting the Easter Gospel* (London: Darton, Longman and Todd, 2002), pp. 91–112.

10 Niall McLaughlin, 'Lecture on Architecture and Memory', RIBA Annual Address, 2019.

11 Shelly Rambo, *Resurrecting Wounds: Living in the Afterlife of Trauma* (Waco, TX: Baylor University Press, 2017), pp. 83–118.

12 Giles, *Re-pitching the Tent*.

13 https://www.gloucesterblackfriars.co.uk, accessed 28.08.2025.

14 https://www.all-saints.org.uk, accessed 28.08.2025.

15 Jürgen Moltmann, *Theology of Hope: On the Ground and the Implications*

of a Christian Eschatology, trans. James W. Leitch (London: SCM Press, 1967), pp. 1–5.

16 https://www.pinakothek.de/en/the-museums, accessed 28.08.2025.

17 https://en.wikipedia.org/wiki/Kaiser_Wilhelm_Memorial_Church, accessed 10.09.2025.

18 https://www.kolumba.de, accessed 28.08.2025.

19 Rowan Williams, 'The Body's Grace', in *Theology and Sexuality: Classic and Contemporary Readings*, ed. Eugene F. Rogers Jr. (Oxford: Blackwell, 2002), p. 309–21.

20 https://stjohnswaterloo.org, accessed 28.08.2025.

21 Nancy L. Eiesland, *The Disabled God: Toward a Liberatory Theology of Disability* (Nashville, TN: Abingdon Press, 1994), pp. 98–106.

8

Power, Priesthood and the Performance of the Ideal: Ableism in the Liturgies of Empire and Ecclesial Authority

Liturgies of power, theologies of flesh

Throughout its history, the Church has not merely articulated doctrine; it has embodied theology through ritual. These rituals, particularly those performed in collaboration with the state, are not passive inheritances of tradition but active performances of theological anthropology. They shape the imagination of the faithful and the watching world. Whether in the solemn grandeur of a coronation, the reverent choreography of a state funeral or the cloistered discernment of a papal conclave, the Church enacts its understanding of human dignity, divine image and ecclesial authority not just through words but through bodies.

In the context of the Church of England as the established Church, these rituals carry an additional dimension: they are heritage acts. They bind the institution not only to its theology but to the nation's memory, identity and constitutional imagination. The Church's role in coronations, state openings of Parliament, jubilees and national funerals is not marginal: it is foundational to the cultural heritage of the United Kingdom. These are not merely ecclesial observances: they are national liturgies. They forge a public memory of who we are, who leads us, and what kind of body is considered worthy of symbolic and political representation. They inscribe ecclesiology into heritage, and heritage into ecclesiology. But this inheritance, shaped through centuries of repetition, carries within it not only beauty and continuity but exclusion and distortion.

Rituals are never neutral. They communicate a vision of holiness and legitimate memory. They declare, with aesthetic precision, what kind of body is welcome at the centre of the Church's life and the nation's stage. And too often, both the Church of England and the Roman Catholic Church, along with many other traditions, have tacitly proclaimed that sacred power must be embodied in bodies that conform to the unspoken ideal: upright, composed, cognitively fluent, physically strong, male and visually whole. These bodies are granted authority, veneration and symbolic centrality. Others are rendered peripheral, historically unseen, structurally excluded, ritually absent.

This implicit anthropology is not rooted in the gospel but is part of a long legacy of assimilation to Graeco-Roman ideals of perfection, control and transcendence. As the early Christian movement became increasingly enmeshed with state power, its theological imagination was restructured around ideals of order, purity and coherence; values that resonated with imperial aesthetics but distorted the scandalous particularity of the Incarnation. We should not be surprised therefore that liturgical memory of the Church too became aligned with the aesthetic and political logic of empire. These national liturgies of the Church of England, in its role as the established Church of the state, are the most public displays of this warped liturgical memory.

But in doing so, the Church exchanged a storied anthropology, one that sees the human as narrative, relational, time-bound and marked by contingency, for a static and visual ideal. The public rituals of the established Church, particularly those that carry high heritage value, are often effaced by a spectacle of bodily control and perfection, one that reinscribes ableist norms as national and ecclesial virtues.

Liturgies of power, such as those I will examine in this chapter, do more than commemorate theological claims. They shape ecclesial memory, curate legitimacy and instruct the community in what bodies are permitted to carry authority. They encode theology into tradition and tradition into heritage. In doing so, they not only reflect the Church's anthropology but embed ableist assumptions into its most sacred performances. The result is that disabled bodies are not only excluded from leadership but are also absented from the very theological imagination that undergirds sacrament, priesthood and presence. This is particularly acute in the Church of England's ceremonial alignment with statecraft, where ecclesial and civic identity converge in events watched by millions. The choreography of these national liturgies canonizes an image of Britishness that is steeped in bodily normativity.

This exclusion is not merely ethical, it is theological. It reveals a misunderstanding of the Incarnation, a distortion of resurrection, and a betrayal of the Spirit's groaning witness within the vulnerable. As I have already argued, the disabled body does not lack the *imago Dei* but fully manifests it, often in ways that expose the Church's own spiritual limitations. When the Church enacts power through perfected forms, it abandons the God who chose to dwell in fragility, be broken on a cross and rise with scars still visible.

Therefore, in this chapter I will explore how the Church's public rituals – coronations, ordinations, state funerals, conclaves and other ceremonial performances across various traditions – not only participate in the theological formation of Christian communities but inscribe exclusion into the performance of sacred memory. I will argue that these rituals are not just liturgies of belief but are also architectures of heritage: encoded memories of power, legitimacy and normativity. Drawing upon risen body theology, liberation theology and critical disability studies, it calls the Church not to accommodation, but to conversion. For only by reconfiguring these liturgies in the light of a scarred, risen Christ can the Church reclaim its calling to be a body in which all members are honoured and where power is no longer disguised ableism but becomes grace-in-flesh.

The Church of England and the theatre of the state

Coronation: anointing the normate body

The coronation of a British monarch is one of the most elaborately theological ceremonies performed by the state in partnership with the Church. Rooted in a vision of sacred kingship, the rite is replete with symbolism: robes of righteousness, sceptres of justice, orbs of divine sovereignty. In Westminster Abbey, the monarch is not only crowned but anointed, set apart in a liturgy that deliberately echoes biblical priestly and prophetic ordinations. The anointing, conducted by the Archbishop of Canterbury in the most intimate and sanctified portion of the rite, positions the monarch as both the representative of the people and the recipient of divine commission. For a moment, the body of the sovereign is liturgically transfigured: oil becomes the vehicle of consecration, and the human form becomes a vessel of spiritual and national identity.

Yet beneath the grandeur of this theological performance lies a deeply ableist anthropology. The body prepared for coronation is a carefully curated spectacle, clothed, postured and choreographed to signify wholeness, strength, dignity and command. It is a body that walks unaided, ascends steps, receives regalia with steady hands and gazes forward with composed resolve. The expectation is unspoken but universal: the sovereign must appear visually whole, physically upright, cognitively fluent, emotionally stable and capable of enacting the script of monarchy without visible disruption. This is not a neutral expectation, it is an embodied theology that aligns sacred authority with normative physicality.

Ableism is therefore expressed in the very structure of the rite: the assumption that anointing and coronation require an unassisted gait, the positioning of throne and altar to necessitate symmetrical movement and the absence of liturgical adaptations for diverse neurocognitive or communicative expressions. There is no provision during a coronation for a monarch who uses mobility aids, has involuntary movements, communicates with assistive technology or expresses affect atypically. Even the invisibility of such imagined possibilities in public discourse signals the extent to which ecclesial heritage, performed in state ritual, depends on a theology of ideal embodiment. It is not simply that disabled monarchs are unrepresented: it is that the very possibility of their full liturgical participation has been excluded from the theological imagination.

The theological underpinnings of this exclusion are manifold. Drawing on the classical inheritance of Graeco-Roman aesthetics, Christian liturgical practice has historically equated physical composure with spiritual authority. Moral purity and bodily control have been entwined through centuries of theological reflection, producing an implicit ecclesiology in which the ideal leader is imagined as physically coherent and emotionally contained. This ideal is perpetuated not only in ecclesial documents but in the symbolic weight of ritual performance, particularly those aligned with national identity and sacred heritage.

Theologians such as Hans Reinders and Deborah Creamer have demonstrated that much of Christian theology has failed to decouple moral worth from bodily capacity.[1] The monarch's body becomes, in this rite, a symbol not only of governance but of sanctity; a vessel of divine right whose authority is underwritten by its conformity to cultural norms of ability. The liturgy thus baptizes ableism, transfiguring it into tradition, and rendering it invisible by virtue of repetition.

Moreover, the coronation operates as a heritage event, repeated across generations, filmed and archived, embedded in the collective memory of nation and Church. It performs not only theology but continuity, not only ecclesiology but cultural permanence. This heritage function amplifies its theological consequences, for what is inscribed in the liturgy of kingship becomes a template for other rituals of authority: ordination, enthronement, commemoration. The coronation becomes a master-script, rehearsed across centuries, in which disabled bodies are written out before they are ever written in.

This is not merely an aesthetic failure; it is a theological distortion. The risen Christ appears in the Gospels not as a healed and perfected form, but as a wounded and recognizable body; scarred yet glorified. To perform the anointing of sovereigns without imagining a theology capacious enough for disabled leadership is to reject the very body through which God chose to be known. The Church, by participating in and sanctifying such a rite, reveals the extent to which its understanding of divine vocation has been shaped not by the gospel of Christ crucified and risen, but by the spectacle of bodily idealism.

A coronation that cannot imagine the sovereign anointed in a wheelchair, or processing with a tremor, or communicating through nonnormative speech, is not simply a failure of imagination. It is a failure of Christology. And it calls for a radical conversion of ecclesial heritage, from spectacle to witness, from perfection to presence, from symmetry to scar.

State funerals and national mourning

The funeral of Queen Elizabeth II in 2022 was one of the most widely viewed events in global broadcast history. The liturgy, meticulously choreographed and steeped in ecclesial heritage, featured military procession, evensong chants and sermon themes focused on duty, strength, service and national continuity. In many ways, it was a deeply moving act of public mourning. Yet while the event carried immense cultural and pastoral weight, its theological implications merit careful scrutiny, particularly when examined through the lens of disability theology and the anthropology of grief.

State funerals, especially those endorsed by the established Church, do not merely commemorate the dead. They perform national memory through theological ritual. In doing so, they become agents of public catechesis, ritualizing what the nation believes about death, the body and human worth. In the case of Queen Elizabeth II's funeral, the emphasis on noble service, unwavering strength and peaceful resolution to a life well-lived reinforced an idealized eschatology, one in which sanctity is demonstrated through performance, coherence and personal control. There was no liturgical space for weakness, no theological acknowledgment of chronic pain, cognitive decline or relational dependency. Yet the Queen, like all human beings, experienced bodily fragility and the indignities of age. That such dimensions were omitted from the ritual memory suggests a liturgical ableism woven deep into the fabric of public Christian mourning.

Ableism here is not expressed through overt exclusion but through ritual erasure. The funeral did not exclude disabled people by name; rather, it performed a theological anthropology in which bodily vulnerability is rendered invisible, inconvenient or aesthetically discordant with the tone of national reverence. The catafalque was guarded by symmetry and precision. The liturgical language avoided lament. The body was never spoken of as fragile, aged or mortal in its messiness, but rather as honoured, complete and transcendent. The eschatology on display was not of the scarred Christ who dies abandoned and rises still wounded, but of a monarch who exits history in near-divine composure.

This aesthetic of closure is rooted in a theology that associates dignity with distance from disruption. A vision of death shaped by military order, ecclesial splendour and composure undercuts the core Christian proclamation that God embraced weakness, entered suffering and refused to sanitize death's disorder. Thomas Reynolds has argued that the Church often resists vulnerability because it destabilizes the myth of self-mastery, a myth which we have inherited as much from Enlightenment ideals as Graeco-Roman ones.[2] John Swinton's work on memory and personhood reframes dignity not as something earned by cognition, clarity or continuity but as conferred by love, presence and sacrament.[3] Yet these insights remain marginalized in the spectacle of state mourning, where the aesthetics of composure become proxies for theological hope.

Such rituals imply that only certain kinds of death are grievable, and only certain kinds of bodies are worthy of public remembrance. Christine Pohl's work on hospitality and presence challenges the idea that worth is tied to cultural contribution.[4] In contrast, state funerals often present a functional anthropology, one that celebrates lives of visible service while erasing those whose holiness was marked by limits, silence, or unrecognized fidelity. The danger of such performances is that they turn heritage into hagiography: not the truthful telling of a life shaped by God's grace, but the sanctification of strength, the canonization of composure.

This has ecclesiological consequences. The Church's participation in these rituals not only reflects but reinforces an image of the body politic in which disabled lives are made absent. The liturgy becomes an agent of social memory that canonizes a mythic ideal of Britishness: unwavering, stoic, unbending to suffering. And yet, in Christian theology, the Church is not built on such bodies but on wounded flesh, tears of lament and the Spirit's groaning within weakness. A funeral that cannot acknowledge vulnerability is not a sign of honour; it is a theological disinheritance. It tells the watching world that sanctity is incompatible with dependence, that memory must be curated through strength alone.

If the Church is to be faithful in public grief, it must resist this ableist inheritance. Its funeral liturgies, especially those broadcast to the world, must tell the truth about death, the body and the gospel. They must make room for decline, for suffering, for ambiguity and for grace unaccompanied by grandeur. Only then will ecclesial heritage serve not as a monument to power, but as a witness to resurrection.

State openings and the architecture of power

The State Opening of Parliament is among the most iconic expressions of church–state partnership in the United Kingdom. Framed in prayer, as each session of Parliament is, it is an annual ritual that not only inaugurates legislative activity but enshrines constitutional memory through choreography. It unfolds as liturgical theatre: the monarch, robed and adorned with regalia, processes down the royal gallery of the Palace of Westminster, flanked by guards, heralds and attendants. Bishops in parliamentary robes sit on benches in hierarchical sequence. The Woolsack and throne stand as architectural focal points, embodying a visual theology of symmetry, sovereignty and inherited authority.

Yet beneath its ceremony lies a profound theological problem. The Opening teaches through space, posture, movement and silence. The body of the monarch must be unassisted. The bishops must appear dignified. The choreography must unfold without interruption. There is no room, liturgically or architecturally, for ramps, interpreters, alternative pacing, or non-verbal communication. It is not simply that disabled bodies are absent; it is that the ritual itself renders them theologically incompatible with sacred performance.

Ableism is not a logistical oversight here; it is a theological aesthetic. Yet again we are being offered a space which declares that power must be symmetrical, coherent, fluent and contained. Bodies that do not conform to these standards are rendered anomalous, not merely inconvenient but incongruous with the sacred-political image being projected. The very architecture of the Palace of Westminster, with its narrow thresholds and tiered balconies, reinforces this anthropology; to be seen as sovereign, ecclesial or authoritative, one must pass through spaces designed for unmarked, able bodies. The liturgy of Parliament does not merely exclude the disabled; it makes their presence unintelligible within its frame.

Theologically, this spectacle rehearses a long-inherited anthropology rooted in Graeco-Roman ideals of bodily order and imperial perfection. This illusion is not neutral; it is performative. The Church's visible presence in this ceremony, especially through its bishops, aligns ecclesial holiness with imperial decorum. As Judith Butler has argued in philosophical terms, bodies that disrupt dominant norms of movement, rhythm or presence are rendered socially unintelligible.[5] When applied to ecclesial performance, this becomes a matter of sacramentality: what kind of body is allowed to signify divine presence, and what kind is not?

Rosemarie Garland Thomson's insight that public rituals create values rather than merely reflecting them becomes particularly pertinent within this context.[6] The State Opening teaches a theology of embodiment, one in which dignity is conferred through uninterrupted movement, fluent speech and self-containment. It ritualizes the belief that theological and political legitimacy depend on bodily normativity. This is not an incidental message; it is a foundational one. The absence of disabled bodies in the ritual imagination of the state, and the Church's uncritical participation in this absence, signals that certain bodies are incompatible with sacred representation.

The absence of ramps or visible accommodations is not merely a failure of inclusion; it is a public denial of the risen Christ's wounded form. Instead we need a pneumatology which embraces interruption and improvisation, where the Spirit works not through the performance of control but through the presence of those who disrupt it. In ceremonies like the State Opening, such theology remains absent. The Spirit's wildness is domesticated, and the groaning body is hidden from view.

This ritual also serves a heritage function: it enshrines the constitutional identity of Church and state as fused through bodily performance. Its repetition each year reinforces a memory of nationhood and holiness that is defined by bodily symmetry and imperial legacy. As such, it does not merely reflect the past; it canonizes ableism into the memory of the nation. It makes normativity sacred.

If the Church is to be faithful within the structures of state, it must name and resist the theological violence of such spectacles. Participation must no longer mean complicity in a choreography of exclusion. It must mean prophetic interruption, architectural reimagination and a public theology in which the bishop with a tremor, the monarch with a cane, or the minister who signs their prayer is not a disruption but a sacrament.

Roman Catholicism and the machinery of perfection

Papal authority and the infallible body

The figure of the pope occupies a unique space within global Christianity: both a theological teacher and a visual icon, both a successor of Peter and a sovereign of the smallest state on earth. The papacy functions not only through doctrinal pronouncements but through the theatre of presence, by the pope's body being seen, elevated, encircled by ritual and venerated as a focal point of ecclesial unity. The liturgies surrounding papal appearances, travel and pronouncements rely on a consistent visual grammar: the pope as the centre of attention, coherent in movement, fluent in address, contained in gesture, and elevated in status. This theological visibility, however, is underwritten by a profound unease with bodily vulnerability.

Even when a pontiff becomes physically frail, as both Pope John Paul II and Pope Francis did in their final years, the institutional response has been to manage and contain the optics of decline. Their tremors, bowed posture and altered speech were framed as heroic endurance, almost saintly in their defiance of weakness. Yet these changes were rarely interpreted publicly as signs of grace in fragility. Instead, they were handled through a combination of reverent silence and tightly managed media, avoiding theological engagement with their disabled embodiment. Rather than allowing vulnerability to speak theologically, the Vatican narrative translated visible impairment into spectacle, with their suffering becoming meaningful only insofar as it was heroic, offered up, or eventually overcome.

This response reveals a deeper problem in Catholic theology: the conflation of authority with visible coherence. Papal infallibility, while narrowly defined in doctrine, has accrued an aesthetic and performative extension. The body of the pope is not expected to stutter, stumble or require translation. Theological authority becomes embodied in normative physical presence. This is not merely a matter of personal health; it is a sacramental imagination in which certainty, unity and divine guidance are tied to bodily composure and speech fluency. Such a performance implicitly excludes disabled forms of presence from being seen as legitimate vehicles of magisterial authority.

Ableism is thus expressed in the very structure of papal representation. The Vatican balcony is high and unreachable, designed for visual dominance. The papal throne is symmetrically carved and requires bodily poise. The Swiss Guard's rituals echo military precision. Even the traditional white cassock assumes cleanliness, purity and perfection. These visual elements combine to construct a theology in which ecclesial authority is rendered incompatible with uncontainable or unpredictable bodies. Disability becomes unrepresentable in papal space, not because the Church theologically rejects it, but because the Church's visual theology has no language for it.

This is not a neutral absence; it is the result of a longstanding theological anthropology that values transcendence over immanence, rationality over affect, order over relational contingency. When papal leadership is imagined as infallible not only in doctrine but in physical presence, it departs from this Christology and risks returning to an imperial aesthetic of power.

And yet in a risen body pneumatology, a pope who uses a wheelchair, requires an interpreter or is unable to speak publicly is not a diminished vessel of God's grace but a visible sign of the Spirit's radical hospitality. Yet this vision remains almost wholly absent from Vatican practice. Even Pope Francis, who explicitly called for a theology of inclusion, presided over liturgies that remained inaccessible, performatively rigid and visually ableist.

The sacramental implications are profound. If the papal body is the visible expression of unity, and that body must conform to able-bodied norms, then the Church has enshrined ableism at the very heart of its ecclesiology. Liturgical theology, as Susan Ross has shown, must wrestle with how ritual acts reinforce or resist cultural assumptions.[7] In the case of the papacy, the theological body is rendered holy through exclusion, not of doctrine, but of difference.

Until the Church can reimagine papal presence as capable of bearing the marks of disability, not merely as heroic suffering but as theological richness, its witness to the gospel of a wounded and risen Lord will remain compromised. To confess a disabled God while requiring an able-bodied pontiff is not only a contradiction, it is a refusal of the Incarnation in all its disruptive grace.

The priesthood and the illusion of ontological superiority

The priesthood, across many Christian traditions, has long been constructed not only as a sacramental vocation but as a performance of ontological distinction. In Roman Catholic theology, ordination is understood to impart an *indelible character*, a spiritual mark that configures the priest to Christ in a unique and unrepeatable way. While this theological formulation intends to honour the gravity of ministerial responsibility, it has historically become enmeshed with cultural ideals of purity, strength and bodily control. The result is a deeply ableist imagination of who can be a priest and, more profoundly, what kind of body is believed capable of mediating grace.

Canon law, for centuries, explicitly excluded those with physical or cognitive impairments from priestly ordination, categorizing them as possessing a 'defect' that rendered them unfit to stand at the altar or exercise the duties of pastoral leadership.[8] While revisions to canon law and theological discourse have softened some of these restrictions, the legacy of disqualification lingers in ecclesial imagination. The priest is still tacitly imagined as upright, visually whole and capable of executing liturgical and pastoral functions without visible support. The assumption persists: sacramental mediation requires physical coherence and communicative fluency. My own ordained ministry, as a visible disabled person, has been called into question on more than one occasion when it has been approached through this particular lens.

Ableism is embedded in this imagination not simply as prejudice but as theological aesthetics. The normative priestly body is one that can process smoothly, genuflect with grace, elevate the host with steady hands, and speak without pause or repetition. Assistive devices, such as wheelchairs, hearing aids, speech-to-text tools, are not accommodated as sacred instruments but treated as awkward intrusions. Churches are often architecturally designed to presume that the one who presides does so from a central, elevated and physically accessible place, usually a pulpit, altar or chancel with stairs and thresholds. The embodied presence of a priest with tremors, mobility constraints or neurodivergent behaviours is often perceived not as a liturgical expression of the body of Christ, but as a disruption to liturgical flow.

This exclusionary logic is not merely practical, it is theological. It stems from an anthropology in which sacramentality is conflated with performative mastery. The priest becomes the exemplar of control, the visual centre of ecclesial life and the conduit of divine order. This ecclesiology is deeply at odds with the biblical and theological witness of Christ, who emptied himself of divine status, embraced the wounded, and enacted ministry through dependence and shared vulnerability.

Priesthood urgently needs to be reimagined not as the performance of idealized holiness but as the public practice of mutuality, where weakness becomes sacrament and not shame, so that the exclusion from ordination on the basis of disability is one that not only diminishes the Church's inclusivity, but violates the very theology it proclaims; that God is most fully known in broken, relational flesh.

Yet this vision remains largely absent in ecclesial formation. Seminaries, diocesan discernment processes and canonical norms continue to reflect an unspoken bias against bodies and minds that require adaptation. Candidates for ordination are assessed not just for theological insight or pastoral compassion, but for stamina, vocal clarity, physical appearance and perceived 'leadership presence', criteria that disproportionately disadvantage disabled people. Liturgical training often assumes a singular template for presiding, with little attention to how gestures, voice or posture might be reimagined through diverse embodiment.

The theological underpinning of this bias is a distorted understanding of priestly ontology, one that equates nearness to Christ with distance from need. But this is not the ontology of the Eucharist, in which Christ offers himself in breaking bread, nor the ontology of baptism, where the Spirit moves through water, not perfection. Ecclesial inclusion requires not just practical adaptation but a theological conversion, away from mastery and toward where all bodies are recognized as sacramental agents.

Moreover, the illusion of priestly self-sufficiency has consequences beyond ordination. It informs how congregations view holiness, how they imagine leadership, and how they receive the sacraments. If only able-bodied priests are seen at the altar, the theology of the body of Christ becomes disfigured: Eucharist is separated from breaking, ministry from mutuality, authority from interdependence. This produces not a stronger Church, but a spiritually impoverished one.

To confront this, the Church must recover a theology of priesthood grounded not in ontological superiority but in kenotic presence, where presiding becomes a form of witness, not performance; where the trembling hand lifts the host in solidarity with the suffering Christ; and where the voice that stammers echoes the God who speaks through burning bushes and silences alike.[9]

The conclave and the liturgy of secrecy

The papal conclave is among the most secretive and symbolically charged rituals in contemporary Christianity. It is the liturgical heart of Roman Catholic governance: a ritual of transition, discernment and divine election enacted within the Sistine Chapel. The very space of the conclave – elevated, cloistered and historically inaccessible – reinforces the gravity of the event. Yet it also reflects a theological anthropology in which participation is predicated upon physical endurance, cognitive fluency and bodily conformity.

POWER, PRIESTHOOD AND THE PERFORMANCE OF THE IDEAL

Though there are no formal canonical exclusions of disabled cardinals from the conclave, the practical architecture and liturgical choreography of the process render many forms of disabled embodiment incompatible with participation. Cardinals must physically process into the chapel, take a solemn oath while standing, cast their vote by hand at a designated altar, and remain sequestered for potentially long periods under intense physical and cognitive demands. Those who require interpreters, rest periods, ramps, assistive technology or carers encounter unspoken barriers; barriers not legislated but embedded in the ceremony's assumed normativity.

Ableism in the conclave is expressed through liturgical design and spatial symbolism. The entire process presumes a particular kind of ecclesial body; one that is autonomous, mobile, discrete and disciplined. The aesthetic of secrecy, rooted in solemn silence, ritual purity and uninterrupted continuity, resists any form of disruption. Disabled presence, particularly when it involves non-verbal communication, visible support or uneven temporal rhythms, is subtly framed as a threat to the dignity or legitimacy of the discernment. In practice, the conclave enacts a liturgy in which theological clarity is tied to bodily regularity.

This is undergirded by a theology of unity that confuses agreement with uniformity. The early Church discerned the movement of the Spirit not through consensus alone, but through disruption: in the voices of widows, eunuchs, Gentiles and others whom the ecclesial authorities had not anticipated.[10] Yet the modern conclave is choreographed as a closed circle; visually, ritually and theologically. It is designed to reinforce a sense of magisterial continuity, with little room for bodies that deviate from established norms.

The theology behind this is not merely procedural but sacramental. The conclave is seen as the location of the Spirit's guidance. But when the participants are drawn only from a particular class of bodily and cognitive experience, the discernment risks becoming self-referential rather than pneumatologically open. True discernment surely must begin with attentiveness to bodies that are typically marginalized, since the Spirit often reveals God's purposes precisely through the unexpected. A conclave that cannot accommodate or welcome disabled cardinals renders itself resistant to such movements of grace.

We need to call attention to the Church's frequent desire for control, a desire that surfaces in rituals where the illusion of mastery is privileged over the embrace of relational vulnerability. The conclave ritualizes this desire. Its guardedness, solemnity and exclusionary aesthetic function to preserve ecclesial stability, but at the cost of excluding theological alternatives. Bodies that shake, pause, require care or need translation are implicitly framed as incompatible with divine election, though the gospel proclaims otherwise.

The Sistine Chapel, with its iconic fresco of Michelangelo's *The Last Judgement*, becomes not only a backdrop but an icon of idealized flesh. The bodies depicted on its ceiling are strong, youthful, proportionate and free from blemish. That these are the images surrounding one of the most theologically weighty decisions in the Church's life is no accident. The visual and architectural context of the conclave reinforces a specific anthropology: divine election is mediated through aesthetically ideal bodies. The very space becomes a liturgical act of exclusion.

The implications are not only ecclesiological but eschatological. When the conclave enacts a ritual of discernment that omits bodily diversity, it not only distorts the theology of leadership, it misrepresents the Church's eschatological hope. And yet surely the Spirit breathes most powerfully where rigid systems are broken open by compassion, vulnerability and relationality. In this vision, the conclave should be less like a sealed fortress and more like Pentecost, marked by disorientation, mutual dependence and unexpected speech.

To reimagine the conclave in light of risen body theology would not mean abandoning its solemnity but transforming its imagination. A space where a wheelchair user could preside. A process where silence includes alternative forms of expression. A ritual where dependence is not seen as failure, but as fidelity to the crucified Christ. Only then might the election of a pope become not merely a succession of governance, but a prophetic sign of the Church's openness to the Spirit's disruptive grace.

Eastern Orthodoxy: beauty, *theosis* and the invisible body

Eastern Orthodoxy has long rooted its theological identity in beauty – *kallos* – not as aesthetic superficiality, but as a deep expression of divine harmony and transfigured creation. The Orthodox tradition elevates the vision of the transfigured Christ, the veneration of icons and the process of *theosis*, becoming by grace what God is by nature. This soteriological and liturgical vision is profoundly incarnational, sacramental and cosmic. Yet precisely in its emphasis on transcendent beauty, Orthodox liturgical and visual culture often renders disabled bodies invisible, absent or incongruent with the anticipated *telos* of divine likeness.

Icons, central to Orthodox piety and theology, depict the saints and

Christ in stylized, unblemished form: frontal, symmetrical, still and luminous. The theology behind this style seeks to portray not the fallen flesh, but the eschatological human; the one transfigured in divine light. However, this visual grammar communicates, intentionally or not, a theology in which visible impairment has no place in redeemed humanity. Wounds are hidden, deformity abstracted, difference spiritualized or erased. Disability is therefore not incorporated into the sacred image but set aside as pre-transfiguration. The message is clear: to be like God is to be visually unmarked by fragility.

This exclusion extends to the liturgical realm. Orthodox liturgies are deeply embodied, chanted, censed, processional and multi-sensory. But they are choreographed around normative bodies. Clergy are expected to stand and bow, to move with ritual grace and to chant without interruption. The layout of the iconostasis, the narrow spaces of sanctuaries and the lack of sensory alternatives (such as visual cues for Deaf worshippers or tactile access for blind communicants) all reinforce an implicit anthropology. Participation in divine beauty becomes associated with bodily fluency.

Ableism within Eastern Orthodoxy thus emerges not from explicit prohibition, but from the fusion of theology and aesthetics. The tradition's emphasis on divine beauty, understood as order, balance and radiant clarity, leaves little space for asymmetry, disruption or bodily unpredictability. Yet this aesthetic theology is not merely about liturgical taste, it communicates deep anthropological assumptions. The glorified human is expected to reflect divine *kallos*, but what happens when *kallos* becomes a screen through which only idealized flesh is seen as capable of communion?

This tension is particularly acute given that Orthodox theology has also affirmed, in the work of figures like John Zizioulas, that personhood is constituted in communion, not in autonomy or perfection, but in relational being. Zizioulas insists that the true image of God is not the self-contained individual, but the person in relationship.[11] Yet in practice, the ecclesial hierarchy remains visually homogeneous: male, elderly and able-bodied. The theological affirmation of relationality has not yet broken through into liturgical design, visual representation or ministerial diversity. The anthropology performed remains idealized, not storied, resistant to the marks of time, trauma or disability.

Elizabeth Theokritoff and Alexander Schmemann have both emphasized the cosmic and communal dimensions of Orthodox worship, affirming the liturgy as the transfiguration of all creation.[12] Yet creation includes the disabled body. A truly cosmic liturgy would not render it invisible but lift it into full presence. As it stands, however, the Orthodox liturgical space often functions as a theatre of perfected form, with little room for wheelchairs, interpreters, altered pacing or non-verbal prayer. The theological imagination enacted is that of *anástasis* without *stigmata*, resurrection without scars.

The implications extend to how holiness is recognized. Saints canonized in the Orthodox Church are typically remembered for ascetic strength, healing power or martyrdom. Rarely are disabled saints canonized for having lived with impairment in faith and joy. The one exception often cited, St Paul the Simple, remains theologically marginal, seen more as a fool-for-Christ than a theologically rich witness to disability. The Church's hagiography and iconography alike fail to present disability as intrinsic to sanctity. In this way, the tradition's *theosis* becomes unreachable for many, not because of sin, but because of embodiment.

To challenge this, Orthodox theology must rediscover the wounded body of Christ, not as a prelude to resurrection, but as its ongoing revelation. The risen Lord appears with scars not erased but glorified. The Transfiguration is not a shedding of flesh, but its illumination. If *kallos* is to remain the goal of Orthodox worship, it must be expanded to include the radiant asymmetry of grace; where stammering voices chant truth, where wheelchairs pass through the royal doors, where icons are written in diverse flesh and where *theosis* embraces not the ideal but the real.

Pentecostalism

Pentecostalism's global reach and theological vitality have positioned it as one of the most influential Christian movements of the modern era. Its emphasis on the immediacy of the Holy Spirit, embodied worship and charismatic transformation has empowered millions. Yet alongside its liberating potential, Pentecostalism also participates in the transmission of cultural and theological norms that render some bodies invisible, suspect or spiritually deficient. While healing theologies are the most visible site of ableism, they are not the only one. Pentecostalism often embeds ableist assumptions in its liturgical style, anthropological ideals and increasingly in its entanglements with national identity and Christian heritage.

Liturgical ableism and the inherited aesthetic of energetic praise

Pentecostal worship is intensely embodied and performative. Services are loud, immersive and often physically demanding, featuring prolonged standing, rhythmic movement, impromptu dance, raised arms and emotional expressiveness. In many contexts, this aesthetic of energetic praise is valorized as the highest expression of authentic worship and a sign of the Spirit's presence. But in practice, it functions as a kind of liturgical sorting, in which bodies that cannot conform to this rhythm, due to mobility impairments, chronic fatigue, sensory sensitivity or cognitive difference, are rendered out of place or spiritually muted.

This liturgical norm is not a neutral form of expression. It is inherited, shaped by revivalist traditions that associate faith with bodily vitality, and revival with explosive physicality. It becomes, over time, a kind of heritage practice: a repeated choreography that shapes the ecclesial memory of what worship should look like. Those who do not move fast, sing loud or respond with extroverted immediacy are subtly cast as spiritually incomplete. Worship becomes not an open table but a performance of theological able-bodiedness.

When these aesthetic norms are sacralized, they reproduce a deeply ableist anthropology, one that sees wholeness in kinetic fluency, sanctity in emotional overflow and holiness in noise. Yet Pentecostal theologians have begun to suggest that such norms are more culturally inherited than divinely mandated.[13] They call for an expanded liturgical imagination that honours silence, stillness and stimming; where worship is no longer bound to revivalist spectacle but shaped by a deeper theology of mutual presence.

Pneumatological ableism and the nationalized body

In many Pentecostal contexts, especially in the Global South and in nationalist expressions of Pentecostalism in the United States, Brazil, Nigeria and elsewhere, the Spirit is invoked not only in personal transformation but in the sanctification of national destiny. 'Spirit-filled' becomes synonymous not just with personal anointing but with cultural and national exceptionalism. The healed body, the upright family, the prosperous citizen and the strong nation all become intertwined symbols in a charismatic-patriotic imaginary.[14]

In this vision, the normative Pentecostal subject is not only healed, but productive, coherent and representative of national strength. Disability, particularly visible disability or cognitive difference, disrupts this image. It challenges the triumphant anthropology upon which both spiritual power and national pride rest. The disabled body risks becoming a theological embarrassment, one that is either ignored, explained away or turned into a site of miraculous deliverance to reinforce the larger national narrative of divine favour.

This is not merely a theological error. It is a form of liturgical nationalism, in which the Spirit is conscripted into a story of collective perfection. The disabled body, unable to carry this story without remainder, is left out of the liturgical frame. The result is an ableism that is both spiritual and political; the nation, like the Church, must be strong, whole and unblemished. Pentecostal heritage becomes a tale not of radical inclusion, but of triumph over weakness.

Yet this is a betrayal of Pentecost itself. The biblical Pentecost is not a liturgy of national coherence, but a disruption of monolingual power.[15] It is the Spirit poured out on all flesh, men and women, young and old, slave and free. It is a disordered, multilingual and multi-embodied eruption of divine presence that undoes imperial homogeneity. A true Pentecostal theology would not erase disabled difference to preserve a spiritual or national ideal: it would proclaim it as the locus of divine presence.

Ecclesiology, urgency and the exclusion of slowness

Pentecostalism's revivalist roots often create a sense of urgency: the Spirit is moving now, the time is short, the harvest is ready. This eschatological energy produces a high-octane ecclesiology in which ministry is fast, mobile and reactive. While this dynamism has empowered lay leadership and decentralized ecclesial structures, it also embeds a myth of spiritual readiness that excludes those who cannot respond with immediacy.

Disabled people, especially those with fluctuating conditions, sensory processing differences or chronic mental health needs, are often seen as pastorally dependent rather than theologically generative. They are recipients of ministry, not bearers of vision. Pentecostal ecclesiology, under the weight of revival urgency, frequently fails to accommodate the slowness of crip time, the quiet of non-verbal theology or the faithfulness of lives lived with ongoing need.

Moreover, Pentecostal churches frequently present leadership as hyper-functional. The preacher is expected to pace the stage, speak extemporaneously, hear and interpret words of knowledge and manage sensory-rich environments. These performance-based expectations reinforce ableist standards of visibility and coherence. They also establish a form of spiritual heritage in which leadership is remembered and replicated through bodies that display power, not vulnerability.

A different ecclesiology is possible, one in which leadership is shared, mutual and adaptive; one where the call to preach includes the voice box and the speech device, the whisper and the stutter; one where presence is not judged by performance, but by love. Pentecostal heritage must be reconfigured to include those who have always been present but never recognized.

Eschatology and the myth of completion

Pentecostal eschatology often revolves around victory. God's kingdom is breaking in. Miracles are signs of what will be. Healing, deliverance and empowerment are foretastes of the age to come. But in this theology of imminent transformation, disability is frequently framed as a prelude to healing, as a condition that testifies to the power of God only when it is undone.

The result is a theological displacement of disabled bodies into a future where they no longer exist. The eschatological imagination, rather than embracing wounds as eternal, rewrites them as temporary detours. This displaces not just disabled people but their stories, their gifts and their place in the unfolding narrative of grace. Pentecostalism must learn from risen body theology: the Christ who returns does so scarred. Completion is not the erasure of pain but the transfiguration of memory.

When Pentecostal communities link bodily wholeness with final redemption, they silence those whose lives are not marked by healing, but by endurance, adaptation and sacred interdependence. In doing so, they lose the theological witness that disability bears: that perfection is not symmetry, and that grace is not efficiency.

Reclaiming Pentecost as crip heritage

Pentecostalism's rich theology of Spirit, testimony, and transformation holds profound potential for the reimagining of ecclesial inclusion. But to realize this, it must confront its embedded ableism, not just in healing narratives, but in its inherited aesthetics, nationalist imaginaries, and liturgical heritage. The Spirit does not anoint only those who move fast, speak loudly or walk unaided. The Spirit also rests on the paralyzed, the neurodivergent, the exhausted and the non-verbal.

The heritage of Pentecost must become crip heritage: not a triumph over weakness but a theology shaped by wound, slowness and interdependence. Pentecost was not a celebration of strength – it was the undoing of spiritual monopoly. Today, that undoing must include the dismantling of ableist assumptions and the embrace of bodies long kept at the edge of the flame.

Indigenous and non-Western Christianity: theologies of scar and survival

Non-Western and Indigenous Christianity: crip wisdom and ancestral theologies

Following on from Chapter 2, non-Western and Indigenous expressions of Christianity frequently carry anthropologies that challenge the dominant Western theological grammar of the idealized, able and independent body. While these traditions are far from monolithic and can contain their own ableist tendencies, they often preserve or recover theological frameworks in which disability is not deficit, but vocation; not a deviation from human fullness, but an honoured form of embodiment interwoven with land, ancestry and spiritual responsibility. Yet even these traditions have been pressured by colonial Christianity to conform to Western ideals of bodily coherence, healing and liturgical respectability, producing a complex theological inheritance where crip wisdom is both remembered and resisted.

African Independent and Spirit Churches: spiritual power and embodied difference

In many African Independent Churches (AICs), disability is interpreted through the lens of spiritual presence rather than lack. People with physical or cognitive disabilities are often seen as having particular spiritual sensitivities or prophetic vocations. Their bodies are not disqualified from the sacred but located within it. Yet this affirmation sits in tension with the increasing influence of neo-Pentecostal prosperity theology, which has globalized Western ideals of productivity, healing and bodily perfection.[16]

In urban megachurches across Nigeria, Kenya, South Africa and elsewhere, disability is often reframed as a site of deliverance. The disabled body becomes a liturgical prop, evidence of spiritual warfare or a canvas for divine intervention. Here, healing is not merely pastoral but nationalistic; a sign of God's favour upon a rising nation, a body politic that must be strong, unified and productive.

Thus, heritage becomes contested. Traditional African cosmologies that valued liminality, slowness or ancestral connection are increasingly displaced by televised performances of healing and wealth. This colonial theological residue reframes disability as a symbol of regression or curse rather than connection or call. The tension lies between two heritages: one Indigenous and relational, the other imported and individualized. Only by recovering the former can African theologies resist the ableist norms embedded in both colonial Christianity and global capitalist spirituality.

Latin American theology and the wounded God of history

Liberation theology in Latin America, especially in the work of Gustavo Gutiérrez and others, places the suffering and wounded body at the theological centre. God is revealed not in power but in solidarity with those rendered marginal by empire: peasants, the sick, the disabled, the disappeared. This theological vision affirms that pain is not to be spiritualized away but recognized as the site of divine encounter. In this framework, disability becomes part of the theological narrative of resistance: a lived expression of the *crucified people*, in whom Christ continues to suffer and rise.

However, even here, tensions persist. The liberationist emphasis on social transformation can sometimes mirror secular ideals of productivity and coherence. The disabled poor may be centred symbolically, yet excluded practically from leadership, liturgy and theological production. Moreover, the pressure of national Catholic identities, especially in contexts where religious ritual is tied to patriotic spectacle (e.g. processions, Marian festivals, civic Masses), can produce a heritage aesthetic that erases disabled presence. These rites, like their European counterparts, often privilege symmetry, solemnity and sensory control, leaving little space for bodies that move differently, speak unpredictably or require adaptation.

Yet in base communities and feminist liberation theology, a different ecclesiology emerges, one that honours embodiment as storied, wounded and interdependent. Disability is no longer a problem to solve but a lens through which theology must be reformed. As such, national Christian heritage in Latin America stands at a crossroads: it can either deepen its liberationist roots by embracing embodied diversity, or collapse into a performance of pious normativity that conceals its exclusions.

Pacific Islander and other Indigenous theologies: weaving disability into sacred memory

In Indigenous and Pacific Islander Christianity, the body is not an isolated unit but part of a broader sacred ecology. Theological anthropology is shaped by land, water, story and ancestral relation. Embodiment is understood not in terms of independence but interdependence, not normativity but continuity. Disability, in this view, is not a break in identity, but a thread in the communal weave of being, a mark of spiritual depth and ancestral presence.

For many First Nations theologians in Australia, Canada and the United States, the sacred is found in brokenness and endurance. Survival itself becomes a theological category, particularly in the face of colonial genocide, stolen land and cultural erasure. Disability, especially when inherited through intergenerational trauma or environmental displacement, is not seen as external to faith but intrinsic to the lived story of Indigenous Christianity.

Yet ableism still infiltrates. Mission schools and colonial churches imposed a visual and behavioural orthodoxy: bodies must be silent in pews, emotions subdued, movement choreographed. These imported expectations devalued traditional forms of expression – chant, dance, visual storytelling – and framed disabled embodiment as uncivilized or spiritually deficient.[17]

Today, Indigenous Christian leaders are reweaving liturgies that centre disabled experience: creating storytelling circles, inclusive ceremonies and theologies grounded in the wounded earth. This is not merely pastoral; it is an act of decolonial heritage recovery, asserting that disability is not a Western medical issue but a spiritual location within Indigenous cosmology. Crip embodiment becomes a form of witness, a carrier of memory, and a site of sacred continuity.

Crip resistance and the decolonization of theological heritage

Non-Western and Indigenous Christianity bear witness to theological possibilities long suppressed in Western traditions. They remind the global Church that the *imago Dei* is not confined to Graeco-Roman ideals or Constantinian aesthetics. Yet they also reveal how colonial Christianity exported ableism, embedding it within nationalist projects, civic religion and ecclesial architecture.

Whether in African prosperity churches, Latin American state liturgies or postcolonial Indigenous communities, the struggle for crip inclusion is a struggle for theological heritage: who tells the story, whose body is remembered and which rituals shape the imagination of the faithful.

In these diverse contexts, the Church must choose. Either it continues to replicate a heritage that privileges wholeness, control and patriotic spectacle, or it allows itself to be reformed by the Spirit who speaks through silence, scarred bodies and land-storied lives.

From spectacle to witness: rethinking ecclesial power

Reimagining ecclesial rituals through the lens of risen body theology demands not minor adjustment but structural, aesthetic and liturgical transfiguration. It requires the Church to confront how its public acts of worship and state-aligned ceremonies perform a theology of exclusion. Far too often, these rituals are curated around assumptions of bodily perfection, cognitive fluidity, visual order and choreographic control. These assumptions are not simply practical; they are theological assertions, embedding a soteriology of strength, an ecclesiology of symmetry, and an anthropology of exclusion into the heritage life of the Church.

Ableism in ecclesial ritual is expressed in multiple layers. First, it manifests structurally, in the physical inaccessibility of sacred spaces: steps to chancels, tightly packed pews, pulpits without lifts. Second, it appears aesthetically, in the curated visual performance of able bodies: clergy who stand unaided, bishops who process in hierarchical rank, choristers who sing in perfect pitch and formation. Finally, it is enacted liturgically, in the expectation that participation requires verbal fluency, physical stamina or neurotypical focus. These exclusions are not incidental. They perform a theology in which the sacred is imagined to reside only in bodies that appear whole, contained and unbroken.

The theological root of this exclusion is a lingering Christology of perfection, a misreading of the Incarnation and Resurrection that imagines

God as restoring humanity to a normative, pristine ideal. In this vision, the resurrected Christ is falsely imagined as purged of scars, his brokenness erased. This sanitized Christ then becomes the unspoken prototype for priesthood, liturgy and sacrament: strong, articulate, symmetrical and male. The consequences are far-reaching: disabled people are not only excluded from ministry; they are rendered theologically unimaginable within the Church's symbolic centre.

To resist this, the Church must embrace a risen body theology – one that insists that Christ's resurrected form is not the obliteration of his suffering, but its glorification. The wounds are not undone; they are transfigured. This Christology does not erase brokenness but hallows it. In this vision, disability is not something the Spirit must heal before it can inhabit; it is something through which the Spirit is already speaking.

What might this mean for the Church's most public rituals?

Coronations, long seen as the zenith of sacred-national theatre, must shift from displays of imperial wholeness to participatory liturgies of interdependence. Disabled people must not simply be accommodated on the margins, they must stand at the centre: blessing, proclaiming, anointing, interpreting. This would challenge the deeply held assumption that divine right is linked to hereditary or bodily strength and affirm instead that kingship in the kingdom of God is always cruciform, always shared.

State funerals, traditionally choreographed as stately departures wrapped in dignity and triumph, could become occasions for honest theological witness to mortality, fragility and finitude. The liturgy could make space for remembrance of cognitive loss, chronic illness, relational dependence and pain, elements often edited out of national commemoration. In doing so, the funeral becomes not a spectacle of the strong departing but a communal recognition that all flesh is grass, and all glory like the flower of the field.

Papal conclaves and episcopal elections, traditionally held in elevated and symbolically cloistered spaces, must be reimagined to include those whose discernment may be non-verbal, whose wisdom may come through assistive technology, whose theological insight emerges from neurodivergent ways of knowing. Such spaces are not less sacred; they are more so, because they resist the idol of perfection and embody the Church's claim to be a body where every member is indispensable.

Priestly ordinations, frequently performed as liturgical perfectionism, processions, vows, laying on of hands and movements to and from the altar, must be recast to honour those who cannot kneel, who speak using electronic devices, who move with crutches, who tremble. The priesthood of Christ is not defined by composure, but by pierced hands offering broken bread. The ontological change of ordination must be severed from visual norms and recast as embodied solidarity with Christ's wounded presence.

In all of these, the aesthetics of power must yield to liturgies of wounded witness. Ecclesial authority must no longer be based on resemblance to a Graeco-Roman ideal of masculinity and symmetry, but on faithful likeness to the Christ who appeared with scars, breathed peace into fearful rooms and refused to ascend until his broken body had been touched and recognized.

This reframing demands a new ecclesiology, one that views the Church not as a theatre of perfected performance, but as a gathering of scarred bodies around a scarred God. It is only by embracing this vision that the Church's public rituals will become what they claim to be: sacraments of divine grace, bearers of hope for all bodies and witnesses to a God who is not above fragility but glorified through it.

The body at the centre

If the Church is to be the body of Christ, it must centre not the geometry of empire but the scars of grace. Its ceremonies must not mimic state pageantry, military discipline or regal restraint, but must echo the messy, interruptive and often painful reality of embodied life. A risen body ecclesiology will not hide wheelchairs behind columns or refuse the ministry of those who stammer or twitch. It will not treat sensory difference or mental illness as theological embarrassments to be managed offstage. Instead, it will affirm that scarred bodies belong at the centre of the Church's liturgy, not as metaphors but as ministers, not as tokens but as theologians in flesh.

The Church must ask again, with all seriousness: whose bodies narrate our national theology? Whose presence is permitted to shape our collective liturgical memory? Until our national and ecclesial ceremonies reflect the full spectrum of human embodiment, including its pain, interdependence, neurodiversity and physical diversity, we will remain bound to a performative gospel we do not live.

Nowhere is this challenge more urgent than in the national and international liturgies that define the public identity of the Church of England, the Roman Catholic Church and the Orthodox Church. For the Church of England, coronations, state funerals, royal weddings and commemorative services do not merely reflect national unity; they construct it. For the Roman Catholic Church, globally televised papal Masses, canonizations and World Youth Day liturgies become visible proclamations of universal Catholic identity. And in Eastern Orthodoxy, the grandeur of Paschal liturgies and the symmetry of iconostasis rituals communicate sacred order and ontological hierarchy. But in each case, these rites are often crafted through an aesthetic that excludes bodies marked by disability; not only practically but symbolically. The result is an international heritage of worship that canonizes a specific body type: able, ordered, whole, self-contained.

Yet the theology of the wounded Christ shatters that illusion. It confronts us with the truth that divine glory is not found in untarnished flesh, but in wounds remembered and redeemed. The risen Jesus does not ascend in imperial splendour; he stands among the frightened, breathes peace into their fear and extends scarred hands for recognition. He is not the god of empires, but of broken rooms and disrupted expectations. And if the Church is to proclaim this Christ in its most public, national and visible acts, it must become willing to embody him, not through displays of aesthetic power, but through liturgies of shared human vulnerability.

The transformation required is profound. It will involve redesigning liturgies, rebuilding spaces, reconfiguring processions, rewriting prayers and repenting of unspoken theologies that have harmed, excluded and erased. It will involve seeing the disabled body not as deviation but as divine witness, not as anomaly but as the very site through which Christ reveals himself to a watching world.

The Church, especially the established Church and its global counterparts, must lead this transformation. Because if we continue to rehearse the gospel through idealized bodies, we proclaim a lie about the Incarnation. If we persist in preserving heritage at the cost of presence, we worship the past and not the risen Lord. But if we honour the risen Christ as he truly is, scarred, wounded, glorified, then we will finally begin to construct national and global liturgies worthy of the gospel we preach.

So we pivot.

From ecclesial stone, and the liturgies they inhabit, to human flesh. From the history housed in artefacts and liturgies to the living archive carried in disabled bodies, bodies that remember what the Church has tried to forget, bodies that teach what pulpits have failed to preach, bodies that do not demand healing, but offer it.

What if the blind reader, the non-verbal intercessor, the chronically ill minister or the neurodivergent teacher is not at the margins of the Church's story, but at its centre?

What if wholeness begins here? The stones have spoken. The liturgies have performed. Now the bodies will sing.

Notes

1 Hans S. Reinders, *Receiving the Gift of Friendship: Profound Disability, Theological Anthropology, and Ethics* (Grand Rapids, MI: Eerdmans, 2008); Deborah Beth Creamer, *Disability and Christian Theology: Embodied Limits and Constructive Possibilities* (Oxford: Oxford University Press, 2009).

2 Thomas E. Reynolds, *Vulnerable Communion: A Theology of Disability and Hospitality* (Grand Rapids, MI: Brazos Press, 2008), pp. 73–97.

3 John Swinton, *Dementia: Living in the Memories of God* (London: SCM Press, 2017), pp. 257–87.

4 Christine D. Pohl, *Making Room: Recovering Hospitality as a Christian Tradition* (Grand Rapids, MI: Eerdmans, 1999), pp. 3–15.

5 Judith Butler, *Bodies That Matter: On the Discursive Limits of 'Sex'* (London: Routledge, 1993), pp. 81–99.

6 Rosemarie Garland Thomson, *Staring: How We Look* (Oxford: Oxford University Press, 2009), pp. 61–76.

7 Susan A. Ross, *Extravagant Affections: A Feminist Sacramental Theology* (New York: Continuum, 1998), pp. 203–32.

8 Code of Canon Law (CIC 1983), Canon 1041 §1.

9 Exodus 4.10–12.

10 Acts 10; Acts 15; cf. Galatians 3.28.

11 John D. Zizioulas, *Being as Communion: Studies in Personhood and the Church* (Crestwood, NY: St Vladimir's Seminary Press, 1985), pp. 27–66.

12 Elizabeth Theokritoff, *Living in God's Creation: Orthodox Perspectives on Ecology* (Crestwood, NY: St Vladimir's Seminary Press, 2009); Alexander Schmemann, *For the Life of the World: Sacraments and Orthodoxy* (Crestwood, NY: St Vladimir's Seminary Press, 1963).

13 Cheryl Bridges Johns, *Pentecostal Formation: A Pedagogy Among the Oppressed* (Sheffield: Sheffield Academic Press, 1993), pp. 111–29.

14 Nimi Wariboko, *The Pentecostal Principle: Ethical Methodology in New Spirit* (Grand Rapids, MI: Eerdmans, 2011), pp. 203–40.

15 Acts 2.1–18; cf. Willie James Jennings, *Acts*, Belief Series (Louisville, KY: WJK Press, 2017).

16 J. Kwabena Asamoah-Gyadu, *African Charismatics: Current Developments Within Independent Indigenous Pentecostalism in Ghana* (Leiden: Brill, 2005), pp. 167–92.

17 Jione Havea (ed.), *Indigenous Australia and the Unfinished Business of Theology: Cross-Cultural Engagement* (London: Palgrave Macmillan, 2014), pp. 25–46.

9

Embodied Heritage: Disabled Bodies as Living Archives

If stone and stained glass bear the weight of ecclesial memory, so too, more radically, more vulnerably, do bodies. Having examined how sacred architecture reflects and perpetuates ableist assumptions, we now shift our focus to the living, breathing, complex reality of human embodiment. For the Church, heritage has too often been located in places: in chancels and carvings, in vestments and vaulted ceilings. But there is a deeper, more dynamic archive of holiness: the body itself. In particular, disabled bodies, long marginalized by architectural and liturgical design, bear witness to an alternative theology of heritage: one written not in permanence but in vulnerability, not in stone but in scarred flesh. This chapter contends that the Church must learn to receive disabled bodies not as obstacles to heritage, but as custodians of it. For in their marks, memories and movements lies a sacred history too long ignored, an archive of suffering, resistance and divine presence that no building alone can contain.

When we speak of heritage, we often picture stone: a cathedral cloaked in age, a monument weathered by time, a reliquary sealed behind glass. These external artefacts dominate our cultural imagination of the sacred. They are revered, observed, catalogued and protected. But such a view narrows what heritage is and can be. It turns tradition into a relic, detaching it from the living, breathing bodies who carry and reinterpret it every day.

For disabled people, whose lives have frequently been excluded from the dominant expressions of ecclesial memory, this narrowing is not merely unfortunate; it is erasure. The stories of disabled lives rarely appear in stained glass, liturgical calendars or official histories. But absence from these archives does not equate to absence from heritage. In fact, disabled people bear an alternative archive. Our bodies – tremoring, stimming, limping, resting – carry deep histories of survival, community, resistance and faithfulness. We are not supplementary to the Church's memory. We are its living continuity.

This chapter is a call to reframe what counts as sacred heritage. It is not a metaphor. It is a theological proposition. Disabled bodies are not symbols of brokenness awaiting redemption. Our bodies are sites of divine presence. We bear the imprint of liturgical participation, of communal creativity, of the Spirit's enduring work. We are living, improvising archives of Christian life.

My own theological work arises from living within such a body. I write this not only as a theologian but as someone whose body has carried and continues to carry pain and joy, protest and sacrament, into inaccessible sanctuaries and beyond. My theology is not an abstraction from my embodiment; it is formed by it. This is not a method to be justified; it is a witness to be heard.

Theologian Jennie Weiss Block writes of 'copious hosting', a graceful, generous and liberating vision of the Church where disabled bodies are not only welcomed but entrusted with leadership, interpretation and blessing.[1] To embrace this is to reject the fantasy of the ideal Christian body, one marked by independence, control and aesthetic conformity. It is to recognize that the disabled body is not a disruption to be managed, but a revelation to be received.

Such a shift requires confronting inherited theologies that enshrined bodily perfection as a marker of holiness. As previous chapters have traced, thinkers like Origen, Augustine and Aquinas helped form an intellectual framework in which impairment was allegorized, marginalized or interpreted as moral deficiency. What remains to be said here is how that legacy shapes not only liturgy and architecture, but ecclesial memory itself.

Against this, Christ's own body offers a counter-testimony. The incarnate God does not bypass vulnerability: he dwells in it. The resurrected Christ bears the wounds of crucifixion not as blemishes, but as the very marks of glory. The body of Jesus does not conform to idealized form: it subverts it. It is through this body – scarred, broken and glorified – that we come to know God.

This theological claim should reshape how we understand heritage. Scholars such as Laurajane Smith and Rodney Harrison remind us that heritage is not about preserving the untouchable past – it is an active cultural process that involves decisions about value, memory and identity.[2] When disabled bodies are excluded from that process, when ramps, aids or alternative worship practices are seen as inauthentic, it reveals a theology that equates sanctity with stasis. But the tradition we inherit is not meant to be static. It is meant to live.

Disabled people already embody this living heritage. We gather for

Eucharist at bedside tables. We offer praise through adapted gesture and technology. We participate in sacred time through rest, slowness and silence. These practices are not second-rate. They are sacred. They reveal that the heart of Christian tradition has never been about uniformity of form, but fidelity to God's presence in diverse and disrupted lives.

This calls for a re-examination of temporality itself. The rhythms of disabled life – nonlinear, interruptible and cyclical – are not departures from liturgical time but deeper revelations of its essence. Alison Kafer's concept of 'crip time' offers a reimagining of what time can hold and how it unfolds, inviting the Church into a more truthful temporal existence, one that honours delay, dwells in lament and welcomes joy without requiring it to be performative.[3]

The point is not simply that disabled people should be remembered in church heritage. The point is that disabled people *are* church heritage. We carry forward ways of being that the official narratives have overlooked. Our bodies remember where the Church has faltered, and where grace has persisted, nonetheless.

So let me be absolutely clear: disabled bodies are not theological puzzles to be solved. We are not exceptions to be accommodated. We are sacred texts to be read with reverence. We hold the Spirit's improvisations. We echo the wisdom of generations past. We are, in the truest sense, living archives of Christian faith.

This heritage does not fit in a reliquary. It cannot be catalogued. It is not pristine. But it is holy. And it is ours.

The body as sacred archive

In Christian theology, the body has always held profound significance, not as a mere vessel, but as a medium of divine presence. At the heart of the Incarnation lies the radical claim that God took on flesh, not as an abstract gesture, but as a full embrace of human vulnerability. 'The Word became flesh and lived among us' (John 1.14). This theological centre of gravity affirms that God does not dwell in disembodied ideals but in relational, particular and wounded bodies.

And yet, the Church's treatment of certain bodies has long betrayed that truth. Disabled bodies, in particular, have been misread, romanticized, feared or erased. They have been made into metaphors for sin, inspiration or divine correction, anything, it seems, except what they truly are: complex, living vessels of meaning, of holiness, of history.

To reclaim the body as a sacred archive is not an act of sentimentality but a declaration of its role as a site where memory, theology and resistance intersect. Michel Foucault describes the body as an inscribed surface of events, and for disabled individuals, these inscriptions carry theological weight, scars that bear witness to medical interventions, societal exclusion, ecclesial erasure and, above all, radical endurance.[4]

In this sense, disabled embodiment becomes a living liturgy. Our breath, gestures, mobility aids and neurodiverse expressions do not distract from sacred life: they are its proclamation. The disabled body does not interrupt the Church's liturgical performance: it deepens it. It redefines it.

This stands in sharp contrast to a tradition that too often sanctified form over flesh. In the Graeco-Roman philosophical inheritance of Christian thought, the body was subordinated to the rational soul. Augustine's internalized spirituality and Aquinas's aesthetics of order and integrity helped enshrine ideals that marginalized nonconforming bodies.[5] What was irregular, fragile or visibly dependent was seen as lacking the beauty and perfection that supposedly reflected the divine.

But this tradition fails under the weight of lived witness. The actual, breathing, aching, joyful body tells a different story, one echoed in the body of Christ, not as ideal form, but as broken bread. The risen Christ invites Thomas not into abstraction but into tactile encounter: 'Put your finger here' (John 20.27). The glorified body of Jesus is not a rejection of woundedness but its sanctification.

And still, the Church has often failed to learn from this theological centre. Instead, it rehearses liturgies and builds spaces around bodies that are presumed able, bodies that stand unaided, read fluently, kneel on command and perform attention without deviation. All others are adapted for, but rarely centred. We become theological problems to be solved or inspirational footnotes, but not bearers of ecclesial authority.

Yet when our bodies are recognized as sacred archives, we offer something deeper than inclusion. We offer ecclesial reformation. We challenge the norms of time, space, language and leadership. We reshape how we remember, how we worship and how we build.

Nancy Eiesland's understanding of the Disabled God remains a cornerstone of disability theology, affirming that in the resurrected Christ, disability is not a mark of sin nor a condition to be erased but an intrinsic part of identity. This challenges traditional notions of holiness, not by glorifying suffering, but by dismantling the idea that perfection is necessary for divine presence. It is a theological shift that reconfigures embodiment, insisting that wholeness is not found in the absence of wounds but in their integration into redeemed life.[6]

This vision does not deny the reality of pain or the longing for healing. It simply refuses to equate healing with erasure. It honours the possibility that healing might mean being held, being named, being trusted, not being fixed.

In recognizing disabled bodies as sacred archives, we reclaim something the Church has lost: its own woundedness, its own capacity to learn from fragility, its own dependence on grace. We recover the truth that sanctity does not reside in symmetry or strength, but in communion, among those whose very lives reveal the cost and beauty of belonging. And this recognition reshapes not only theology, but heritage. For what is heritage, if not the story of what we choose to carry forward? And if we have silenced these bodies, overlooked their witness, hidden their liturgies, then we have curated not truth, but amnesia.

The task before us is clear. We must learn to read the body, not as an interruption to tradition, but as its deepest source. We must listen to the stammer, the tremor, the absence, the adaptation. We must let the bodies speak, not about how they differ from the Church, but about how they remember it.

Because the Church is not only built in stone. It is built in flesh. And if we listen to these sacred archives, we may yet hear the gospel again.

Healing, wholeness and the bias of the Gospel writers

The healing narratives of Jesus Christ, while central to the Gospel accounts, raise profound theological questions when read through the lens of disability. Were the Gospel writers describing acts of liberation and recognition, or were they subtly reinforcing an ableist imagination in which bodies marked by difference must be 'corrected' to belong? To what extent were these evangelists shaped by their cultural context, by purity codes, Graeco-Roman ideals of physical perfection and inherited Jewish expectations of messianic restoration? And crucially, did they write from the perspective of the idealized other, imagining healing as restoration to a normative body, or from the deeper revelation of Christ's risen, wounded body?

In Mark's Gospel, the earliest and perhaps most visceral account, healing is often immediate, dramatic and framed as a sign of divine authority. In Mark 2.1–12, the healing of the paralyzed man is linked explicitly to the forgiveness of sins, suggesting, at least in its cultural frame, a perceived connection between sin and disability. While Jesus resists this correlation directly ('Which is easier, to say to the paralytic, "Your sins are forgiven," or to say, "Stand up and take your mat and walk"?'), the narrative arc still concludes with a restoration to normative mobility and social function. Disability is not embraced: it is erased.

St Matthew, writing with a more structured theological intent, doubles down on healing as fulfilment of prophecy. In Matthew 11.5, Jesus responds to John's disciples: 'The blind receive their sight, the lame walk, the lepers are cleansed, the deaf hear ...', a litany drawn from Isaiah, used as proof of messianic identity. Here, disability functions rhetorically, as evidence of divine legitimacy. The personhood of the healed is largely irrelevant to the narrative arc; they are signs rather than subjects.

Biblical texts all too often position the disabled body not as an active subject but as a theological device, an illustration of divine power rather than an embodied participant in sacred history. This framing has long shaped theological discourse, reinforcing narratives where disability becomes a metaphor rather than a lived reality; narratives where disabled bodies are not recognized as bearers of theological meaning in their own right.

St Luke, often seen as the evangelist of compassion, offers more narrative detail and social context, yet remains ambiguous. In Luke 14.13, Jesus commands hospitality not to the powerful but 'the poor, the crippled, the lame, and the blind.' Yet even here, the disabled are framed as the passive recipients of charity, not bearers of prophetic witness or divine image. In Luke 17.11–19, the healing of the ten lepers concludes with only one returning in gratitude, again shifting the emphasis from embodiment to response. Luke's theological emphasis on reversal does not necessarily dismantle ableism; rather, it risks baptizing it through acts of pity.

And we finally come to St John's Gospel. The writer here offers the most theologically layered and symbolically rich healings, yet perhaps also the most problematic in terms of ableism. In John 9, the man born blind becomes the focus of a theological dispute rather than a subject with agency. 'Who sinned, this man or his parents, that he was born blind?' the disciples ask. Jesus denies the correlation, stating, 'he was born blind so that God's works might be revealed in him' (John 9.3). The man's blindness becomes a theological object lesson, a means to glorify God through healing. While the narrative concludes with a confrontation that reveals the man's growing agency, the underlying message remains troubling: disability as divine spectacle. The question must be asked: does this story reflect the lived reality of disabled people, or the theological imagination of an able-bodied narrator?

The early Church frequently interpreted these narratives through a spiritual lens, fostering an ideal of healing that risked detaching the breaking body from the risen Christ. Irenaeus of Lyons affirmed a soteriology encompassing all – infants, children, youths and elders – yet within this expansive vision lay an implicit assumption of a normative body. Redemption was often imagined not through woundedness but through an idealized wholeness, reinforcing a theological framework where restoration meant conformity rather than transfigured continuity.[7]

In contrast, contemporary disability theologians have critically engaged these narratives, questioning their underlying assumptions. Nancy Eiesland, in *The Disabled God*, challenges the absence of disabled voices in theological discourse and asks where the God who remains disabled, even in resurrection, can be found. Her critique calls for a radical re-interpretation, one that does not dismiss the healing miracles but situates them within the revelation of the risen Christ. This is a Christ who bears his wounds, rejects bodily perfection and extends an invitation to Thomas, not into unblemished strength, but into the vulnerability of pierced flesh.[8]

Thomas Reynolds builds on this by challenging conventional understandings of healing, reframing wholeness not as the absence of impairment but as the communal embrace of vulnerability. This perspective demands a reassessment of the Gospel healing narratives; not a rejection, but a recontextualization. What if these stories are not about the removal of disability, but about the restoration of agency, dignity and relational belonging? What if Jesus' miracles do not function as divine corrections, but as acts of profound recognition, affirming the worth and presence of those who have been marginalized?[9]

And what if the Gospel writers themselves, limited by the cultural norms of their time, could not fully grasp the theological revolution embodied in the risen Christ, whose glorified body still bore the marks of violence, not as scars to be overcome, but as sacraments of truth?

If we read these narratives through the lens of the risen Christ as the wounded healer who did not shed his impairments, we encounter a different gospel. One in which disabled bodies are not problems to be solved, but icons of the divine. One in which healing is not conformity to a norm, but the deep, difficult resurrection of communion across difference.

Lourdes and the politics of healing

The Marian shrine at Lourdes, nestled in the foothills of the Pyrenees, is among the most iconic pilgrimage sites in global Christianity. Drawing millions of visitors annually, it is revered for its spiritual atmosphere, its rhythm of prayer and processions, and above all its association with miraculous healing. Lourdes also deserves recognition for its remarkable physical accessibility. From medical infrastructure to inclusive liturgical planning, the shrine is intentionally designed to welcome a wide diversity of bodies and needs. It is, in many respects, a material sign of hospitality.

For many disabled pilgrims, Lourdes provides an experience of rare visibility and inclusion. Unlike many heritage sites where disability is marginalized or erased, Lourdes places the disabled body at the centre of its devotional life. Processions are shaped by wheelchairs. Liturgies accommodate a range of access needs. The shrine has cultivated what might be called *sacramental access*, a theology made tangible in the logistics of care and communal embodiment.

And yet, beneath this profound welcome lies an enduring theological tension: the expectation of healing.

The language may be gentle. The intentions may be sincere. But the unspoken script of Lourdes often centres on cure. Pilgrims come in hope, sometimes in desperation. They are prayed for, anointed, immersed in the waters. And while many find solace, community and spiritual renewal, others leave feeling unseen – not because they were not cared for, but because they were not transformed.

This is not a criticism of healing itself. The desire for healing – of body, mind or spirit – is a deeply human and often holy longing. The concern arises when healing is narrowly defined as physical restoration, and when this becomes the implicit measure of a pilgrimage's success. When this expectation is not met, it can generate not only disappointment, but self-doubt and quiet shame. Many pilgrims return home not only with unhealed bodies, but with the burden of wondering whether their faith, or their person, was inadequate.

The theological roots of this expectation are long and complex. Patristic theology frequently linked impairment to divine intervention, treating it as a site of either correction or spectacle.[10] Augustine, while wrestling seriously with the nature of suffering, nonetheless located physical healing within a cosmic narrative of return to a prelapsarian order.[11] In such frameworks, impairment is cast as anomaly, and cure as spiritual alignment.

These ideas continued into the medieval period, when pilgrimage itself was entwined with penitence and miracle. Holy sites like Lourdes emerged within this devotional economy, places where divine grace might be encountered through tangible transformation. In such a paradigm, the disabled pilgrim was either a candidate for healing or a source of spiritual inspiration for the able-bodied. Rarely were they seen as theological agents in their own right.

For many contemporary disabled pilgrims, the echoes of this framework remain. While Lourdes has become far more pastorally aware, the shrine still risks reinforcing a model in which physical change is privileged over spiritual recognition. The absence of supernatural healing can feel like a failure, not of God, but of the person. One pilgrim once shared with me: 'They prayed that I would walk. I prayed they would see that I already stand.'

This dissonance reveals the deeper issue: whose expectations define healing? Who decides what a miracle looks like? Who is allowed to interpret their own body as whole?

When disability is assumed to be suffering, and healing is imagined only as reversal, the complexity of disabled life is flattened. Many disabled people do live with pain, fatigue or limitation. But they also live with creativity, joy and resilience. For some, disability is not something to be overcome, but a mode of being through which they understand the world, and God.

To frame pilgrimage only as a journey toward cure is to miss this truth. A theology of pilgrimage informed by disability liberation would resist the reduction of healing to spectacle. It would make room for healing that emerges not in change, but in encounter. It would honour those who return home in the same bodies they arrived with, but with a deeper sense of being seen, held and known.

Healing, in this vision, may come through laughter at a communal meal, through tears shared in a night vigil, or through the silence of unspectacular faith. It may come in naming grief, in receiving Eucharist from a fellow pilgrim, in realizing that one is not alone. These are not lesser outcomes. They are signs of grace.

Importantly, such a reframing does not pit healing against inclusion. It challenges the assumption that transformation must always be visible to be meaningful. It broadens the imagination of what sacred journeying can be.

Lourdes, then, becomes a site of both possibility and paradox. It welcomes with open arms yet often tells only part of the story. The task ahead is not to strip the shrine of its hope for healing, but to deepen that hope, to make it capacious enough to include every kind of body, every kind of prayer and every kind of outcome.

In this reimagined theology, the waters of Lourdes are holy not because they promise a return to normalcy, but because they testify to God's presence in every body that enters them. Healing is not defined by walking away unaided, but by returning home with the conviction: *I was seen. I was welcomed. I was whole before I ever arrived.*

Healing to the idealized norm

> Then the devil took him to the holy city and placed him on the pinnacle of the temple, saying to him, 'If you are the Son of God, throw yourself down; for it is written,
> "He will command his angels concerning you",
> and "On their hands they will bear you up,
> so that you will not dash your foot against a stone."'
> (Matt. 4.5–6)

The third temptation in the wilderness, an invitation to leap for the sake of spectacle, remains dangerously alive in contemporary Christian approaches to disability and healing. At its heart is a theology that demands performance: prove your faith, demonstrate God's power, be made whole, visibly, dramatically, and now.

It is a theology that equates healing with conformity to able-bodied and neurotypical standards, a liturgy shaped not by the risen Christ but by a cultural fantasy of unblemished strength. When miracles are expected to match this template, those whose bodies remain unchanged are subtly, or not so subtly, deemed insufficient, lacking in faith, gratitude or holiness.

Such expectations are not born of the Gospels themselves but from a deeply embedded ecclesial discomfort with limitation. The Church too often reads healing through the lens of restoration to a normative ideal, rather than the redemptive embrace of woundedness. In this view, the disabled body is a problem to be solved, not a theological witness to be received. Healing becomes spectacle, and inclusion becomes conditional.

But the body of the risen Christ resists this interpretation. It is not perfected into erasure but transfigured through endurance. The wounds remain, not as reminders of failure, but as enduring marks of solidarity and love. As Shelly Rambo writes, resurrection is not about escaping trauma but remaining with it faithfully, gathering 'at the site of wounds to tell difficult truths', making space for its continued presence without being overcome by it.[12]

The healing narratives of Jesus, when read with attentiveness to context, reveal a theology not of conformity but of communion. Those who come to Jesus for healing – lepers, paralytics, haemorrhaging women – are not just seeking a medical cure. They are seeking restoration to community, recognition of dignity and freedom from religious and social stigma. Jesus' response is not simply to fix but to affirm: 'Your faith has made you well.' 'Your sins are forgiven.' These are profound declarations of identity and relationship, not just bodily change.

Moreover, the Gospels themselves, as I have just shared, carry the interpretive fingerprints of their authors; writers shaped by purity codes, Graeco-Roman ideals, and a worldview in which physical difference was often associated with spiritual deficiency. But in spite of all these biases the actions of Jesus, even when shared by these writers, consistently defy the Gospel writers' cultural norms and destabilizes their embedded assumptions. Jesus touches the untouchable, centres the excluded and redirects attention away from public spectacle toward personal relationship. Jesus does not require people to prove themselves worthy of healing; he reveals and affirms that they already are.

This is not a rejection of healing, but a redefinition of what healing is for. It is not to validate theological correctness, but to proclaim divine proximity. Jesus brings the temple not to the mountaintop but to the margins. He makes space holy not by protecting it from impurity as was the cultural norm of that period, but by inhabiting it with mercy.

Healing, in this light, is not a return to an ideal form, but a movement into deeper belonging. It does not erase difference – it honours it. It is not about overcoming embodiment but learning to live faithfully within it. To reduce healing to the performance of normative bodies is to reenact the third temptation, to demand that God prove God's self through power rather than presence.

Disabled people, therefore, do not exist as waiting rooms for miracles. Our lives are not testaments to spiritual delay. We are, already, sacraments of grace. The ramp, the push-pad, the wheelchair, the scooter, crutches, the communication aid, these are not signs of failure but instruments of liturgical truth. They do not disrupt the gospel. They reveal it.

Confession, placed at the heart of Christian worship, is not a transaction for divine fixing but an act of honest return to relationship. It acknowledges not a failed body but a beloved one. The act of being 'healed' is not about shedding mobility aids or stammers, but about being met, known and cherished in the midst of them.

To pray for healing, then, is not to erase the body but to embrace it more fully. It is to align ourselves not with the spectacle of the Temple's pinnacle, but with the Christ who refused to jump, who chose solidarity over display. Theologies of healing must turn from perfectionism toward presence, from triumphalism to tenderness.

As a disabled person, I refuse the lie of performative healing. I am already whole, not in spite of my crutches or scooter, but in and through them. I am whole because I live interdependently, because my body is held in community, because my life has been shaped not only by pain but by purpose. My body is not the site of a delayed miracle; it is a living archive of grace.

Healing must no longer be tethered to the false god of normalcy. It must become the name we give to mutuality, to deep welcome, to the recognition that each body is already fearfully and wonderfully made, not fearfully and flawlessly, but fearfully and tenderly. To persist in the demand for healing-as-spectacle is to fall again into the devil's script. It is to mistake theatrical proof for divine presence. And it is, in the end, to preach a gospel that excludes the very Christ it claims to honour.

Let the Church repent of this idolatry. Let it turn again to the Christ whose glory is wounded, whose power is made perfect not in strength but in shared vulnerability. Let it proclaim not the flawless, but the faithful. Not the normate, but the neighbour. Not the miracle, but the mercy.

And let that be our healing.

Testimony and trauma: the ethics of embodied memory

To speak of disabled bodies as sacred heritage demands a deeper engagement than aesthetic admiration or theological affirmation. It requires the Church to confront histories of exclusion and the realities of trauma, not as detours in the journey of faith, but as its terrain. For many disabled people, the body is not simply a site of identity or theological reflection; it is the place where neglect, coercion and misrecognition have taken flesh. Our liturgies have often been shaped not by welcome but by avoidance. Our doctrines have too often bypassed pain in favour of polished triumph.

Disabled bodies are archives not only of resilience but of injury. They bear the imprint of systemic injustice: from institutionalization and forced sterilization to being excluded from sacraments or subjected to unwanted healing prayers. These are not marginal stories. They are part of the collective inheritance of ecclesial ableism. And they challenge any tradition that would preserve itself without reckoning with the bodies it has harmed.

Shelly Rambo's work in *Spirit and Trauma* is pivotal in reshaping theological engagement with suffering. She emphasizes the necessity of a theology that does not hasten toward resolution but remains present in the unresolved, the 'middle space' between crucifixion and resurrection. This is a theology that dwells in Holy Saturday, where breath is suspended, meaning is uncertain, and the temptation to prematurely claim healing is resisted. It is a call to honour what persists, acknowledging that redemption is not always found in closure but in continued witness.

Such a theology is urgently needed in the Church, where the disabled person is so often expected to either testify to miraculous healing or disappear. This pressure for closure is not just pastorally harmful, it is theologically bankrupt. It turns testimony into spectacle and worship into performance. But testimony is not about completeness: it is about truth. It is the act of naming what has happened, without demand for resolution.

Traditional ecclesial heritage, meanwhile, clings to idealized forms. It celebrates what endures, preserves what impresses, and too often excludes what disrupts. But trauma is disruptive. It refuses the linearity of heritage trails and canonized memory. It does not fit neatly within stained glass or curated exhibition. And disabled people, who carry both bodily and spiritual trauma, do not conform to inherited ecclesial aesthetics. Our presence interrupts the heritage script.

This interruption is not a failure. It is grace.

The risen Christ models this. His body does not return to wholeness as defined by classical perfection. His scars remain, not as blemishes, but as invitations. 'Put your finger here.' He invites Thomas, and us, not to observe a body made pristine, but to witness a body made holy in its memory of pain. This is not spectacle. It is solidarity.

To speak of disabled bodies as sacred heritage, then, is to resist ecclesiologies that demand resolution. It is to proclaim a gospel that honours wounds. It is to see the Eucharist not as polished ritual but as breaking bread, shared in the midst of weariness and grief. In every act of access, every captioned prayer, every quiet space, every act of accommodation, we proclaim a different theology. One in which the wounded body is not erased but held with reverence.

This requires a fundamental shift to:

- tell the story of trauma as integral to Christian witness, not an embarrassment to be managed

- abandon the demand for spiritual neatness and welcome disruption as holy
- curate disabled lives not as inspiration, but as theological witnesses
- name ableism in the Church not as a lapse, but as a structural betrayal of the gospel
- build liturgies that begin, not beyond trauma, but within it

This is not an optional addition to ecclesial life. It is the necessary work of healing a Church that has too often canonized control.

To testify from a disabled body is to live out a liturgy of memory. It is to say: the body remembers, even when the Church does not. And Christ remembers too. The one who breathes peace with pierced hands and feet continues to meet us in our own scars, not to fix us, but to dwell with us. This is not the theology of spectacle. It is the theology of solidarity. And only from there, from that scarred embrace, can resurrection be truly proclaimed.

Ecclesiology and embodied memory

The Church, St Paul declares in 1 Corinthians 12, is the body of Christ. But that image, radical, incarnational and deeply communal, has been dulled and diluted by overuse. Too often it is reduced to metaphor, drained of its ethical force and theological consequence. But when Paul writes, 'The members of the body that seem to be weaker are indispensable,' he is not offering sentiment. He is articulating a foundational claim: that the body of the Church is not whole without those it tends to overlook.

Paul's own theology emerges not from abstract speculation, but from a deeply embodied and humbling encounter. His dramatic experience on the road to Damascus was not only a call to faith but a confrontation with dependency, from a perceived personal identity of independence (1 Cor. 12.22). Blinded, he was led by the hand, an apostle born through weakness, not power. This inversion seeded a new ecclesiology: one in which difference is not a problem to be solved, but a condition of shared life. St Paul's subsequent ministry is a playing-out, and the seeking understanding, of that profound personal experience of disability on the road to Damascus.

In *Vulnerable Communion*, Thomas Reynolds expands on this Pauline vision by naming the ecclesial danger of idealizing independence. The Church, shaped by cultural fantasies of strength and control, often builds itself around homogeneity, masking exclusion with the language of welcome. But as Reynolds argues, real communion begins not with strength but with vulnerability. The Church becomes church not by avoiding difference, but by dwelling within it.[13]

This reframes disabled people's relationship to the Church. We are not tokens of inclusion or subjects of ministry. We are co-creators of ecclesial life. Our presence reconfigures not just the seating plan but the theology of the space. We interrupt aesthetic assumptions, resist linear liturgies and call attention to fragilities the Church would often prefer to ignore. This is not disruption for its own sake. It is theological correction.

To speak of ecclesiology in this way is to speak of memory. A Church shaped by the lives and leadership of disabled people is a Church that remembers differently. It does not preserve tradition as nostalgia or monument. It embodies tradition as faithful, flexible memory, memory attuned to voices and stories that were previously silenced.

This has profound implications for heritage. If the Church is the body of Christ, and disabled people are indispensable members of that body, then disabled history is not supplemental to ecclesial memory. It is central. Sacred memory cannot be confined to relics and rites. It must also take the form of shared life, mutual care and ongoing witness. And that means ecclesial spaces, including physical, liturgical and institutional ones, must reflect this truth.

A cathedral that lacks wheelchair access to its altar or neurodivergent participation in its liturgical life does not merely have a logistical oversight. It carries a theological contradiction. Its architecture may be majestic, but its ecclesiology is fractured. When disabled people are absent from stained glass, marginal in leadership or excluded from the sacramental table, the Church forgets its own gospel.

Heritage without the presence of disabled lives is a curated myth. It sacralizes exclusion. It creates a hagiography of strength while ignoring the holiness of weakness, slowness, silence and adaptation. And this misremembering is not benign. It distorts the Church's self-understanding and perpetuates harm.

True ecclesial memory is not tidy. It is honest. It names the scars. It mourns the exclusions. And then it re-members – literally puts back together – the fragmented body of Christ. It builds ramps not for charity, but for coherence. It tells stories that include pain and protest. It welcomes the tremor, the stutter, the stim, not as interruptions, but as liturgies of their own.

To be the body of Christ is to be unfinished, wounded, interdependent. Ecclesiology rooted in embodied memory dares to believe that holiness is not found in uniformity, but in difference held together by grace. It is a Church that does not merely tolerate disability but confesses its own need for disabled wisdom.

This is not a renovation. It is a reformation. It is not about compliance or aesthetics. It is about conversion. A turning back to the Christ whose body still bears the marks of pain, whose resurrection did not erase history but transfigured it.

To be the Church is to remember truthfully. To welcome with integrity. To honour the wounded members of the body not as anomalies, but as guides. And to say with our architecture, our liturgy, our leadership and our love: you are not an interruption to our heritage. You are its revelation.

Disabled saints and forgotten legacies

Throughout Christian history, disabled people have been part of the story of sanctity. But their presence has often been misrepresented, misremembered or omitted altogether. In ecclesial memory, their impairments have too frequently been framed as obstacles to overcome rather than realities through which holiness was lived. When these stories are preserved, they are too often retold in ableist terms – sanitized, moralized or spiritualized – rather than honoured as faithful lives shaped in and through disabled embodiment.

But the historical record, when approached with care, offers a more complex and truthful witness.

Take St Margaret of Castello (1287–1320). Born blind and with a form of dwarfism, Margaret was imprisoned by her own family because of her difference. Later embraced by a lay Dominican community, she became a woman of deep prayer and radical hospitality. Margaret was not canonized because she transcended her disability. She was canonized because she lived the gospel with fierce fidelity within it.

Or consider St Servulus of Rome, a man who lived with severe physical impairments and who begged outside the Church of St Clement. Though unable to move unaided, he was remembered for his joy, generosity and intercessory prayer. His sanctity was not in spite of his condition but expressed through it. Neither Servulus nor Margaret are remembered for miraculous cures. They are remembered for the grace that flowed through bodies others might have dismissed.

Yet even these stories have often been subjected to interpretative distortion. Traditional hagiographies, shaped by theological assumptions that equated holiness with wholeness, often cast disabled saints as figures who achieved sanctity by triumphing over the burden of their embodiment. Disability becomes the prelude to heroism or the stage upon which divine intervention must occur, rather than a meaningful context for discipleship.

This interpretative habit reflects a failure to develop a fully integrated theology of disabled sanctity that stands on its own terms, one which challenges the Church to better learn to recognize sanctity, not despite disability, but within it. That recognition calls for a renewed vision of the communion of saints, one in which disabled lives are not anomalies or exceptions but central witnesses to the gospel's radical inclusivity.

For the implications are not merely historical. They are ecclesiological. They challenge how the Church constructs and preserves its heritage.

To honour disabled saints is to challenge the theological norms that shaped ecclesial architecture, liturgy and iconography. It is to ask: why are crutches, wheelchairs and prosthetics so rarely seen in stained glass or statuary? Why do depictions of sanctity so often conform to classical ideals of aesthetic perfection? Why have disabled saints been remembered only in stories, but rarely in space?

This is not about sentimentality. It is about theological accuracy. If the *imago Dei* shines through disabled lives – and it does – then heritage that omits our lives is not just incomplete. It is untrue.

To centre disabled saints in the Church's memory means designing accessible shrines and feast days that reflect and honour the reality of disability. It means depicting their impairments faithfully in sacred art, not as flaws, but as features of their witness. It means lifting their stories out of obscurity and allowing them to reshape the Church's understanding of holiness.

This recovery is not an act of historical restitution alone. It is an invitation to reimagine sanctity. These saints offer a different model of discipleship: one rooted not in triumph over limitation but in faithful presence amid it. They reflect a holiness that is not about purity or power, but about mercy, justice and joy. They remind the Church that the body of Christ is not abstract, not idealized, but particular, wounded and shared.

The memory of disabled saints should not be tucked away in devotional footnotes. It must be inscribed in the architecture, language and prayer of the Church. Because to honour them truthfully is to affirm that their lives, like the life of the crucified and risen Christ, speak not of lack, but of love.

Collectively, these movements embody what Alison Kafer terms 'crip memory', a way of remembering shaped by resistance, relationality and embodied presence. Crip memory is not at all nostalgic. It is in fact the antithesis of nostalgia; it is disruptive and theological. It does not seek coherence or polish. It bears witness through rupture, fragility, adaptation. It is memory kept alive in retrofitted buildings, in tactile prayers, in silent vigils and shouted protest.

Crip memory resists the monumental impulse of heritage that canonizes only what is beautiful, old and finished. Instead, it mirrors eucharistic anamnesis, memory that is not about perfection but about presence. Just as we remember Christ through breaking bread and poured wine, crip memory invites us to remember the Church through breaking bodies and unfinished stories. In doing so, it reclaims the body of Christ not as idealized, but as interdependent and wounded, yet risen.

Through this liturgy of resistance, disabled people offer the Church more than critique. They offer new ways of being. They model what it means to remember faithfully: not by enshrining an unbroken past, but by inhabiting a shared, scarred, Spirit-filled future.

Crip time, memory and sacred temporality

Time is one of the most pervasive yet invisible forces in our lives. We often experience it as linear, regular and goal-oriented, a sequence of ordered steps toward progress. In Western modernity, this temporal framework is bound up with efficiency, output and predictability. It is built into our schedules, rituals and institutional rhythms, including those of the Church: liturgical calendars, lectionary cycles and sacred seasons structured for orderly participation.

But for many disabled people, time doesn't behave this way.

Disability, whether manifest in chronic illness, sensory difference, neurodivergence or fluctuating energy, can disrupt normative timelines. Time bends, slows, loops or collapses. A day may begin with momentum and end in stillness. Plans dissolve. Recovery lingers. Expectations break. And crucially, this is not a failure to keep pace; it is a different mode of time altogether.

This is where the idea of crip time offers both a cultural critique and a theological opening. Popularized by disability studies scholar Alison Kafer, crip time reframes time not as neutral or universal, but as embodied, political and contingent.[14] It resists the assumption that faster is better or that healing and participation follow linear trajectories. Instead, crip time embraces slowness, uncertainty, adaptation and interruption, not as detours, but as faithful and valuable modes of being.

The implications of this for ecclesial life are profound. Much of church practice assumes regularity, coherence and availability. Worship services are tightly choreographed. Pastoral presence is expected to be punctual. Theologies of healing and sanctification are often future-facing and solution-oriented. These expectations reinforce dominant ideals of stability and control, privileging those who can reliably meet them.

Crip time interrupts this. It insists that divine presence is not predicated on consistency or speed. It honours forms of participation that are sporadic, nonlinear or fragmentary. It affirms that revelation can come not despite delay or disruption, but through them.

This insight profoundly reshapes how we understand memory and, by extension, heritage. Traditional approaches to heritage valorize preservation: keeping things 'as they were', maintaining visual coherence, restoring timelines. Time is treated as something to be held still and made legible. Continuity is prized. But crip time unsettles these assumptions. It asks: whose past are we preserving? At what pace? With what bodies in mind?

For Robert McRuer, crip temporality disrupts linear, normative understandings of time, rejecting the notion that progress must follow a straight and predictable path. Theologically, this reframes memory, not as a neat, chronological archive but as something fragmented, recursive and lived in the present. Memory becomes an active force rather than a fixed record, one that is messy, embodied and sacred in its refusal to conform to polished narratives.[15]

The Gospels themselves resonate with this alternative rhythm. Jesus does not follow the calendar of empire. His ministry is marked by pause, withdrawal and response to interruption. In Mark 5, he stops to engage a bleeding woman while en route to another healing, choosing presence over urgency. He interrupts his travels to visit Zacchaeus in his house (Luke 19.3). These delays are not incidental. They are revelatory. In them, divine grace emerges precisely where normative timelines fracture.

This reframes ecclesial memory not as a polished recollection of success, but as a practice of dwelling with what is unfinished. It invites us to recognize that time, like space, can include or exclude. Whose rhythms govern our gatherings? Who is kept outside by assumptions of regularity or expectations of participation?

Thomas Reynolds' vision of hospitality moves beyond mere invitation; it demands an architectural and temporal transformation where belonging is actively cultivated. This extends to time itself: liturgical rhythms, pastoral presence and communal remembrance must be fluid, responsive and open to interruption. This is not merely accommodation, but a theological assertion that the Church's structuring of space and time must reflect the expansive welcome of God, a welcome that does not require conformity but honours the integrity of diverse bodies, needs and histories, because in crip time, delay is not failure, it is invitation, absence is not emptiness; it is space for grace, and disruption is not a threat; it is an opening.[16]

Heritage shaped by crip time does not seek to restore a past imagined as whole. It learns to return to what was excluded. It honours fragility rather than coherence. It welcomes improvisation. It listens slowly. It remembers not by fixing stories in place, but by returning again and again to what has been silenced.

In this mode, sacred temporality becomes less about preservation and more about faithful presence. The point is not to hold time still, but to inhabit it generously.

Crip time teaches us that the rhythms of holiness are rarely fast, rarely neat, rarely efficient. They are slow, nonlinear, patient and porous. In that tempo, the Church does not simply remember Christ, it becomes more like him: pausing, noticing, remaining with those who move differently through time.

Theological cartographies of memory

Having traversed the intersections of theology, ableism and heritage, we now turn to mapping the terrain. Not as a definitive guide, but as a theological cartography, a constellation of insights to orient us in an uneven landscape. This map does not chart a linear path: it traces disruption, return and the sacred complexity of remembering differently.

What emerges from the dialogue between disability theology, liberation theology, crip theory and critical heritage studies is a shared revelation: ecclesial memory has been shaped by exclusion. Its stained glass, its doctrines, its spatial hierarchies have too often preserved the narratives of the dominant while obscuring the voices and bodies of those relegated to the margins. But memory in Christian theology is not static. It is not reducible to nostalgia or institutional pride. It is sacramental. It is participatory. It is a call to transformation.

Disability theology offers a necessary reorientation, not by restating theological claims already addressed, but by insisting that the lived realities of disabled people are not interruptions to ecclesial life: they are its testimony. They offer a way of reading the body of Christ through fragmentation, persistence and grace. They call the Church not to reflect on inclusion from the outside but to reckon with the memory it has tried to forget.

Liberation theology deepens this by affirming that the memory of suffering must not be sanitized. The Church's integrity lies not in idealized continuity, but in faithful confrontation with what it has silenced. The marginalized are not theological supplements; they are the bearers of revelation. If their witness is excluded from the Church's heritage, then that heritage must be questioned – and changed.

Critical heritage studies, particularly the work of Laurajane Smith, remind us that memory is not neutral. Heritage is not simply inherited: it is curated.[17] It tells us not only what a community remembers, but what it chooses to forget. The theological implications are urgent: if we believe memory to be a locus of divine encounter, then the act of remembering becomes inseparable from the work of justice.

Crip theory further unsettles conventional notions of continuity, coherence and progress. Scholars like Alison Kafer and Robert McRuer challenge the assumption that time unfolds predictably, that memory must be neat, or that knowledge comes only through stability.[18] Crip temporality honours pause, rupture and return. It invites us to resist ecclesial performances of control and instead dwell with the jagged edges of belonging.

These frameworks converge not in uniformity but in invitation. Together, they suggest a renewed ecclesiology, one that understands the Church's memory as contested and unfinished. The question is no longer how to preserve the past but how to inhabit it truthfully. What do our churches remember in stone, in silence, in structure? What remains unspoken? And how might those gaps become spaces for grace?

To reimagine heritage in this way is not to discard it, but to reconsecrate it. Not to tear down, but to look again. We begin to see that what has been curated as holy has often erased the very people whose lives bore it most faithfully. To remember better is to return, not to a perfected past, but to the forgotten fragments that carry the pulse of the gospel.

This is not an abstract exercise. It is eucharistic. This is not just theological principle. It is a pastoral imperative.

I do not speak of this in theory alone. I write as a disabled priest who has been both exiled and embraced, overlooked and ordained. I have encountered theologies that regarded my presence as disruption, and spaces that finally recognized it as renewal. In returning to the altar, I was not merely restored. I became a witness to a deeper memory, a bearer of what the Church had tried to forget.

In those moments, the space changed. Not because I arrived whole, but because the illusion of wholeness was interrupted. That is what sacred memory does when we let it breathe. It reveals not only what the Church has preserved, but what it must become.

And so this cartography does not offer closure. It gestures toward invitation. To walk together in memory's uneven terrain. To let silence speak. To let the architecture of our theology be unsettled. To listen, return, repair. To remember – sacramentally, ethically, theologically. To re-member.

Flesh and memory, crip and Christ

When we look closely at the risen body of Jesus Christ, something astonishing is revealed: Christian anthropology is not grounded in abstract ideals, but in a lived, storied body. The Resurrection does not conceal the Crucifixion: it bears it forward. Jesus' scars are not erased but shown. He invites Thomas to touch them, not to prove his divinity, but to reveal it (John 20.27). The marks of violence become the signs of love.

The risen Christ is not a return to pre-trauma wholeness. He is not polished or perfected in the aesthetic sense. He is transfigured: still bearing pain yet filled with peace. This is not incidental: it is the hermeneutical key to our theology of the body. To be human is not to conform to idealized norms of health or symmetry, but to be known, remembered and loved in our particularity.

In this vision, disabled bodies are not theological anomalies. We are part of the Church's living fabric. Not despite impairment, but through it, disabled people bear witness to a God who chooses presence over power, relation over resolution. Our bodies do not merely illustrate theological points: we are theological texts.

These are bodies that carry memory: memory of exclusion, of perseverance, of joy that lives alongside pain. We hold the truth of ecclesial harm and the promise of re-membering. Not a memory tucked away in plaques or history books, but a memory inscribed in joint pain, in breath control, in stim and scar. A memory that does not resolve but remains.

This is not nostalgia. This is the synthesis of eucharistic anamnesis, the kind of memory that makes the past present again in flesh. In the Eucharist, we don't commemorate Christ abstractly; we meet Christ again in the breaking bread. Likewise, in disabled lives and bodies, the Church is summoned not to admire from a distance, but to encounter, to learn, to change.

To affirm disabled bodies as sacred heritage is to say their presence is not supplementary, it is constitutive. These are not bodies waiting for permission to belong. We are already bearers of the Spirit, already temples of a God who dwells not in perfection but in presence (1 Cor. 6.19). We are teaching the Church not only how to remember, but how to be.

This memory, crip memory, is purposely disruptive. It refuses easy closure. It resists theologies of strength and independence. It pushes back against the silent liturgies of exclusion that have shaped so much of ecclesial history. And in doing so, it invites the Church to conversion, not to sentimentality, but to truth.

Crip memory does not erase the Church's failures. It names them. But it also names grace: in mutual care, in adapted liturgies, in the slow, sacred work of building access. These are acts of remembrance that are not nostalgic, but prophetic. Not neat, but necessary. They are the ongoing unfolding of what it means to be the body of Christ, scarred, storied, shared.

Without disabled bodies, without our stories and liturgies and ways of being, the Church does not just lose inclusion. It loses truth. It loses Christ.

In exploring embodied heritage, we have seen how disabled bodies act as living archives, bearing witness to the exclusions and contestations embedded within ecclesial memory and space. These bodies interrupt the smooth continuity of institutional heritage and insist upon another telling, one marked by rupture, resistance and re-membering. Heritage, as I have argued, is not static; it breathes. But whose breath has been sanctified? And whose has been silenced?

This question leads us directly to pneumatology. For if the Spirit is breath, and breath has been normed, aestheticized and policed, then our theology of the Spirit has also absorbed the logics of ableism and idealized embodiment. What happens when we confront the Spirit not as symmetrical breath, but as disrupted, laboured, mechanical or groaning? What if the Spirit, like heritage, is most fully revealed in the places of fracture?

In our next chapter, I turn to the Spirit's breath, not as a metaphor of calm regulation, but as a theology of interruption. I will explore how breath, in Scripture and tradition, has been misaligned with cultural ideals of the whole and holy body, and how a theology rooted in the risen Christ reframes breath not as conformity, but as divine disruption and liberating groan.

Notes

1 Jennie Weiss Block, *Copious Hosting: A Theology of Access for People with Disabilities* (New York: Continuum, 2002), pp. 151–82.

2 Laurajane Smith, *Uses of Heritage* (London: Routledge, 2006), pp. 44–82; Rodney Harrison, *Heritage: Critical Approaches* (London: Routledge, 2013), pp. 3–34.

3 Alison Kafer, *Feminist, Queer, Crip* (Bloomington, IN: Indiana University Press, 2013), pp. 25–46.

4 Michel Foucault, *Discipline and Punish: The Birth of the Prison*, trans. Alan Sheridan (New York: Vintage Books, 1995), pp. 3–32.

5 See Augustine, *Confessions*, trans. Henry Chadwick (Oxford: Oxford University Press, 1991), Book X; Thomas Aquinas, *Summa Theologiae*, I, q.39, a.8, and I-II, q. 94, a.2.

6 Nancy L. Eiesland, *The Disabled God: Toward a Liberatory Theology of Disability* (Nashville, TN: Abingdon Press, 1994), pp. 89–107.

7 Irenaeus, *Against Heresies*, Book II, ch. 22.

8 Eiesland, *The Disabled God*, pp. 49–68.

9 Thomas E. Reynolds, *Vulnerable Communion: A Theology of Disability and Hospitality* (Grand Rapids, MI: Brazos Press, 2008), pp. 175–210.

10 Irenaeus, *Against Heresies*, Book V; Tertullian, *On the Resurrection of the Flesh*.

11 Augustine, *City of God*, Book XXII, trans. Henry Bettenson (London: Penguin Classics, 2003).

12 Shelly Rambo, *Spirit and Trauma: A Theology of Remaining* (Louisville, KY: Westminster John Knox, 2010), p. 114.

13 Reynolds, *Vulnerable Communion*, pp. 175–210.

14 Kafer, *Feminist, Queer, Crip*, pp. 25–46.

15 Robert McRuer, *Crip Theory: Cultural Signs of Queerness and Disability* (New York: New York University Press, 2006), pp. 146–70.

16 Reynolds, *Vulnerable Communion*, pp. 175–210.

17 Smith, *Uses of Heritage*, pp. 44–82.

18 Kafer, *Feminist, Queer, Crip*; McRuer, *Crip Theory*, pp. 25–46.

10

Breath Disrupted: Pneumatology, Normativity and the Spirit of the Risen Body

Mapping the Spirit, framing the breath

Pneumatology remains one of the most metaphorically potent yet theologically under-examined loci of Christian doctrine, especially when viewed through the lens of disability theology and the contested terrain of Christian heritage. The Spirit is named but seldom seen, evoked yet rarely constrained. It slips through doctrinal frameworks with the same ungraspable quality attributed to its images: wind, fire, dove and, most pervasively, breath. These metaphors, deeply embedded in scriptural witness and liturgical language, invite poetic reverence. But they also carry with them inheritances of normativity.

Breath, so often invoked as the mark of divine life (Gen. 2.7, John 20.22), has always been imagined as rhythmic, stable and autonomous. It is seen as a symbol of life in control; of capacity, not struggle; of clarity, not cognitive difference. In this aesthetic and theological regime, the human subject shaped by the Spirit is assumed to be cognitively coherent, bodily intact and aesthetically harmonious. To be 'filled with the Spirit' is thus unwittingly cast in ableist terms: an untroubled psyche, a fluent voice, a supple body receptive to divine activity. Pentecost becomes not the birth of an unruly, multilingual, barrier-breaking Church, but the celebration of ecstatic symmetry, order mistaken for holiness.

Such theological aesthetics are not neutral. They too are victims of centuries of spiritual, liturgical and anthropological assumptions in which abledness is mistaken for godliness, and where the metaphors of the Spirit have been assimilated into imperial and ecclesial visions of control. The disordered breath of the asthmatic, the laboured exhale of the ventilated, the wordless groan of the non-speaking autistic person: these are rarely imagined as sites of Spirit-bearing life. Instead, they have been excluded from the Church's spiritual imagination and, therefore, I wish to argue, from its pneumatology.

In this chapter, I will interrogate how pneumatology has been constrained by what I've named the idealized norm, the Graeco-Roman inheritance baptized by Western theology and embedded in liturgical life, sacramental access and ecclesial aesthetics. I will argue that the metaphors of the Spirit, when uncritically received, perpetuate exclusion. Yet when re-read through the wounded, risen body of Christ, these very metaphors, be they breath, interruption or groaning, become signs of divine disruption and new creation.

Breath and the myth of rhythmic wholeness

In much Christian spirituality, breath is aligned with serenity. It is a symbol of spiritual openness, liturgical attentiveness and monastic discipline. From the steady inhale of contemplative prayer to the measured chant of monastic worship, breath becomes synonymous with peace, attentiveness and readiness for divine encounter. This image, however, hides a deeper anthropology shaped not by theological necessity but by culturally embedded norms, particularly those privileging bodies that are regulated, symmetrical and cognitively coherent.

Breath, as spiritual metaphor, is thus often reserved for bodies that conform to what disability theorists call the 'normate' ideal: bodies that breathe steadily, speak clearly and self-regulate without assistance. This norm is rarely named but constantly reinforced through ecclesial aesthetics: in the cadence of liturgy, the assumptions of choral participation and the silence expected in worship. The Spirit is subtly associated with those who breathe 'correctly', able-bodied, neurotypical and emotionally regulated persons whose breath supports speech, stillness and song.

But what of those whose breath is laboured, erratic, interrupted or mediated by technology? What of those whose bodies exhale in gasps, whose vocal cords do not cooperate with liturgical expectation, whose breath cannot be synchronized with chant or suppressed in silence?

Too often, their breath is seen not as spiritual, but as a disruption. A ventilator hissing during prayer may provoke discomfort; an autistic person's stimming breath or vocalizations may be seen as distracting. This aesthetic discomfort translates, often unconsciously, into theological marginalization. The Spirit is presumed to breathe most freely in calm, still places, in temples of tranquillity and regulated respiration.

Sharon V. Betcher's critique confronts the deep-seated ableist assumptions embedded in theological imaginaries, challenging a construction of God that upholds autonomy and economic utility as spiritual ideals. In contrast, she insists that the Spirit moves within disabled flesh, disrupting conventional notions of wholeness and productivity. Her analysis dismantles the aesthetic-spiritual equation that has long prioritized silence over sighing, symmetry over interruption and self-sufficiency over interdependence. Even the notion of an idealized breath, one that is a smooth, deep, symmetrical inhale, emerges not as a theological imperative but as a cultural fabrication, revealing how embodiment itself has been subjected to theological gatekeeping.[1]

Indeed, when breath is equated with control, we risk creating a spirituality that is hostile to fragility. We risk imagining that God's Spirit can only dwell in 'whole' bodies, rather than bodies marked by trauma, exhaustion or disability. We reinforce a soteriology of exclusion, where the disordered breath is seen not as part of divine image-bearing but as a deviation from it.

But if we begin, instead, with the breath of the wounded Christ, the breath of one who gasped, bled and expired, we are offered a radically different anthropology. This is not the breath of meditative calm, but the breath of one hanging between heaven and earth. It is this breath, expelled in agony, that gives the Spirit to the world.

A true theology of the breath of the Holy Spirit must begin not with the idealized norm but with the breaking and beloved body; not breath as rhythm, but breath as witness. To achieve this, I will call on three biblical breaths of the Spirit, each one a random, rhythmically broken breath, unregulated and disruptive.

1 Christ's final breath – Spirit through pain

To speak of the Spirit as breath is not only to evoke origin (Gen. 2.7) or renewal (John 20.22), but to confront the profound mystery of breath in suffering and death. Nowhere is this more theologically charged than in the final breath of Christ on the cross, a breath not serene but agonized, not life-giving in its biological form but life-bearing through redemptive rupture.

In Luke 23.46, Jesus cries out with a loud voice, 'Father, into your hands I commend my spirit,' and then 'having said this, he breathed his last.' This final grasping breath is not incidental. The Gospel writers mark it as a deliberate theological moment, not a passive cessation of bodily function but a willed surrender. In John 19.30, the language is even more explicit: 'He bowed his head and gave up his spirit.' The breath of God departs not with silence but with a declaration: 'It is finished.'

This final breath is not metaphorical. It is a gasp forced through collapsing lungs, a cry from a body suspended and suffocating. The breath of the crucified Christ is not composed or contained; it is ruptured, strained and poured out. It is the very antithesis of the normate breath. Yet it is this breath that inaugurates the new creation.

Traditional theology has often bypassed this moment, leaping from crucifixion to resurrection, from agony to triumph. But the crucified breath is crucial. The resurrection breath of John 20.22, in which the risen Christ breathes on the disciples and says, 'Receive the Holy Spirit,' is inseparable from the breath he last drew on Calvary. These are not two breaths but one rhythm, kenotic exhalation and pneumatic renewal.

Eiesland's vision resonates powerfully here. The breath of the cross does not dissipate into silence but becomes the Church's first inhale. The Spirit is not confined to undisturbed tranquillity; it moves through brokenness, through wounds that do not disappear but reshape the very fabric of resurrection. This breath is not a retreat from suffering but its transformation for it is exhaled through torn flesh, carried forward in the scarred yet risen body. It does not bypass affliction; it dwells within it, ensuring that resurrection is not a forgetting but a continuation.

The disabled God, as Eiesland declares, breathes new life into the Church, not by erasing the body's history but by making it the dwelling place of grace.[2]

The Spirit, then, is also marked by wounds. It proceeds not from perfection but from pain. Christ's final breath becomes a pneumatological protest against every theology that demands bodily regulation as the condition for holiness.

This has profound implications for how we understand who may bear or embody the Spirit. The child with a tracheostomy. The adult whose breath is controlled by a machine. The person dying with rattling breath. These are not sites of divine absence. These are, if we follow the Gospel texts, the precise locations where the Spirit most intimately dwells.

Breath, in this context, becomes not only a symbol of vitality but a sacrament of suffering. The Church must learn again how to see holiness in breath that is not smooth. It must learn to hear the Spirit not only in tongues of fire, but in the gasps of crucifixion, the sighs of ventilation and the broken wheeze of the dying.

The crucified Christ teaches us this: the Spirit can be exhaled in pain and remain profoundly holy.

2 Groaning breath – the Psalms and Romans 8

To breathe is to live, but to groan is to tell the truth. In the Psalms and in Paul's letter to the Romans, breath is not only a vehicle of prayer or praise, but a medium of pain, a form of expression that transcends vocabulary. Here, groaning is not a sign of failure but of profound participation in the Spirit's own yearning.

In Psalm 6.6, the psalmist writes: 'I am weary with my moaning; every night I flood my bed with tears; I drench my couch with my weeping.' Psalm 38.8 intensifies the lament: 'I am utterly spent and crushed; I groan because of the tumult of my heart.' And again, in Psalm 102.5: 'Because of my loud groaning my bones cling to my skin.'

These psalms are not polite prayers: they are unrestrained exhalations of distress. Their breath is heavy, turbulent and embodied. The groaning is physiological, not metaphorical. These are prayers that begin in the lungs, not the liturgy. They are profound, holy, spirit-filled expressions of pain that precede coherence. And yet, even in this disarray, the Psalms declare: 'Let everything that breathes praise the LORD' (Ps. 150.6).

Note, not everything that can articulate, not everything that sings on pitch, not everything that speaks clearly, but *everything that breathes*. This radical affirmation means that every kind of breath – disordered, shallow, rapid, non-verbal, mechanical – is fit for praising. The theology here is not aesthetic but ontological: breath itself is a site of worship, no matter its form.

The Apostle Paul echoes and deepens this theology in Romans 8.22–26:

> We know that the whole creation has been groaning in labour pains until now; and not only the creation, but we ourselves ... groan inwardly while we wait for adoption ... Likewise the Spirit helps us in our weakness; for we do not know how to pray as we ought, but that very Spirit intercedes with sighs too deep for words.

This is one of the most profound pneumatological passages in all of Scripture. It makes clear that the Spirit is not only breath that gives life, but breath that shares in our struggle. The Spirit does not translate our groaning into neat theological language: it joins in our groaning. The Spirit breathes with us, in us, even as us, in forms of expression beyond articulation. For it is all too tempting to slip into thinking of spiritual maturity as the ability to pray fluently. But in Romans 8, the deepest prayer is the one we cannot say. The Spirit is most present in what we cannot speak.

For people who cannot form speech in conventional ways, or whose breath is strained or assisted, this is a crucial affirmation: your groaning is not a disqualification, it is participation in the Spirit's own voice.

Groaning, in this theology, is not sub-spiritual. It is eschatological speech. It carries within it both protest and promise, suffering and hope. It bears witness to a world not yet redeemed, and to a God who is not ashamed of our frailty.

The Church must therefore recover a liturgical and architectural space for groaning breath. Too often, silence has been equated with holiness, and noise with disruption. But if the Spirit groans, then disruption is divine. The gasp, the sigh, the sob, all become part of the Spirit's movement.

Pneumatology, then, must move beyond the polished breath of cathedral choirs and into the groaning breath of hospital wards, care homes and trauma centres. The breath of the Spirit is heard in ventilators as well as vespers.

In the Psalms and Romans, we are invited to reimagine breath not as composure but as communion, breath that aches, breath that stutters, breath that testifies.

3 Ruach *in the valley – Ezekiel's prophetic breath*

Among the most vivid pneumatological visions in Scripture is found in Ezekiel 37, where the prophet is taken to a valley full of dry bones. The vision begins in silence and desolation: the bones are 'very dry', long disconnected from life, memory or dignity. It is a field of forgotten bodies – unburied, unnamed, unmourned. This is not just a metaphor for death; it is a metaphor for dismemberment, for social erasure, for those whose bodies no longer register on the liturgical radar of the living.

And yet, this is where *ruach*, the Spirit-breath of God, is commanded to go. 'Then he said to me, "Prophesy to the breath, prophesy, mortal, and say to the breath: Thus says the Lord GOD: Come from the four winds, O breath, and breathe upon these slain, that they may live"' (Ezek. 37.9).

Here, the Spirit is not imagined as gentle or local. It is a breath summoned from the four winds, uncontained, sweeping, public and chaotic. It is summoned to those who cannot breathe for themselves. The bones are passive, lifeless, silenced. Yet when the Spirit breathes, they rise. Ligaments reconnect. Flesh returns. Breath enters. And they stand on their feet, 'a vast multitude'.

This reading of Ezekiel's vision unfolds into a theology of reclamation, where resurrection is not a passive event but an active, public reconstitution. The Spirit does not merely lift individuals into life: it restores the erased and disregarded, re-membering what empire has dismembered. Ezekiel's valley of bones is populated not simply by the dead, but by those whom systems of power have discarded – the forgotten disabled saints, the ventilated bodies denied sanctuary, the unbaptized infants who were buried without liturgical witness. And yet, the Spirit calls them back into the body of grace.

Thomas Reynolds' reflection illuminates this dynamic. To be remembered by God is not merely to persist, but to belong, to be gathered into community, affirmed and loved. This is a theology that resists mere survival and insists on justice, on presence, on a resurrection that is neither sentimental nor triumphalist but deeply embodied. It is a movement that holds the fractures of history, refusing their erasure and instead drawing them into the life of the Church.³

Ezekiel's vision is not about bodily perfection: it is about bodily participation. The Spirit gives breath not to restore idealized forms, but to gather lives torn apart. Breath becomes the medium of resistance against annihilation. This breath is not antiseptic. It passes through trauma, history and bones.

Moreover, this scene critiques a heritage theology that only curates saints who are beautiful, whole and vocal. Ezekiel's bones push back against heritage practices that venerate only normative icons. The Spirit's breath enters into disabled, disarticulated, unnamed bodies and calls them not defective – but divinely desired.

The ecclesial implication is urgent: if the Spirit breathes among the bones, the Church must do likewise. Liturgy must make room for broken breath. Architecture must echo with the memory of the slain. Heritage must remember that those most excluded from history are precisely those the Spirit revives first.

In Ezekiel, we find a vision of a Spirit that does not reinforce bodily norms but reconfigures them entirely. It breathes not into the powerful, but into the powerless. It does not reward control; it raises the forgotten.

Breath and the heritage of the Church

Building directly upon my earlier critiques of how ableism and imperial theological anthropology have shaped Christian heritage, where I traced how both ecclesial memory and architectural design have privileged the normate body, nowhere is this more insidiously evident than in the Church's pneumatological imagination. Breath – perhaps the most primal and universal sign of life – has been coded within the Church's heritage to align with a narrow ideal of able-bodied sanctity.

Across history, the Church has colluded and collaborated, choreographing its sacred spaces and liturgical aesthetics around particular assumptions about breath. From the vaulted acoustics of medieval cathedrals to the disciplined rhythm of Gregorian chant, breath is presumed to be steady, vocal and controllable. It is not merely spiritual; it is aestheticized, governed by a legacy that equates the Spirit with composure, volume and silence on demand.

As I have already expressed, heritage is not neutral; it is performed, and breath has become a significant part of that performance. The fact that heritage operates through exclusion and power finds direct expression in ecclesial life: who breathes freely in worship? Who stirs the space with groaning or stimming breath and is deemed disruptive? Whose respiratory irregularity is accommodated, and whose is silenced or not even acknowledged?

This breath-regulated heritage places neurodivergent, disabled and ventilated bodies outside the aesthetic liturgy of holiness. It enshrines a spiritualized normativity in which the breath of the Spirit is imagined flowing most freely through smooth cadences and uninterrupted silence, when, as I have shown throughout this chapter, Scripture reveals precisely the opposite.

To inherit such a tradition uncritically is to baptize ableism as orthodoxy. But the wounded, risen Christ refuses this inheritance. His breath is not calm but cruciform. His breath on Easter evening (John 20.22) is the same breath he relinquishes in a cry on the cross (John 19.30). These breaths are not separated by aesthetics: they are joined by theological continuity. To breathe in the Spirit is to inhale the wounds of Christ, and to exhale not smooth serenity but radical inclusion.

Therefore, to reimagine the Church's heritage of breath is not to reject tradition, it is to return it to its cruciform root. It is to remember that the Church's very birth, at Pentecost, was marked by breath as fire, noise, chaos and multilingual disruption. It is to declare, with Psalm 150.6, that 'everything that has breath' shall praise the Lord, including bodies that breathe differently, unpredictably and imperfectly.

Just as John Hull drew attention to the Church's creation of a visual theology, where the unseen, the unheard, the irregular, the uncomfortable have all been gently edged out of the realm of the sacred,[4] so too has the Church created a respiratory theology, a liturgical architecture of exclusion, in which some breaths are canonized and others disqualified. But the Spirit groans where we cannot speak (Rom. 8.26), and the dry bones rise where there is no breath at all (Ezek. 37). These are not exceptions; they are the pattern of redemption.

The challenge before us therefore is whether the Church is brave enough to allow and enable the Spirit's heritage to shape the Church's heritage, so that in the future we will curate a liturgy, an architecture and a memory that begin not with ableist normativity but with the ruptured spirit-filled breath of God.

Notes

1 Sharon V. Betcher, *Spirit and the Politics of Disablement* (Minneapolis, MN: Fortress Press, 2007), pp. 68–121.

2 Nancy L. Eiesland, *The Disabled God: Toward a Liberatory Theology of Disability* (Nashville, TN: Abingdon Press, 1994), pp. 107–20.

3 Thomas E. Reynolds, *Vulnerable Communion: A Theology of Disability and Hospitality* (Grand Rapids, MI: Brazos Press, 2008), pp. 175–213.

4 John M. Hull, *In the Beginning There Was Darkness: A Blind Person's Conversations with the Bible* (London: SCM Press, 2001), pp. 67–75.

11

Cracked Chalices, Overflowing Grace: Disability, Sacrament and the Neurodivergent Body of Christ

If, as we have seen, the Spirit groans with us, not above us, and breathes not in the perfected but in the pierced, then the same pneumatological truth must shape how we encounter God in the sacraments. Just as we reimagined breath, interruption and groaning through the risen body rather than the idealized norm, so too must our theology of sacrament undergo a similar transformation. The sacraments are not distant echoes of purity but living witnesses of grace in breaking time and scarred flesh. What follows, then, is a re-examination of the Church's sacramental life; not as a pristine inheritance, but as a contested and prophetic space in which disabled bodies have too often been erased. It is time to re-member what the Church has dis-membered.

The sacraments are the tangible rhythms of Christian life, where flesh meets grace, and memory becomes presence. But for disabled people, these moments of divine encounter have often been sites of exclusion, misrecognition or harm. This is not because the sacraments themselves are deficient, but because the Church has administered them through the lens of ableism, a theology and practice that privileges normative bodies, minds and behaviours, not simply a social prejudice but a theological distortion. It imagines grace as symmetrical, holiness as coherent, and participation as conditioned upon bodily decorum and cognitive alignment. It treats the sacraments therefore as the reward of the disciplined rather than the gift of the crucified.

In this chapter I will undertake a twofold movement. First, I will critique the sacramental tradition where ableist assumptions have shaped baptism, Eucharist and anointing. Second, I will reimagine these sacraments through a theology grounded in the risen, still-wounded body of Christ, offering a vision of ecclesial life that honours all narrative, temporal and storied bodies, especially disabled ones. In doing so, I also interrogate how Christian heritage has curated sacraments through a static and exclusionary aesthetic, and propose a new, time-formed anthropology that makes space for eucharistic grace in every body.

The wounds of exclusion – sacrament and the idealized norm

1 Ecclesial beauty and the aesthetic of wholeness

Since the fourth century, the ableist idealized norm assimilated itself into virtually every area of the Church's consciousness, including its sacramental imagination, which found itself shaped not only by theology but by imperial aesthetics. Sacred buildings were constructed to reflect Graeco-Roman ideals of symmetry, order and hierarchized access. The sacramental body naturally followed suit and was presumed to be upright, composed, rational and whole. The very space of sanctity, the raised altars, narrow chancels, linear pews of our sacred buildings, reflected an anthropological norm that excluded disabled bodies from full sacramental participation.

This legacy persists in practice and perception. A child who stims at the font, a neurodivergent adult who flinches at liturgical sound, a wheelchair user navigating stone steps, all are subtly, and sometimes overtly, positioned as 'other'. The God we purport to worship is not the crucified one, but a heretical idol of control.

Theological frameworks like Aquinas's *ex opere operato* preserved sacramental efficacy, but ecclesial applications often demanded 'right disposition', implying a moral, cognitive or aesthetic suitability. The result? Sacraments were guarded by a theology of fitness rather than hospitality, performance rather than presence.

2 Baptism and cognitive gatekeeping

Baptism, as the gateway to Christian belonging, has frequently become a site of cognitive ableism. In traditions requiring personal confession, intellectual assent becomes a prerequisite; in traditions of infant baptism, developmental norms are assumed as guarantees of future understanding.

But the New Testament presents baptism as a radically inclusive act of divine initiative. In Acts 8, Philip baptizes the Ethiopian eunuch with no catechism, no delay, just a desire to belong. In Acts 16, entire households are baptized, irrespective of age or cognition. Grace precedes comprehension. They respond to the Common Worship baptismal statement of belonging and investment, that 'in God we have a new dignity, and God calls us to fullness of life.'

The Spirit does not demand cognitive conformity before moving, nor does it restrict belonging to those who can articulate belief in conventionally recognized ways. Baptism, as an act of divine welcome, should never be contingent upon intellectual ability; its denial in such cases is not theological caution but sacramental violence.

This exclusion stands in direct contradiction to the baptismal commitments expressed in *Common Worship*'s introduction, where grace is affirmed as freely given, not earned or verified. Theologically, this exposes how ecclesial practices can subtly reinforce ableist assumptions, treating cognitive difference as a barrier rather than a testament to the breadth of God's inclusivity. In this sense, baptism should not function as an act of sorting, of deciding whose embodiment is 'ready' for grace, but rather as a declaration of God's unreserved embrace, a re-membering into the body of Christ that acknowledges all forms of knowing, sensing and being as sacred.

The font must be reclaimed as a place where water meets skin without condition. Baptism should not require performance. It is God's act, not ours. It is the Church that must adjust its imagination, not the disabled body. Not any body.

3 Eucharist and the politics of access

The Eucharist rightly stands at the heart of the Christian faith and Christian worship, not merely as a ritual to be observed, but as a transformative act of communal memory and becoming. In partaking of the broken bread and shared cup, the Church embodies the wounded yet risen body of Christ, embracing vulnerability and grace.

St Paul reminds us, 'Because there is one bread, we who are many are one body' (1 Cor. 10.17). This unity is not predicated on perfection but on the shared experience of breaking and redemption. The Eucharist teaches that holiness is found not in flawlessness but in the communal sharing of Christ's body, through the act of breaking, marked by scars and sustained by hope.

For disabled Christians, the Eucharist resonates deeply. It affirms that Christ meets us in our vulnerabilities, not despite them. The sacrament becomes a space where disability is not marginalized but recognized as a site of divine encounter.

This understanding challenges traditional liturgical practices. Consider at a service of benediction, the display of the consecrated Host in a monstrance, unbroken and elevated. Here we meet the heresy of the idealized norm, with its implicit reference to a socially and theologically constructed standard of human embodiment; one that privileges physical wholeness, autonomy, rationality and aesthetic symmetry; rooted in cultural, medical and religious assumptions; one that imagines the 'perfect' body as able-bodied, neurotypical, visually unmarked by difference and functionally independent.

Now reimagine this practice by presenting the breaking bread; not the flawless unbroken bread, but the bread now sharing the visible response to the act of breaking – the fault line – the place where we encounter both suffering and creation, the wounded and glorified body of Christ, the storied body, the resurrected body which aligns with the lived realities of the faithful. The body of Christ in the monstrance now becomes the paradox of glory and wounding, presence and fragmentation. Displayed in gleaming gold and radiant rays, the consecrated breaking Host is lifted before the faithful as the *corpus verum*, the true body, of the risen Christ. Yet what it represents is not triumphant perfection, but a body breaking, and sharing. It becomes the embodiment of the eucharistic action: 'We break this bread to share in the body of Christ'. 'Breaking' does not result in the bread being broken, as in needing to be fixed, but is rather the action of 'sharing', of the building of community, of becoming the body of Christ.

The eucharistic Christ is not the flawless ideal, but the wounded one: pierced hands, torn flesh, side still open. Held aloft in the monstrance is not merely divinity concealed in bread, but the ongoing memory of a body given, bruised and yet glorified. The monstrance thus becomes a sacred contradiction, an ornate vessel housing the radical claim that resurrection does not erase wounding but transfigures it. In this breaking yet risen body, disabled believers find not exclusion, but profound recognition: a God who does not transcend suffering but bears it, hallows it and offers it as the site of communion.

However, many churches inadvertently exclude disabled individuals through inaccessible architecture and unaccommodating liturgies. Altars elevated by steps, narrow chancels and the absence of accommodations for various disabilities contradict the inclusive nature of the Eucharist. These barriers transform the table of grace into a symbol of exclusion.

Gordon Lathrop observes that the Eucharist sanctifies the ordinary.[1] Yet, when the ordinary needs of disabled individuals, such as mobility aids or alternative communication methods, are overlooked, the sacrament's sanctity is compromised. True inclusion requires intentional design and practice that welcome all to the table.

Reimagining the eucharistic table involves more than physical adjustments; it demands a theological commitment to inclusivity. This includes designing spaces that accommodate mobility devices, offering gluten-free wafers, and embracing diverse expressions of participation. Yet it is too often choreographed for the able-bodied and neurotypical: steps to climb, stillness to maintain, gestures to master, silences to preserve, attention spans to extend. Sensory environments are frequently unforgiving, such as bright lights, crowded spaces, loud echoes, while theological assumptions prove even more so. In many churches, to be deemed 'ready' to receive communion still implies an ability to sit still, process theological concepts and receive reverently with regulated gestures and facial composure. These criteria are soaked in ableism and neurotypical normativity.

But what of the autistic child who rocks or flaps while receiving the Host? What of the adult with ADHD whose gaze wanders during the liturgy? What of the person with a cognitive disability who cannot articulate belief but who loves Jesus with fierce simplicity? What of the worshipper who stims in joy or fidgets in anxiety? What of those for whom eye contact is painful or bread texture unbearable? If the Eucharist is only accessible to those who conform to regulated expressions of reverence, then what has become of the sacrament? It has become a heretical sacrament of exclusion rather than a life-giving sacrament of grace.

The Gospels, as always, offer us a different, grace-filled vision. In Luke 14, Jesus rebukes the elite who refuse his invitation and insists that the banquet of the kingdom be filled instead with 'the poor, the crippled, the blind, and the lame' (Luke 14.21). These are not metaphors: they are real people whose bodies and social presence disrupted the norms of temple and table. In Jesus' vision, these are not mere afterthoughts; they are the welcomed intended guests.

And in Luke 24, the disciples on the road to Emmaus journey with the risen Christ for hours, unable to comprehend him. Only in the breaking of the bread – note, not in teaching, not in rational explanation – do they comprehend the risen Christ in their midst and recognition occurs (Luke 24.30–31). The risen Christ is not discerned by intellectual mastery but through shared action, gesture and embodied presence. The Eucharist is not a test of comprehension but a revelation in vulnerability. Participation in the sacrament is not contingent upon doctrinal precision or controlled posture: it simply asks for presence. Hunger itself becomes a confession, an embodied theology that speaks without words.

Neurodivergent worshippers challenge the Church's long-held assumptions about reverence and understanding. Too often, faith has been equated with cognitive assent, while worship has been measured by its conformity to quietude and restraint. Yet reverence does not always manifest in stillness, and faith is not confined to the structures of articulated doctrine. Movement, sensory experience, nonlinear engagement; these, too, are liturgical languages.

The theology of eucharistic welcome dismantles the barriers of liturgical elitism, reminding us that participation is not measured by comprehension but by presence. Neurodivergent worshippers are not outsiders accommodated at a table not meant for them: their presence reshapes the very meaning of the feast, revealing a capacious faith that refuses exclusion. The liturgical demands of silence, stillness and cognitive articulation expose an ecclesial ableism that has too long dictated the conditions of belonging. Yet the Eucharist subverts these conditions, it does not demand qualification, it does not weigh intellectual assent, it does not privilege polished prayers. It feeds first.

For the eucharistic body is not an image of perfection but a body with holes in it, one that bears scars which are not erased but transfigured, not corrected but consecrated. This is a theology that refuses to equate wholeness with flawlessness. Jesus' body does not transcend disability but communes through it, affirming that sanctity is not about escaping vulnerability but about dwelling within it.

In this light, eucharistic practice must resist exclusion in all its forms, not as an act of tolerance but as the recognition that God's presence is found precisely in those the Church has too often overlooked. Worship is not performance. It is embodiment. It is witness. It is the radical proclamation that in this meal, all belong.

The Church must therefore abandon its ableist and neurotypical performance of sacramentality and reimagine the Eucharist as an act of radical hospitality. It must be willing to break bread with trembling hands, with stimming bodies, with neurodivergent minds and with all those who disrupt the performative liturgies of control.

To do this is not to dilute the sacrament but to deeply honour its truth: that in Christ, God gives not perfection, but presence. And that this presence is discerned most clearly not in purity but in mutual dependence, open hands and the shared vulnerability of breaking bread.

In centring disabled bodies within eucharistic practice, the Church moves beyond acts of charity toward a deeper embodiment of eschatological hope. The Eucharist becomes a foretaste of the heavenly banquet, a gathering where every scar and adaptation is honoured, and every individual is joyfully welcomed. The Eucharist is the beating heart of ecclesial life.

Toward a risen body sacramentality

1 Baptism as immersion into shared fragility

Romans 6.4 declares we are 'buried with [Christ] by baptism'. This is not about achieving holiness through development. It is about entering into Christ's death and resurrection with whatever body we have.

Baptism, in this light, is not about conformity to an idealized form but about a radical solidarity, a descent into vulnerability that mirrors Christ's own journey. This radical solidarity reframes baptism as an act of divine recognition rather than correction. It is a ritual not of eligibility but of belonging.

For disabled bodies, this affirmation is profound. Baptism does not wait for coherence, stillness or cognitive articulation; it does not demand alignment with an ableist ideal before bestowing grace. Instead, it proclaims that God's *yes* is immediate, unqualified and fully present. The waters do not filter out difference; they embrace it. The font does not exclude those who enter in ways that are unexpected or unconventional – bodies marked by time in breath, motion, sound, silence – all are gathered into renewal.

This is the Church at its most capacious: not measuring participation by doctrinal precision but recognizing that baptism is, above all, the proclamation that every body belongs. It is not the threshold to an idealized faith: it is the immersion into grace that refuses to erase history, wounds or difference but instead makes them part of the sacred story itself.

2 Eucharist as the feast of cracked bodies

To eat Christ's body is to join a meal not of conquest but of crucified communion. As 1 Corinthians 11 reminds us, those who fail to discern the body exclude the poor, and the disabled, from the table.

Jennie Weiss Block urges us to see access not as generosity but as justice.[2] Eucharistic hospitality must extend to the neurodivergent, the communicatively different, the distracted and the dependent. To receive with a carer, through a tube or in a noisy body is not deviation. It is holy participation. The Eucharist is not a rite of discipline. It is a moment of shared fragility, an altar of grace for cracked chalices.

3 The body of Christ and the narrative of becoming

Traditional eucharistic theology often reflects a static anthropology: Christ's body as fixed, idealized; our bodies as unchanging or 'corrected' by grace. But this misunderstands both the Incarnation and ecclesiology.

Christ's body is the ultimate storied body, born, bruised, crucified and, most significantly of all, risen. It is a body through time. It is a body through life and death. Paul reminds us in 1 Corinthians 11.26 that every Eucharist is a proclamation until Christ comes again. This table, this meal, is temporal, not timeless.

Deborah Creamer's 'limits theology' helps us here by offering a more faithful anthropology: we are dynamic, interdependent and time-bound.[3] Our bodies are becoming, not failing. Our story has not stopped, it continues. The Eucharist, then, must meet us in our becoming. Not at the imagined endpoint of perfection, but in the middle of story, rupture and resistance.

4 Anointing as shared suffering, not fixing

Anointing is often reduced to medical cure. But in the Gospels, healing is not restoration to norm but participation in divine presence. The woman in Mark 5 is healed through touch, risk and testimony. The man in John 9 becomes a theologian before he sees.

Anointing then is not a remedy for suffering but acts as its sanctification. In risen body theology, the oil does not erase but consecrates, marking holiness in chronic pain, grace in mental distress, presence in perceived absence. This is not a theology of escape but of transfiguration, where wounds are not removed but drawn into the life of resurrection, held as testimony rather than corrected into silence.

Heritage, memory and the sacraments we forget

This is a call to liturgical integrity, a demand that the Church's heritage reflect the fullness of those who live within its sacramental life, not merely the polished aesthetics of theological abstraction. Laurajane Smith's insight exposes the reality that heritage is an active construct, shaped by what is chosen to be remembered and what is allowed to fade.[4] The Church has curated its history in ways that often reinforce exclusion, preserving grandeur while neglecting accessibility, naming only those who fit within its predefined vision of belonging.

But the sacramental life does not obey these exclusions. It spills over, defying the barriers placed around it. Fonts drenched in the unruly joy of baptism. Bread fragmented by hands that move unpredictably. Oil pressed onto limbs that do not conform to symmetrical motion. These are not deviations from sacred order: they are its fullest revelations.

To re-member the sacramental body is not to dilute its holiness but to unveil its truth. It is to insist that the Eucharist, the font, the anointing oil, all of it, is meant for the entirety of God's people, not just for those whose bodies fit neatly within tradition's aesthetic boundaries.

The Church has chosen to remember the polished but forgotten the act of breaking.

We must re-member our sacramental life: fonts wet with chaotic joy, bread broken with involuntary movement, oil smeared on paralyzed limbs. This is not a degradation of the sacred. It is its unveiling.

Sacraments of the scars

Ableism has colonized the Church's sacramental imagination. It has hidden the wounded, sanitized the table and curated a memory that forgets real bodies. But the risen Christ still bears his wounds. The sacraments are not icons of control but ruptures of grace.

Baptism for the silent. Eucharist for the stimming. Anointing for the incurable.

This is the sacramental life of the Church we are called to. And it is not new. It is ancient, remembered afresh by the very bodies the Church tried to forget.

But if a risen body sacramental theology shows us what grace looks like in the now, eschatology dares to ask what grace will look like in the not-yet. But what happens when our vision of heaven has already been shaped by ableism? What if our hope has been colonized by the same heritage that erased disabled people from the font and altar?

In the next chapter, I will turn to eschatology, not as escape from the body, but as its glorified witness. I will interrogate how Christian heritage has shaped our imaginations of perfection, healing and resurrection, and ask what it means to long for a kingdom that still bears the wounds of Christ.

Notes

1 Gordon W. Lathrop, *Holy Things: A Liturgical Theology* (Minneapolis, MN: Fortress Press, 1993), pp. 87–138.

2 Jennie Weiss Block, *Copious Hosting: A Theology of Access for People with Disabilities* (New York: Continuum, 2002), pp. 115–17.

3 Deborah Beth Creamer, *Disability and Christian Theology: Embodied Limits and Constructive Possibilities* (Oxford: Oxford University Press, 2009), pp. 93–114.

4 Laurajane Smith, *Uses of Heritage* (London: Routledge, 2006), pp. 44–83.

12

Wounds That Remain: Eschatology, Narrative Bodies and the Kingdom of the Risen Flesh

Eschatology has too often been treated as an escape hatch from the body, as if the *telos* of Christian hope is to shed the skin of history, memory and frailty in favour of a perfected and disembodied bliss. Within this framework, disability yet again becomes a problem to be solved, now and in the hereafter, a tragic footnote in the story of becoming whole. Resurrection, in such traditions, is imagined not as the glorification of the wounded body but as its replacement with a more idealized form.

Christian eschatology does not erase embodiment – it sanctifies it. The longing for resurrection is not a rejection of earthly existence but a hope that everything we carry – our limits, wounds and loves – will be held and transfigured in God. The resurrected body is not a perfected abstraction but a testimony, bearing the marks of survival, relationship and history.

Willie James Jennings affirms this truth, emphasizing that salvation is not a flight from flesh but the renewal of flesh, a redemption that does not discard our scars but consecrates them. The body is not abandoned in resurrection; it is embraced, glorified and woven into the eternal life of God.[1]

Against escapism, toward embodied hope

In this chapter I will name and interrogate the ableist tendencies woven through Christian heritage, traditions that have sanctified a vision of eternal life that is also marked by physical uniformity, cognitive competence and behavioural decorum. These visions have shaped not only theology but also so-called pastoral practice: sermons that promise 'healing in heaven', funerals that deny the meaning of lived disability and sacred art that erases bodily difference from the risen Christ.

By contrast, I will explore how a narrative anthropology, an understanding of the human person as storied, time-bound and socially formed, transforms eschatology. Through this anthropology, disability becomes not a deviation but a dimension of identity, not a detour, but part of the sacred route. And when this anthropology is paired with a risen body theology, a Christology that refuses to erase the wounds of resurrection, but rather holds and shares Christ's whole story, we arrive at a radically inclusive eschatological hope. One in which the kingdom of God is not a realm of idealized bodies but of remembered, glorified ones. Wounded. Whole. True.

Drawing from Scripture, early Church Fathers, medieval mystics, reformation thinkers and contemporary theologians of disability and hope, I will trace a vision of the not-yet that bears faithful witness to the now. In this kingdom, wounds do not disappear; they shine. They are not anomalies to be corrected but testimonies to be transfigured.

We are not heading for a heaven without memory. No, we are journeying toward a world in which our scars are kissed into glory.

Eschatological perfection and the legacy of ableism

From the earliest centuries of the Church, the Christian imagination of heaven has been shaped not only by Scripture but also by the surrounding aesthetics and assumptions of Graeco-Roman culture. The ideal body of the classical world, one which is youthful, symmetrical, rational and controlled, found a troubling theological afterlife in Christian visions of the resurrected body. In this aesthetic regime, disability could only ever be imagined as something to be corrected or cured. This is not a neutral theological error. Here we have a deeply embedded form of eschatological ableism.

And how the early Church Fathers wrestled with what kind of body would be raised. Tertullian asserted that 'the flesh shall rise again, whole in every member,'[2] arguing for anatomical continuity but still under the influence of Roman ideals of bodily integrity. As I have already shown, Augustine took this further in *The City of God*, proposing that the resurrected body would be 'most perfect and most beautiful', suggesting that all deformity would be eliminated.[3] Thomas Aquinas systematized this eschatological perfectionism in the *Summa Theologiae*, teaching that the glorified body would possess clarity, agility, subtlety and impassibility, four qualities that, if we are being honest, effectively exclude every disabled experience.[4]

Of course, such visions were meant to exalt the resurrection; but in doing so, they excluded from glory the very bodies that Christ so often drew near to in his earthly ministry, namely the sick, the lame, the epileptic, the deaf and the mentally distressed; those whom Jesus touched, healed, dignified were completely imagined out of the eschatological picture.

The consequences of these views are not confined to theological abstraction. They have filtered into how Christians preach, teach and pastorally accompany countless disabled Christians, who have heard that they will be 'healed in heaven', with the clear implication that their current embodied state is a problem, a lack or a temporary affliction unworthy of eternity. Such preaching imagines resurrection as a kind of divine edit, erasing any trace of difference that cannot be smoothed into the symmetry of an idealized eternity.

The resurrection does not sanitize suffering; it transfigures it. In John 20.27, Jesus does not erase his wounds but presents them as proof of identity, inviting Thomas not into an idealized form but into a scarred, glorified body. This is the scandal of resurrection: it does not conform to expectations of bodily perfection but insists that wholeness is found in the persistence of wounds, in their integration into redeemed life.

Nancy Eiesland's insight underscores this reality: that her recognition of the *Disabled God* speaks to a theology where disability is neither obstacle nor imperfection but an intrinsic part of divine presence. The risen Christ does not correct embodiment; he consecrates it. His scars are not vestiges of a past affliction but marks of solidarity, witnesses to a God who does not heal by removal but by remaining.[5]

An eschatology that adopts an idealized view of humanity by erasing disability likewise betrays the gospel. It further underlines the claim that God can only dwell in perfection, when in truth, God *chose* incarnation, crucifixion and a resurrection that did not tidy up the evidence of trauma. The Church must recognize that its traditional eschatologies have also been shaped by imperial aesthetics and theological sanitization, and in doing so, must begin the work of unlearning what it means to be made whole.

Resurrection as narrative, not erasure

To imagine resurrection correctly, we must return to first principles by once more rejecting the idea that the body is an object to be restored to a former ideal. Resurrection is not a return to Edenic symmetry or some

Graeco-Roman perfection. Rather, it is the glorification of the particular body, through time, with all its histories, traumas and transformations remembered in love.

This requires a move from a static anthropology, formed through our historical embrace of the imperial body, the Graeco-Roman idealized norm, where the human person is defined by form, function or fixed attributes, to a narrative anthropology, revealed and articulated through the risen body of Jesus Christ; one that understands the self as a story, unfolding through time, marked by events, relationships and embodied change. In this frame, the body is not merely what we are but how we live, how we are remembered, how we are loved. It is the foundation of our incarnational relational theology.

The body of Christ raised from the dead is not returned to a pre-crucifixion state. It is not a reset. It is a body recognizable by its wounds (Luke 24.39–40), and unrecognizable in glory (Luke 24.16). It is a body that confounds static identity and insists instead on a form that holds memory within it. The story is not erased but fulfilled. Thus, it follows that my story of disability will not be erased by the resurrection either, but honoured and valued.

The Apostle Paul captures something of this mystery when he writes of the resurrection body in 1 Corinthians 15. He speaks not of replacement but transformation, of a body 'sown in weakness' and 'raised in power' (v. 43), of continuity that includes change. But the metaphors he uses – seed and plant – signal that what is raised is organically connected to what was sown. The narrative continues. There is no harvest without the seed.

This reimagining of resurrection confronts long-standing assumptions about bodily restoration. Instead of erasing difference or imposing an idealized wholeness, resurrection affirms embodiment as it is – bearing its story, its struggles, its witness. The glorified body is not a perfected abstraction but a testimony to the life it has lived, transformed yet still recognizable.

Deborah Creamer challenges traditional salvific narratives that prioritize normative restoration. Rather than envisioning salvation as the correction of bodily variance, her theology embraces complex embodiment, an affirmation that difference is not an obstacle to grace but a vital part of its expression. Resurrection does not overwrite identity: it reveals the fullness of God's presence within the diversity of human experience.[6]

Resurrection, viewed through the lens of narrative anthropology, is not a process of refinement or erasure but of divine remembrance.

It affirms that identity is not discarded but drawn into renewed life – endurance, relationship and difference are not obstacles to glorification but essential to it. This theological vision insists that nothing of our lived experience is lost in God; rather, it is held, transfigured and re-membered.

John Swinton reinforces this truth, that resurrection is not the granting of new identities but the return of our own, healed by love and remembered into life. Resurrection is not an escape from embodiment but an affirmation that our stories, struggles and wounds remain integral to who we are, gathered into the fullness of grace rather than erased by it.[7]

The apocalyptic witness to wounded glory

Biblical apocalyptic literature, often viewed as obscure, symbolic or overly dramatic, is, in fact, a vital theological genre for confronting suffering. It reveals a divine perspective on history that honours the wounded, remembers the oppressed and refuses to let trauma be the final word. Far from being an escapist fantasy, apocalyptic texts unveil a world where wounds matter, where the suffering body is not erased, but enthroned. Let me share three vital examples from both the Old and New Testaments.

1 Revelation and the slain, yet reigning lamb

In Revelation 5.6, John sees 'a Lamb standing as if it had been slaughtered', positioned at the centre of heaven's throne. The paradox is deliberate and potent: the Lamb is alive, standing, but visibly wounded. The marks of slaughter are not erased by resurrection: they are the very credentials of divine authority. This image dethrones any eschatology that imagines glory as perfection and instead insists that the kingdom is ruled by a wounded body.

This is a profound theological claim, one that refuses to separate divine sovereignty from the realities of embodied suffering. The Lamb is not declared worthy despite his wounds, but because of them (Rev. 5.9). The eschatological centre of Christian hope is not an abstracted perfection but a body bearing its history. Trauma is carried forward into glory, not erased in transcendence.

The resurrected Christ does not abandon impairment but embodies it, fully and visibly. His scarred flesh is not a contradiction to divinity but its fullest expression, the *imago Dei* revealed in wounded, risen presence. This is the disruptive truth at the heart of resurrection: glory is not found in untouched perfection but in the transfigured continuity of suffering and grace.

2 Ezekiel, Daniel and resurrection as re-membering

In Ezekiel 37, the prophet sees a valley of dry bones. The bones come together, sinew and flesh cover them, and finally the breath (*ruach*) of God enters them. But these are not anonymous corpses; they are 'the whole house of Israel' (v. 11), a traumatized community re-embodied in hope. This is not about restoring to an ideal form: it is about remembering a people from within their devastation. The bones speak. Resurrection is about re-membering, not remaking.

In Daniel 7, the Son of Man stands as a radical departure from the imperial visions that precede him. Unlike the beasts that symbolize unchecked power – consuming, trampling and fragmenting creation – the Son of Man emerges not as a conqueror but as one who embodies divine solidarity with the afflicted. His authority is not won through violence but granted through vindication, a revelation of justice that does not erase suffering but transforms it.

The saints in Daniel's vision are those who have been worn down by empire, their existence shaped by marginalization and oppression. Yet their fate is not mere endurance; it is resurrection, an enacted justice that reverses their degradation. This is not a passive deliverance but a re-membering of those whom history has crushed. The eschatological promise here is not detached from lived experience: it is woven into the reality of imperial violence, insisting that redemption unfolds *within* history, not beyond it.

The imagery of the Son of Man speaks directly into the theology of risen bodies, not as perfected abstractions but as scarred testimonies. Resurrection, in this framework, is not an escape from history but its reclamation. It declares that empire does not have the final word, that those erased by power are seen, that justice does not come through domination but through divine presence with the suffering. This vindication does not erase wounds; rather it ensures that they are carried forward, that the bodies history sought to break are restored, lifted up in the presence of God, not as proof of their resilience alone but as witnesses to a justice that refuses to forget.

3 Revelation 21 and the descent of the city

In Revelation's final vision (21.1–4), the new heaven and earth are revealed not as an escape from the world but as its transformation. The descent of the New Jerusalem signifies that redemption does not pull creation upward into abstraction but brings God's presence downward into embodied reality. The eschatological promise is not separation but communion – God's dwelling is with humanity, intimately near, wiping away every tear in an act of profound tenderness.

The removal of the sea – a recurring biblical motif of chaos and division – is not a negation of diversity but an undoing of the forces that fracture and endanger. This is not a future of uniformity but of restored wholeness, where barriers cease to separate and harm no longer has dominion.

Laurajane Smith's work on heritage studies illuminates this theological movement, for memory is never about the past alone but about the narratives we choose to bring into the present and future. Revelation's vision is deeply tied to this idea; redemption is not amnesia but restoration. The wounds of history are not erased but carried forward into divine presence, woven into a new creation where they are seen, acknowledged and healed. The future does not abandon the past – it re-members it into glory.[8]

Toward a theology of remaining wounds

If the apocalyptic texts unveil the wounded Christ at the heart of eschatological glory, then Christian theology must develop a vocabulary and vision for what might be called a theology of remaining wounds. This is a theology that neither idolizes suffering nor seeks to erase it, but instead allows wounds – bodily, historical, communal – to bear truthful witness to both trauma and transformation.

In traditional soteriologies, wounds are often seen as marks of sin, weakness or the need for healing. This has become the most prevalent and popular contemporary understanding of the atonement, where the cross becomes a moment of substitution, after which suffering is no longer relevant to the resurrected state. But in a theology of remaining wounds, resurrection does not obliterate suffering: it redeems it by making it visible and glorious. This is not to say that pain itself is eternal, but that its marks, its stories, are held, honoured and transfigured in the risen body of Christ, and, therefore, in the bodies of all who rise with him.

A theology of remaining wounds reframes resurrection not as the final erasure of embodied difference but as God's radical inclusion of every wounded story. The resurrected body of Christ does not walk away from suffering but carries its history into the future of God.

Jürgen Moltmann and the crucified God raised

Jürgen Moltmann offers a pivotal contribution to an eschatology grounded in the memory of suffering and the transfiguration of the body. His theology refuses both utopian optimism and passive resignation, insisting instead on a hope that arises precisely from the wounds of history. For Moltmann, hope is not the projection of fantasy, but the transformation of reality through God's faithful remembering. Resurrection, in this theological vision, does not bypass the cross but confirms its enduring significance. The risen body is not a reversal of pain, nor a negation of the crucified one, but the glorification of the very body that suffered. In *The Coming of God*, Moltmann describes resurrection not as a rupture with the created body, but as its transfiguration, a re-creation in which continuity, not erasure, is central. The marks of trauma are not wiped clean: they are taken up into glory. The flesh is not discarded, but renewed; its story is preserved, not denied.[9]

In *The Crucified God*, Moltmann articulates a Christology in which God does not remain above suffering but enters it fully. The crucifixion is not simply an event in salvation history: it is the definitive self-revelation of a God who chooses solidarity with the vulnerable. This theological choice has profound implications for how we imagine the resurrection. The body that is raised is not untouched by death but carries the memory of it. It is not the body of the idealized norm, but the body that has borne injustice and pain, now vindicated in divine life. The risen Christ remains the crucified one. His wounds are not anomalies to be erased, but permanent features of his glorified identity.[10]

For disabled people, this eschatological realism offers more than abstract consolation: it offers ontological dignity. In a world that so often portrays disability as something to be overcome or healed away, Moltmann's vision proclaims the opposite: that the fullness of redemption does not require the erasure of difference, but its transfiguration. Disabled bodies are not temporarily tolerated until perfection comes: they are the very sites where God's redeeming work is most visible. The promise is not a body that forgets the struggle, but a body that remembers it truthfully, and furthermore, carries those memories not with shame, but with splendour. In this vision, scars become signs of grace, impairments become liturgies of perseverance, and every body, however fragile, is drawn into the resurrection not as a copy of some ideal, but as the beloved original made radiant.

Memory, justice and mutual recognition

The Church must recover a vision of resurrection in which justice is not abstract, but embodied recognition. The wounds that remain in the risen body of Christ are not signs of defeat but guarantees that the oppressed will not be forgotten.

This theology bears fruit in practices of mutual recognition. It honours those whose bodies have borne injustice and says, 'we are seen, we are known, and nothing of our story will be lost'. In Luke 24.39–40, Jesus shows his hands and feet to his disciples, not to prove power, but to confirm identity. The same is true for all of us. Our wounds and our vulnerabilities, when held in love, become sites of recognition.

This is not mere poetic metaphor. It has liturgical and pastoral consequences. Funerals that speak of 'release from the broken body' perpetuate ableist theology. Sermons that proclaim heavenly wholeness while ignoring embodied justice in the present betray the gospel. A theology of remaining wounds calls us instead to preach resurrection with memory, to promise that nothing of our lived experience is wasted in God.

Implications for Church and hope

If the eschatological future promised by God is not one of bodily erasure but of wounded glory, then the implications for ecclesial life are profound. The Church cannot speak of resurrection apart from bodies, and it cannot proclaim bodies without wrestling with the conditions of their exclusion. The Church's own liturgy, architecture, preaching and pastoral practice must be shaped not by the myth of perfection, but by the reality of remembered wounds. What would it mean for the Church to be a community formed in the image of the disabled, risen Christ?

A Church of storied bodies

The Church, as the body of Christ, is not a collection of perfect individuals. It is a communion of wounded witnesses. Each member carries their history in their flesh. A theology of resurrection grounded in narrative anthropology insists that we are not saved from our bodies, but in them, as they are remembered, transformed and glorified by God.

This narrative understanding calls the Church to resist all forms of static or idealized anthropology. Our bodies are not fixed monuments: they are stories in motion. The Church, therefore, must be a community where bodies in process, bodies that age, change, rupture and adapt, are welcomed as bearers of sacred meaning.

Our eucharistic theology must resist abstraction, especially when it comes to the realities of embodiment. The Eucharist is not simply a symbolic representation of unity: it is a deep and tangible participation in Christ's breaking-yet-glorified body. To receive this body is to enter a mystery that does not erase difference but sanctifies it, affirming that every single body carries its own history, its own wounds, its own story.

Radical hospitality is at the heart of this sacrament. The table is not a place where limitation is denied but where it is held, blessed and brought into communion. Eucharistic participation is not about conformity to an idealized wholeness but about the divine joining of every single body, across time, ability and experience.

The Eucharist now becomes the site where boundaries dissolve, where flesh is gathered into God's embrace and where the fullness of human difference is not a barrier but the very texture of grace. This is not a feast of perfection but of presence. To partake is to be drawn into a love that does not filter out fragility but holds it as holy.

Funeral liturgies and the theology of the body

In moments of death and mourning, eschatology becomes most palpable. Yet funeral liturgies often revert to an ableist subtext: that the deceased has finally 'escaped' their disabled body, that heaven has made them 'whole'. Such language, however comforting to some, betrays the theological truth of the gospel.

A theology of remaining wounds insists instead that the disabled body is not a mistake to be corrected in heaven, but a sacred story to be honoured in eternity. The Church must learn to speak of resurrection not as restoration to an ideal but as glorification of the actual, lived body, with every scar transfigured into a testimony of love.

This requires liturgical creativity, theological courage and pastoral care that is rooted in the full dignity of embodied life. It asks that the Church become a people who can grieve without denial and hope without distortion.

Preaching and catechesis

The pulpit is a powerful site of theological formation. It is here that eschatological hope is offered or denied. Preachers must move beyond sentimental visions of 'perfect healing' and instead proclaim the risen, wounded Christ as the pattern of our own resurrection. Catechesis should include stories of disabled saints, biblical figures who bear physical and cognitive difference, and theological visions that embrace rupture as revelation.

To teach resurrection is to teach memory. And to teach memory is to honour the God who remembers us into being, not by undoing our stories but by bringing them to radiant completion.

Scars in glory, memory in motion

The gospel proclaims that Christ is risen. But it does not say he is unmarked. The risen Lord stands in the upper room, his hands and side pierced, his body bearing testimony to the trauma of crucifixion. These are not blemishes on an otherwise perfected body. They are sacramental signs, visible, tactile and glorified. They are wounds that speak.

This image of a disabled, risen Christ radically reorients the Christian imagination. It refuses to conform to the eschatology of the idealized norm, that long and powerful tradition in which eternity is imagined as a realm without scars, without stutter, without struggle. Instead, it offers us a vision of a kingdom where difference is not defeated but transfigured; where memory is not wiped away but made luminous; where our embodied stories are not left behind but raised in glory.

Such a vision critiques not only individual piety but the whole heritage of Christian theology and practice. It exposes how much our doctrines of resurrection have been shaped by the aesthetics of empire, the values of utility and the cult of symmetry. It challenges us to unlearn what we have too often assumed: that wholeness means erasure, and that salvation is the suppression of the disabled self. And it beckons us forward.

The eschatological hope offered by narrative anthropology and risen body theology is not a hope that denies suffering, but rather a hope that draws suffering into the heart of divine justice. It is a hope that says: nothing of your true self will be lost. Not your limp. Not your silence. Not your seizures. Not your scars. All of it, every single fragment, will be gathered and redeemed, not erased but re-membered, re-fashioned, re-glorified in the body of Christ.

This is a hope grounded not in perfection but in promise. Not in escape, but in deep solidarity. Not in a fantasy of wholeness, but in the truth of a wounded God.

This eschatological vision, of memory, woundedness and transformation, challenges not only theology but also heritage: the way the Church remembers itself. If resurrection involves the re-membering of every wounded story, then the Church must ask: whose stories have been left behind? Whose bodies have been forgotten? And how might our theology of resurrection reshape the Church's memory, its monuments, its art and its imagination?

The scars of Christ are not just personal. They are prophetic. And they call the Church to a future in which every body is honoured, every wound remembered, and every life raised, just as it was, just as it is, and just as God shall glorify it.

It is through these prophetic voices that we now turn to those who, in their lives and scholarship, have insisted that the Church must be rebuilt not *despite* disability, but through it. If buildings can be storied, so too can bodies. If architecture can rise through remembered trauma, so too can ecclesiology. The next chapter traces the theological and prophetic ministry of disabled theologians whose work offers a new foundation, not for a Church that erases the past, but for one that *remembers in hope*.

Notes

1 Willie James Jennings, *The Christian Imagination: Theology and the Origins of Race* (New Haven, CT: Yale University Press, 2010), pp. 270–312.

2 Tertullian, *On the Resurrection of the Flesh*, ch. 63, in *Ante-Nicene Fathers*, vol. 3.

3 Augustine, *City of God*, Book XXII.

4 Thomas Aquinas, *Summa Theologiae*, Supplementum Tertiae Partis.

5 Nancy L. Eiesland, *The Disabled God: Toward a Liberatory Theology of Disability* (Nashville, TN: Abingdon Press, 1994), pp. 89–107.

6 Deborah Beth Creamer, *Disability and Christian Theology: Embodied Limits and Constructive Possibilities* (Oxford: Oxford University Press, 2009), pp. 107–32.

7 John Swinton, *Becoming Friends of Time: Disability, Timefullness, and Gentle Discipleship* (Waco, TX: Baylor University Press, 2016), pp. 235–64.

8 Laurajane Smith, *Uses of Heritage* (London: Routledge, 2006), pp. 82–109.

9 Jürgen Moltmann, *The Coming of God: Christian Eschatology*, trans. Margaret Kohl (Minneapolis, MN: Fortress Press, 1996), pp. 58–76.

10 Jürgen Moltmann, *The Crucified God: The Cross of Christ as the Foundation and Criticism of Christian Theology*, trans. R. A. Wilson and John Bowden (Minneapolis, MN: Fortress Press, 1993), pp. 200–90.

13

Heritage as Contestation: Crip Interventions and the Reconfiguration of Sacred Memory

Having reimagined the body, the Holy Spirit and the Risen Body as sacred heritage and the site of divine memory, we now turn to the disruptive and redemptive witness of disabled people as prophets in the Church. Too often confined to the role of recipients – of care, of healing, of charity – disabled people have been denied the theological agency to speak, challenge and lead. Yet throughout Scripture and Christian history, it is precisely those on the margins who bear the clearest vision of God's justice. In this chapter, we explore the prophetic ministry of disabled people: not as metaphor, but as embodied truth-telling. Their lives confront the Church with uncomfortable questions about access, worth and who gets to define holiness. Like the biblical prophets who spoke from wildernesses and exile, disabled people expose the idolatries of ableism, call the community to repentance and reveal a vision of the body of Christ shaped not by perfection, but by participation.

Heritage is never just what we inherit. It is what we choose to remember. It is an act of curation, narration and power. When it comes to sacred heritage, especially within ecclesial contexts, this curation takes on theological weight. The stories we tell, the saints we venerate, the architecture we preserve, all these form a liturgical imagination of who belongs and why.

Yet for generations, disabled people have found themselves omitted from these sacred narratives. Not just forgotten, but actively unremembered. When we appear, it is usually as passive recipients of charity, metaphors for sin or inspiration or targets of healing. Rarely are we remembered as theologians, leaders, creators or core members of the ecclesial body.

This is more than neglect: it is a form of theological and cultural violence. To be absent from the stained glass, the hagiographies, the liturgical scripts and the theological curricula is to be told, again and again, that our lives are peripheral to the story of salvation.

But disabled people have never stopped remembering. In the face of exclusion, we have cultivated alternative archives: memory that lives in bodies, in access rituals, in mutual care, in liturgies of resistance. These are not mere corrections. They are counter-liturgies. What we call 'crip interventions' are not simply additions to heritage: they expose its omissions. They reconfigure memory by unsettling assumptions of normativity, aesthetic cohesion and theological purity.

Prophetic crip interventions arise wherever disabled people make visible what has long been erased. They show up in architecture prophetically redesigned to communicate access not as an afterthought but as a sacrament. They show up in worship practices that prophetically centre stimming, silence, alternative pacing and interdependence. They show up in art, protest and storytelling that prophetically insist disabled lives are not inspirational exceptions, but central theological witnesses.

These practices contest heritage at its roots. They challenge the very logic of traditional memory-making, which has often prioritized preservation over justice, and continuity over truth. Heritage, in its dominant ecclesial form, has canonized stability and marginalized disruption. But crip memory, like anamnesis, does not aim to restore a pristine past; it recalls the breaking body, makes it present and calls it holy.

It exposes the structures that canonize some lives while rendering others ungrievable. It insists that the rhythm of disabled time, nonlinear, interrupted, fragile, is not an obstacle to memory but a mode of remembering that echoes the very heart of the gospel.

This is not about adding disabled saints to an existing ledger. It is about rethinking the ledger entirely. It is about recognizing that the body of Christ is not whole until its forgotten limbs are restored, not in triumphalism, but in tenderness.

Thus, crip interventions are not acts of protest alone. They are theological acts of re-membering. They confront ecclesial nostalgia with prophetic truth. They demand that the Church stop curating perfection and start consecrating presence.

These prophetic interventions are happening now, in parish halls, in online ministries, in community art, in liturgical experimentation. Disabled people are not waiting for permission. We are shaping the future of the Church from within, by refusing to be invisible. And through our memory practices, our stories, scars, tools, liturgies, we prophetically proclaim a new kind of sacred heritage: one that is relational, embodied and resistant to erasure.

Heritage is not what survives untouched, it is what survives loved. And the most faithful acts of preservation may well be the ones that begin by breaking, bread, silence and stone, to make room for every member of Christ's body.

Crip aesthetics and the reformation of space

To enter a cathedral is often to enter a world of soaring arches, symmetrical design and carefully measured lines. These visual languages, drawn from classical and Renaissance principles, speak of order, balance and harmony, qualities long equated with holiness. But as beautiful as these spaces are, they often communicate a hidden liturgy of exclusion. Sacred architecture has historically privileged not only certain forms of worship, but certain kinds of bodies – those that can walk, climb, hear clearly and take in grandeur from a visual height.

Yet theology does not reside only in doctrine. It is also built into stone and steel. The design of churches is itself a theological act, one that has too often sanctified aesthetic ideals derived from Graeco-Roman norms rather than the wounded, risen body of Christ. When beauty is narrowly defined by proportion and symmetry, the result is not merely architectural but anthropological: disabled bodies are made to feel out of place, anomalies in a space meant to signify divine perfection.

Disability aesthetics offers a compelling alternative. Rather than resisting change to protect inherited ideals, it invites us to ask different questions: what if sacred space was designed not around an image of the ideal body, but around the full spectrum of embodied life? What if ramps, hearing loops, tactile guides and sensory adaptation were not corrections, but sacramental gestures, declarations that all bodies are liturgically central?

Tobin Siebers' concept of disability aesthetics fundamentally disrupts the traditional frameworks of beauty, extending them beyond symmetry and wholeness into a realm where the non-normative becomes revelatory. In ecclesial spaces, this shift is particularly urgent. Ramps are not merely pragmatic solutions; they are theological articulations, bearing witness to a grace that does not impose conditions on belonging. The built environment of the Church speaks, whether intentionally or not, and its architectural language must reflect the inclusivity it professes.[1]

Sara Hendren's vision of accessibility as an expansion of design rather than a constraint reinforces this. Spaces do not merely accommodate bodies; they actively shape them. Liturgical architecture, from the placement of altars to the height of fonts, carries implicit messages about who is welcomed and who is overlooked. This is not peripheral to theology, it is theology embodied.[2]

To rethink ecclesial space through the lens of disability aesthetics is to ask what kind of embodiment the Church truly honours. It moves beyond accommodation into a theological interrogation of presence, inviting communities to confront the question: *whose movement is assumed? Whose stillness is required? Whose access is unquestioned?* In this reckoning, true hospitality is not an addendum; it is a transformation of space, an architectural confession of grace.

But the reformation of sacred space is not limited to architecture. Disabled people have already been prophetically remaking the Church's imagination through art, music, story and leadership. The textured fibre sculptures of Judith Scott, created from within the silence of profound communicative difference, speak a theology of mystery and resilience more evocatively than many creeds.[3] Her work embodies the Spirit's sighs that are too deep for words (Rom. 8.26), enfleshing a theology of expression where verbal articulation fails.

Beethoven's deafness is often romanticized as triumph over adversity, but his late works suggest a more complex witness: one of persistence, lament and sacred insistence on beauty within breaking. His music, often dissonant and searching, becomes a kind of doxological refusal to be silenced, echoing a eucharistic theology of offering what we have, however incomplete.

Theatre and film also open ecclesial imagination. Works like *Children of a Lesser God* or *The Miracle Worker* complicate cultural narratives around communication and control. They offer spaces where the divine is encountered not in resolution, but in relationship, spaces where silence is not absence, but possibility.[4]

Meanwhile, disabled leadership continues to widen the frame of ecclesial possibility. Recent appointments of visibly disabled clergy to senior positions are not symbolic victories, but theological recalibrations. We are challenging the assumption that spiritual authority must be mediated through physical conformity. True ecclesial inclusion is not simply about proximity; it is about power, sacramental presence and narrative ownership.

These transformations are not accidental. They are often the result of years of advocacy, protest and prophetic disruption. Activism, both inside and outside the Church, has forced new conversations, dismantled old idols and demanded new practices. Such efforts are not aesthetic accommodations: they are incarnational interventions. They echo the gospel itself: God entering the world not in idealized form but in fragility and flesh.

Crip aesthetics, then, is not about compromise. It is a reformation. It is theologically disruptive because it does not seek to fit disabled people into existing frameworks of sacred space. It asks us to change those frameworks altogether. It expands our ecclesial imagination, compelling the Church to witness more faithfully to the wounded, risen Christ.

When we allow disability to prophetically reshape architecture, music, leadership and memory, we enact a more authentic theology, one that recognizes that sacredness is not the absence of disruption, but the holy presence of difference.

Reclaiming memory: participatory heritage and the prophetic witness of disabled curators

Christian institutions often describe themselves as 'guardians of tradition' or 'stewards of sacred story', underscoring the responsibility of preserving spiritual legacies. However, memory is not neutral: it is shaped by those who control narratives, determining whose experiences are acknowledged.

Historically, disabled individuals have been marginalized within ecclesial memory. Their contributions are frequently absent from stained glass, archives and theological discourse. This exclusion is not merely an oversight but aligns with what philosopher Miranda Fricker terms 'epistemic injustice', where individuals are wronged specifically in their capacity as knowers.[5]

The inaccessibility of theological archives and sacred spaces extends beyond physical barriers to include epistemic ones. Disabled individuals often lack representation in the interpretation and curation of religious heritage, leading to a skewed understanding of the faith community's history.

Moreover, disabled people have sometimes been portrayed not as integral members of the faith community but as subjects requiring correction. For instance, institutions like the Royal Earlswood Asylum operated under Christian auspices, housing disabled individuals in segregated conditions under the guise of moral improvement.

In response, a transformative approach known as participatory heritage has emerged. This model positions disabled individuals not as passive subjects but as active curators and theologians, reshaping collective memory. Projects like the UK's 'History of Place', led by the national programme Accentuate, exemplify this shift by involving disabled people in reinterpreting heritage sites connected to disability history.[6]

Through such initiatives, architectural spaces become sites of liturgical reflection:

- Walls bear witness to previously untold stories.
- Thresholds symbolize transitions toward inclusivity.
- Inaccessible altars prompt theological reconsideration of sacred spaces.

The annual Conference on Disability and Church at St Martin-in-the-Fields in London further illustrates this participatory model, where disabled individuals lead worship and theological discussions, embodying a living ecclesiology. Grassroots movements like Deaf Anglicans Together[7] advocate for liturgical and spatial reforms, ensuring that language and worship practices reflect the diversity of the faith community.

Participatory heritage thus represents a theological reformation. It challenges the Church to embrace a memory that is complex and inclusive, recognizing that true ecclesial remembrance must honour the diverse embodiments of the body of Christ.

Rewriting iconography: redeeming the image of God in sacred art

Christianity has long communicated its theology not only through words but also through images. Cathedrals, chapels and shrines are adorned with visual narratives: saints depicted in stained glass, Christ portrayed in gilded domes and Mary rendered in frescoes. These artworks constitute a 'visual theology', engaging believers in a participatory experience of the divine.

However, traditional Christian art often presents an idealized vision of holiness; figures are symmetrical, youthful and able-bodied. Even the resurrected Christ is frequently depicted with minimal wounds, resembling a Graeco-Roman deity more than a Jewish carpenter from occupied Palestine. Such portrayals can inadvertently suggest that sanctity is synonymous with physical perfection.

This perspective overlooks the profound theological truth that the risen Christ retains his wounds, presenting his impaired hands and feet to his disciples, and revealing in the process a God who embodies both woundedness and divinity. This challenges the notion that holiness is contingent upon physical wholeness.

Contemporary disabled artists are reshaping sacred art to reflect this inclusive theology. Sunaura Taylor, in her work and writings, emphasizes that disability is a form of embodied difference, not a deficit. Her art invites viewers to recognize beauty in diverse bodily experiences.[8] Similarly, Hannah Ensor's illustrations, informed by her experience with Ehlers-Danlos syndrome, capture the nuances of vulnerability and resilience, offering a liturgical resonance that speaks to the complexities of disabled life.[9]

Lauren Wright Pittman, a founding member of Sanctified Art, creates pieces that depict biblical figures with diverse bodily features, emphasizing emotional depth and authenticity. Her series 'Bodies Are Good' challenges conventional portrayals, inviting a reimagining of sacred narratives.[10]

Churches are beginning to commission disabled artists to contribute to their visual landscapes. In 2018, the Anglican Church of Canada collaborated with Jesse Thistle, a disabled artist, to create iconography for a national reconciliation liturgy. His work integrates Indigenous symbolism and theological reflection, resisting sanitized narratives of healing.[11] In the UK, Fiona MacDonald, working under the name Feral Practice, partners with churches to reinterpret sacred spaces through installations that embrace ecological vulnerability and neurodiversity.[12]

These artistic endeavours are not mere additions to existing traditions but are transformative theological interventions. By embracing diverse embodiments, sacred art can more fully reflect the image of a God who encompasses all forms of human experience.

Rewriting iconography in this manner invites all believers to see themselves within the sacred narrative. It proclaims that every body, in its uniqueness, is a vessel of divine grace. In doing so, the Church moves closer to embodying the inclusive love at the heart of the gospel.

The risen body and the golden fracture: the idealized norm and the *kintsugi* Christ

In John's Gospel, the risen Jesus appears to the disciples and shows them his hands and his side (John 20.20). A week later, he invites Thomas to touch his wounds. The scars are not symbolic. They are physical and present. They are not marks of failure. They are marks of love.

Such an image fundamentally challenges normative anthropologies. If the risen Christ retains his scars, then resurrection is not the undoing of brokenness, but its redemption. Theology, then, must make space for bodies that do not conform to idealized norms, not as temporary states to be fixed, but as eternal bearers of divine presence.

Here the art of *kintsugi* offers a potent theological metaphor. Developed in Japan during the fifteenth century, *kintsugi*, 'gold joinery', is the practice of repairing broken pottery by filling the cracks with lacquer mixed with gold, silver or platinum. Rather than hiding the fracture, *kintsugi* beautifies it. The break becomes the site of radiance.

Kintsugi is not a naïve romanticization of suffering. The pot is broken. The repair is real. The cracks remain. But the philosophy behind *kintsugi*, drawn from *wabi-sabi*, the Japanese appreciation of imperfection and impermanence, offers us a striking contrast to the Western pursuit of flawlessness.[13] The repaired object is not restored to a previous ideal. It is made more beautiful because of what it has endured.

Shelly Rambo's theology reframes resurrection not as immediate resolution but as endurance, an unfolding presence within wounds that have not disappeared. Holy Saturday becomes not simply a transitional space; it becomes the lingering reality of suffering, where resurrection emerges not as triumphal escape but as survival. In this vision, restoration does not mean erasure; it means remaining, carrying forward and witnessing to the continuation of life within and beyond pain.

Kintsugi further deepens this understanding. Just as broken pottery is repaired in a way that highlights, rather than conceals, its fractures, so resurrection does not erase wounds but transfigures them. In both, the rupture does not signal loss but transformation: the scar is not merely healed, it gleams. Resurrection, then, is not a return to wholeness as imagined in conventional terms but a sacred emergence, one that acknowledges the past even as it moves into renewed life. Resurrection, for Rambo, is not a flip of the switch from death to life, but a slow, sacred emergence, a trace of presence through pain. This resonates deeply with *kintsugi*: the wound does not disappear, it gleams.[14]

Leonard Cohen captures this in his haunting line: 'There is a crack in everything, that's how the light gets in.'[15] Cohen does not deny the crack. He insists upon it. The crack is not a detour from beauty: it is its very entry point. In the same way, the scars of Christ are not divine inconveniences. They are the glory of God refracted through pain.

This anthropology invites us to see our own bodies differently. In a world saturated with impossible ideals, beauty standards, fitness culture, surgical perfection, the risen body of Christ offers an alternative grammar: one where scars are not shameful but sacred.

This vision is not just comforting. It is revolutionary. It invites the Church to embody a new kind of welcome; one where disabled, aged and transfigured bodies are not pitied or fixed but honoured as Christ-bearing. It calls for liturgies that centre fragility, altars that accommodate wheelchairs, Eucharists spoken in sign language, images of Christ with a stoma bag or using a cane.

This is not about inclusion. It is about redefinition.

In sacred art, the metaphor of *kintsugi* is beginning to appear. Contemporary Christian artists have begun depicting the wounded Christ with golden seams, not to romanticize suffering, but to resist its erasure. In one notable example, British artist Hannah Rose Thomas's portraits of Yazidi women who survived trauma depict not only pain, but luminous strength etched into their faces with gold leaf, clearly inspired by *kintsugi*.[16]

Similarly, the artist Paige Payne's painting 'Broken for Us' portrays Christ's body cracked with gold, inviting us to engage with our vulnerability as gift.[17] These images are not only theological statements: they are visual resistance to perfectionism, to shame, to the false gospel of strength.

In these icons, worship becomes an act of truth-telling. The broken is blessed. The cracked is crowned.

What might a *kintsugi* ecclesiology look like? It would begin by admitting that the Church is breaking, institutionally, morally, historically. But instead of hiding its failures behind polished stone and polite liturgies, it would fill those fractures with gold, stories of survival, repentance and grace. It would stop trying to be impressive. It would start trying to be honest.

Practically, this means listening to disabled voices not as inspirational footnotes, but as theological authorities. It means curating heritage that honours impaired bodies, commissioning art that breaks with idealization and building spaces that reflect the reality of interdependence.

It means refusing the myth of the seamless saint and worshipping instead the risen Christ whose wounds shine.

Resurrection is not reversal. It is not the undoing of pain. It is the transformation of pain into glory. In the risen body of Christ, we see a new anthropology, one that defies perfectionism and honours brokenness. Through the lens of *kintsugi*, we learn to see our wounds not as defects, but as places of divine artistry.

Leonard Cohen was right. The crack is not the failure of the vessel. It is the very site of its becoming.

As the Church seeks to recover its identity in an age of fracture – ecological, political, institutional, personal – we must stop striving for flawless restoration. Instead, we must allow the gold of grace to fill the cracks. This is what the *kintsugi* Christ teaches us: that holiness is not found in the absence of scars, but in the presence of love that refuses to erase them.

The digital sanctuary: crip presence, virtual theology and the future of ecclesial memory

The internet has evolved beyond a mere communication tool for the Church. Since the Covid-19 pandemic of 2020, it has become a sanctuary, a site of worship, community and theological innovation, particularly for disabled individuals who have long faced barriers in traditional sacred spaces.

For decades, disabled worshippers have encountered obstacles such as steep steps, narrow pews and sensory-unfriendly environments, making participation challenging or even hazardous. The pandemic-induced shift to digital platforms unexpectedly rendered the Church more accessible for many, as physical barriers were replaced with virtual inclusivity.

This movement was not simply a response to exclusion: it was a defiant creation of new sacred spaces. Disabled individuals, long forced to adapt to physical inaccessibility, turned to digital platforms not as a compromise but as a reclamation of worship and theological discourse. What was historically sidelined became central: livestreamed liturgies, podcasts exploring theology from embodied perspectives, online exhibitions amplifying marginalized voices, virtual choirs weaving communal song across distances and captioned Eucharists ensuring participation beyond traditional barriers.

For theologian Heidi Campbell, the virtual church is not a diminished version of the physical church: it is a fully realized ecclesial body where real communities form, and faith is nurtured in meaningful ways. These spaces have not replaced the traditional Church but have expanded its reach, proving that sacred connection is not confined to pews and pulpits: it flourishes wherever people gather in Christ's name. Digital liturgies are not accommodations: they have become sites of theological innovation, places where accessibility shapes a vision of Church that is truly inclusive.[18]

Institutions like York Minster and Canterbury Cathedral have exemplified this inclusivity by consistently livestreaming services, allowing those who are housebound, chronically ill, disabled or geographically distant to participate fully in the spiritual life of the cathedral, drawing in the online congregation to the in-person worship.[19]

However, digital spaces are not inherently accessible. Many church websites lack features like alt text for images, closed captions for videos and screen reader compatibility. Such oversights are not just technical issues but theological ones, reflecting a limited understanding of the body of Christ.

Despite these challenges, disabled individuals have been proactive in creating inclusive digital spaces. The 2020 documentary *Crip Camp: A Disability Revolution* chronicled the rise of the US disability rights movement and became a digital liturgy of memory and resistance, sparking online discussions, vigils and worship services.[20]

Similarly, *Not Going Quietly* (2021) follows activist Ady Barkan's journey with the terminal neurodegenerative disease amyotrophic lateral sclerosis (ALS, also known as motor neuron disease), highlighting how digital platforms can amplify voices and foster community.[21]

Platforms like Chronically Academic, Crip HumAnimal, Autistic Empire and Mad Covid are more than advocacy spaces: they are sites of intellectual resistance, reshaping the discourse around disability, neurodivergence and embodied theology.[22] Here, theological reflection is not bound by conventional gatekeeping but emerges in conversation, experience and shared inquiry. These communities are rewriting the relationship between faith, accessibility and scholarship, not as a concession but as an assertion that the richest theological insights often arise from those historically pushed to the edges.

This is the Church reimagined, not as a church constrained by walls or institutional validation, but enacted in presence, in dialogue and in radical hospitality. The margins do not dilute theology, rather they expand its vision, revealing that sacred discourse is most transformative when rooted in lived realities. Shane Clifton's 'ecclesiology of the edge' speaks to this dynamic, an understanding of church not as centralized hierarchy but as lived practice, cultivated where people gather in mutual recognition and solidarity.[23]

Theology in digital spaces is not secondary or derivative: it is deeply lived, shaped by the immediacy and relationality of online interactions. Memes, hashtags, Twitter liturgies and comment section dialogues are not mere artefacts of internet culture: they are manifestations of theological praxis, unfolding in real time. In these spaces, theology is participatory and dynamic, responsive to the experiences of those engaging with it.

Digital communities are not less ecclesial simply because they exist online; rather, they often echo the earliest Christian gatherings, small, intimate and deeply embodied in vulnerability. Theological reflection here is not confined to traditional academic discourse but emerges in shared storytelling, moments of pastoral care exchanged in threads, and liturgical creativity that breaks beyond conventional formats.

This is theology without fixed walls, expanding the ways faith is expressed and encountered. It does not dilute the sacred but multiplies its presence across new forms of connection. Online spaces have become sanctuaries where voices historically marginalized in institutional settings find resonance, where accessibility reshapes the liturgical imagination, and where participation is no longer determined by physical proximity but by shared engagement in a continually unfolding conversation.

The post-pandemic retreat from digital ministry reflects a failure to fully grasp the radical theological implications of presence beyond physical space. Many churches, eager to return to traditional structures, have overlooked the profound accessibility digital worship provided, the spaces where disabled, chronically ill and neurodivergent individuals could fully participate without navigating architectural and social barriers. This regression exposes our narrow theology of presence, one that privileges embodiment in conventional terms rather than embracing the Spirit-filled solidarity crip theology champions.

The body of Christ is not defined by proximity but by inclusion. Distance does not diminish communion, exclusion does. To abandon digital ministries is not merely a logistical shift: it is a theological failure to recognize that presence unfolds across difference, across screens, across breaths shared in virtual liturgy. The Church's ecclesiology must surely expand to honour the realities of complex embodiment, ensuring that its future is shaped not by nostalgia for pre-pandemic worship but by a deep commitment to radical hospitality. Digital sacred space was not a temporary measure: it was a revelation. The question remains whether the Church will listen.

Virtual spaces, when thoughtfully shaped, are not lacking embodiment but reimagining it. They do not forsake heritage – they extend it. Just as sacred narratives have been carried through illuminated manuscripts, frescoed walls and stained-glass windows, they now move through video calls, hyperlinks, captioned sermons and digital sacraments. These are not lesser mediums but new vessels of transmission, ensuring that theology remains a living, evolving presence.

Virtual space is not sacred by default; it becomes so through intentional gathering, relational depth and prayerful engagement. These platforms are not an abstraction of worship but an expansion of it, shaping new forms of presence that resist exclusion and affirm that the sacred does not require proximity to remain profound.

Therefore, the future of ecclesial memory is being written now in digital formats. Churches and heritage organizations must not only accommodate this shift but be transformed by it, curating digital theology with the same reverence as ancient stonework. Failing to do so risks losing the most prophetic archives of our time.

A theology of crip digitality insists that wherever disabled individuals gather to remember, resist, worship and create, there the Church must be also, because there the Spirit already is.

Chrononormativity and the gospel of crip time: reimagining heritage through the sacred pause

Heritage often draws its power from the illusion of continuity, unbroken stones, preserved rituals, seamless transitions from past to present. In this frame, sacred value is measured by endurance and resistance to change. Churches, cathedrals and liturgies are frequently cherished for their perceived immunity to interruption. But this very understanding of time, as linear, progressive and disciplined, is itself a theological construct. And for disabled people, it is often a violent one.

Elizabeth Freeman calls this regulatory framework chrononormativity: the use of time to organize bodies in service of productivity, conformity and legibility.[24] In this schema, heritage becomes a curated narrative of control. Only what can be sustained and repeated without disruption is considered worthy of preservation. Cracks in ritual or architecture, like those made for ramps, captions or stammered prayers, are viewed as flaws rather than revelations.

Chrononormativity has long dominated ecclesial and architectural thinking. Stone is trusted more than silence, tradition more than transformation. Heritage grant frameworks reward aesthetic consistency, not pastoral responsiveness. Inaccessibility is often excused as necessary to protect the past. But whose past is being protected? And at what cost?

The Incarnation breaks the logic of managed time. Jesus lives and moves in divine detour: pausing for children, weeping with friends, interrupting power. His ministry unfolds in sacred slowness, not strategic sequence. The haemorrhaging woman does not wait her turn: her interruption is received as faith (Mark 5.25–34).

Resurrection unsettles expectation, for it is not a neat conclusion but an unfolding presence that lingers in ambiguity and persistence. Shelly Rambo's *middle space* challenges the assumption that resurrection is simply a reversal of suffering, insisting instead that wounds remain, carried into new life as testimony rather than erased in triumph. The risen Christ does not return in perfected form but in scarred continuity, embodying divine patience rather than immediate resolution.[25]

Crip time amplifies this theological rhythm. Rooted in disability theory and lived experience, it resists the demand for speed and efficiency, moving instead with attentiveness, adjustment and relational depth. Theologies that presume seamlessness overlook the complexity of actual bodies – bodies shaped by endurance, by interruptions, by the rhythms of pain and healing that do not conform to linear expectation. In crip time, delay is not failure. It is a deepening of presence, a refusal to force resolution where patience is sacred.

Heritage built on chrononormativity resists this. It fears deviation, suspects accommodation and canonizes sameness. But a theology formed by crip time honours interruption as invitation. It celebrates adaptation not as compromise, but as the clearest expression of communion.

To welcome crip time into sacred architecture and liturgy is not to abandon tradition. It is to fulfil it. Not to destroy continuity, but to expand it to include every pace and all bodies. This is heritage that remembers not what stood longest, but who was welcomed. Not what survived untouched, but what changed in love.

Notes

1 Tobin Siebers, *Disability Aesthetics* (Ann Arbor, MI: University of Michigan Press, 2010), pp. 17–43.

2 Sara Hendren, *What Can a Body Do? How We Meet the Built World* (New York: Riverhead Books, 2020), pp. 33–64.

3 John M. MacGregor, *Metamorphosis: The Fiber Art of Judith Scott; The Outsider Artist and the Experience of Down's Syndrome* (Oakland, CA: Creative Growth Art Centre, 1999).

4 Harold Krents, *To Race the Wind: An Autobiography* (New York: Putnam, 1972); Mark Medoff, *Children of a Lesser God* (New York: Dramatists Play Service, 1980); and *The Miracle Worker* (1962), a film about Helen Keller, by Arthur Penn (director) and William Gibson (writer), https://en.wikipedia.org/wiki/The_Miracle_Worker_(1962_film), accessed 10.09.2025.

5 Fricker, Miranda, *Epistemic Injustice: Power and the Ethics of Knowing* (Oxford: Oxford University Press, 2007), pp. 17–29.

6 Accentuate, 'History of Place', *Accentuate*, https://www.accentuateuk.org/Accentuate-History-of-Place, accessed 07.07.2025.

7 Deaf Anglicans Together, https://deafanglicanstogether.org.uk, accessed 07.07.2025.

8 Sunaura Taylor, *Beasts of Burden: Animal and Disability Liberation* (New York: The New Press, 2017).

9 Hannah Ensor, 'Pages', *Stickman Communications Blog*, https://stickmancommunications.blogspot.com, accessed 07.08.2025.

10 Lauren Wright Pittman, 'Who Will You Listen To? Digital painting by Lauren Wright Pittman', *Sanctified Art*, https://sanctifiedart.org/prints-by-lauren-wright-pittman/who-will-you-listen-to, accessed 07.08.2025.

11 Jesse Thistle, https://jessethistle.com, accessed 07.08.2025.

12 Fiona MacDonald, 'Fiona MacDonald: Feral Practice (CV)', *Feral Practice*, https://www.feralpractice.com/W-About/Fiona-MacDonald-CV.pdf, accessed 07.08.2025.

13 Alexandra Kitty, *The Art of Kintsugi: Learning the Japanese Craft of Beautiful Repair* (Atglen, PA: Schiffer Publishing, 2020), pp. 10–17.

14 Shelly Rambo, *Spirit and Trauma: A Theology of Remaining* (Louisville, KY: Westminster John Knox, 2010).

15 Leonard Cohen, 'Anthem', *The Future*, Columbia Records, 1992.

16 Hannah Rose Thomas, *Tears of Gold: Portraits of Yazidi, Rohingya, and Nigerian Women* (New York: Plough, 2024), http://hannahrosethomas.com, accessed 07.08.2025.

17 Paige Payne, 'Broken for Us', https://paigepaynecreations.com/products/broken-for-us-canvas-print, accessed 03.11.2025.

18 Heidi A. Campbell, ed., *The Distanced Church: Reflections on Doing Church Online* (n. p.: Digital Religion Publications, 2020), pp. 3–6.

19 York Minster, 'Ways to Worship', https://yorkminster.org/worship/ways-to-worship, accessed 15.08.2025.

20 *Crip Camp: A Disability Revolution*, directed by James LeBrecht and Nicole Newnham (Netflix, 2020).

21 *Not Going Quietly*, directed by Nicholas Bruckman (Greenwich Entertainment, 2021).

22 See Chronically Academic, https://chronicallyacademic.org, accessed 15.08.2025, a collective of disabled and chronically ill academics advocating for inclusive scholarship and institutional change. Crip HumAnimal is a project exploring intersections of disability, critical animal studies, and embodiment; see https://criphumanimal.org, accessed 15.08.2025, for project details and related publications. Autistic Empire is a self-advocacy organization promoting autistic-led governance, language reform and social innovation; see https://www.autisticempire.com, accessed 15.08.2025. Mad Covid is a user-led platform created in response to the Covid-19 pandemic by and for people with lived experience of mental distress, aiming to centre mad knowledge and mutual aid; see https://madcovid.com, accessed 15.08.2025.

23 Shane Clifton, *Crippled Grace: Disability, Virtue Ethics, and the Good Life* (Waco, TX: Baylor University Press, 2018).

24 Elizabeth Freeman, *Time Binds: Queer Temporalities, Queer Histories* (Durham, NC: Duke University Press, 2010), pp. 1–20.

25 Rambo, *Spirit and Trauma*, pp. 6–8.

14

The Disruptive Grace of Disabled Witness

The body is breaking. The heritage is fragmented. The memory is incomplete. This is not a metaphor. It is a theological diagnosis.

This book has traced how ableism is not a peripheral issue for the Church but a deep theological crisis. It has distorted the Church's imagination, how it conceives of God, constructs beauty, builds community and preserves memory. Its reach has shaped architecture, art, liturgy, theology and institutional power in ways that continue to harm, silence and marginalize disabled people. Yet ableism is not the final word.

Across generations, disabled people have borne witness not only to their survival but to a profound graceful reimagining of ecclesial life. Through resistance, creativity, scholarship and prayer, they have invited the Church into deeper faithfulness. This is not just protest. It is prophecy.

And yet, disability theology is often treated as a modern innovation, a recent corrective to centuries of ecclesial neglect. Yet if only we had been alert to our conscious and unconscious biases we would have recognized that Scripture has long borne witness to a theology of disability through the lives of its prophets. The Bible does not merely include disabled figures; it centres them in God's redemptive work. Moses, who protests that he is 'slow of speech and slow of tongue', becomes the voice of liberation (Ex. 4.10). Jeremiah, overwhelmed by grief and youth, is called to speak hard truths to a collapsing kingdom (Jer. 1.6–9). Ezekiel lies bound and mute, embodying divine judgement in his immobilized frame (Ezek. 3.26; 4.8). Paul, afflicted by a mysterious 'thorn in the flesh', testifies that God's grace is sufficient and made perfect in weakness (2 Cor. 12.7–9). These, as we shall discover, are not exceptions to a norm; they *are* the norm of prophetic vocation. Their impairments are not obstacles to God's work, but the very medium through which divine power is made manifest. The Church's rediscovery of disability theology, then, is not a departure from Scripture, but a long-overdue return to it, a reawakening to the disruptive grace of disabled witness already woven into the sacred text.

Christian tradition has always valued the figure of the prophet, the one who speaks divine truth into human systems, often at great cost. But the prophetic witness has never been merely rhetorical. It has always been flesh and word, pain and promise. And it has often come from the margins.

Jesus, as the culmination of the prophetic tradition, does not simply declare truth; he enacts it in his body. His ministry is not performed from a place of institutional power, but through vulnerable presence. He touches lepers (Mark 1.40–45), heals on the Sabbath (Luke 13.10–17) and reveals divine glory not by ascending to power but through descent into woundedness and death. His resurrection does not erase this body. It reveals it, scarred and alive (John 20.27).

This prophetic inheritance has been embraced and embodied by disabled Christians today. Too often sidelined by ecclesial norms, they now offer the Church a summons: not toward mere inclusion, but toward conversion. Their witness exposes the idols that still lurk beneath liturgical beauty and architectural grandeur, the idol of perfection, the idolatry of autonomy, the mistaken conflation of normative ability with spiritual virtue.

Disabled Christians confront these assumptions not only with critique but with vision. They imagine and build churches that reflect God's justice and presence in radically accessible, interdependent and theologically expansive ways:

- a liturgy shaped by access, silence and embodiment
- an architecture that centres welcome, not preservation
- a theology grounded not in triumph, but in mutual need
- a pace of church life governed not by efficiency, but by grace-filled time

Their very presence, whether through assistive technology, non-verbal expression, bodily movement, or sacred stillness, interrupts the idol of the seamless and the polished. It reminds the Church that the gospel was never about appearance, but always about presence. About truth.

Prophetic graceful witness is not only about identifying what is wrong, but also about gesturing toward what could be. Disabled people are not merely asking for remembrance in ecclesial history. They are actively reshaping the future of the Church through theology, art, leadership and communal life. Their lives do not merely reflect the gospel, they embody it.

This witness is not sentimental. It is not about inspiration. It is about Christ. It is about recognizing that if the Church is truly to be the body of Christ, it must reckon with bodies that are wounded, interdependent and gloriously nonconforming.

To honour disabled people only as saints or sufferers is to miss the call. The Church must learn to see them as prophets, calling the body back to its most foundational truth: that holiness is not found in strength, but in grace; not in perfection, but in presence; not in control, but in communion.

This is not accommodation. It is salvation. And it is the Church's only way home.

Prophets from the margins: disability and the biblical vocation of truth-telling

The prophets of Scripture rarely emerge from institutional centres. They arrive instead from deserts and doorways, from exile and obscurity. Their voices rise not with polish but with urgency. These are not figures of prestige, but of interruption, people whose lives themselves are declarations of divine protest. From Amos the herdsman to Jeremiah the trembling youth, from Isaiah undone by holiness to Ezekiel lying on his side in the street, the prophetic tradition bears witness to a God who speaks through disruption, not decorum.

Amos disclaims professional prophecy, claiming no lineage or training, only divine compulsion: 'I am no prophet, nor a prophet's son; but I am a herdsman, and a dresser of sycamore trees' (Amos 7.14). Jeremiah resists his calling with a cry of inadequacy, 'I do not know how to speak, for I am only a boy,' only to be told that his very fear is the context for his commissioning (Jer. 1.6–9). Isaiah, overwhelmed by glory, confesses 'unclean lips', yet is made ready not through strength but purification (Isa. 6.5–7). Their hesitancy is not a hindrance. It is the holy ground on which vocation takes root.

Prophetic imagination resists stagnation – it is disruptive, embodied and fiercely rooted in history. Prophecy does not merely critique injustice: it *shatters* realities that have become calcified into exclusion. This is particularly urgent in confronting ableist norms, which have long shaped theological and ecclesial life by determining which bodies are fully seen, which voices are taken seriously and which presences are dismissed as peripheral.

True prophetic work refuses abstraction. It does not engage in vague sentimentality but in concrete transformation. It insists that theology is not neutral: it is always either reinforcing oppressive structures or dismantling them. When accessibility is treated as an afterthought, when liturgies assume cognitive and physical conformity, when church spaces remain hostile to certain bodies, prophecy demands reckoning. It calls for a vision where presence is not conditional and belonging is not measured by the ability to fit into inherited forms.

This is not reform, it is upheaval. It is the work of re-membering, of refusing theological frameworks that erase disabled experiences, of recognizing that divine presence is revealed not in the maintenance of tradition alone but in the radical disruption of what excludes. The prophetic call is not to accommodate difference; it is to remake the table, the sanctuary, the language of faith itself so that no body is rendered disposable.

Disability, far from being a contradiction of prophecy, becomes one of its crucibles. Disabled people live within structures of exclusion that echo the very injustices the prophets condemned: the reduction of persons to productivity, the equation of value with conformity, the silencing of those who do not fit liturgical norms.

In this context, disabled prophets rise. Not always welcomed, rarely canonized, often accused of anger or ingratitude, they nonetheless name the truth with a clarity born of suffering. They are not anomalies. They are the rightful heirs of the prophetic tradition that honours wounds as witnesses.

Jesus himself embodies this tradition fully. He touches the untouchable, listens to the disruptive, dignifies those whom the religious elite have excluded. The blind man who refuses to be silenced (Mark 10.46–52), the haemorrhaging woman who interrupts (Mark 5.25–34), the paralytic whose friends dismantle a building for access (Mark 2.1–12). All these are not passive recipients of healing. They are prophets. Their actions reveal what community must become. And Jesus meets them not as problems to be solved but as bearers of faith and revelation.

In the Gospel of John, Jesus explicitly rejects the idea that disability is punishment, insisting that the man born blind is not the result of sin, but a site of divine work (John 9.3). And when healing does occur, it is not toward able-bodied norms, but toward restored participation and belonging.

This thread continues with Paul, whose 'thorn in the flesh' is neither removed nor explained away (2 Cor. 12.7–9). It becomes instead the locus of divine strength: 'My grace is sufficient for you, for power is made perfect in weakness.' Holiness does not arise from resolution. It arises from relinquishment. From truth-telling. From embodied grace.

Throughout Christian history, disabled voices have emerged in prophetic power, though too often forgotten. The Desert Fathers and Mothers, early monastics with physical and mental impairments, were revered for their raw spiritual wisdom, not institutional credentials. Abba Moses the Black, a scarred former bandit, became a prophet of humility whose embodied penitence was his greatest sermon.

Today, that witness continues.

Naomi Lawson Jacobs and Emily Richardson, in their research on disability and ecclesiology, expose how many church 'inclusion' strategies still presume normative power structures. Disabled people may be invited in, but rarely invited to lead, to theologize, to reshape the tradition.[1]

Amy Kenny's searing book, *My Body Is Not a Prayer Request*, confronts the weaponization of prayer in the name of healing.[2] Kenny's voice is not an outlier. It is prophetic fire, naming the idolatry of a Church that still equates holiness with health.

Fiona MacMillan and the team at St Martin-in-the-Fields curate not only accessible worship but worship formed in the rhythms of disabled life: allowing for silence, medication breaks, sensory variation. These are not accommodations. They are theological practices. They declare with their very structure: *God is here. In the pause. In the breath. In the broken voice.*[3]

This is not romanticizing disability. It is resisting the romanticization of triumph. Disabled prophets do not speak to inspire. They speak to interrupt. They do not request polite inclusion. They demand ecclesial transformation.

Prophets may be unpredictable, hard to categorize, disruptive in their presence, but we must test their fruit, not their form. For to embrace the prophetic witness of disabled people is to hear again the cry of the bleeding woman, the trembling prophet, the scarred Messiah. It is to make room in our churches not only for access, but for fire. It is to rebuild heritage not only as memory, but as movement. It is to realize, perhaps for the first time, that the margins have never been marginal to God.

They have always been the birthplace of revelation.

The disabled prophet and the disruption of norms

Disabled prophets do not merely seek to be included; we expose the very structures of exclusion. We do not simply request a seat at the table. We question who built it, whom it serves, and what it demands of those who approach it.

Our presence unsettles the Church, not accidentally, but prophetically. Because the disabled body, in all its specificity and unpredictability, testifies to a different kind of holiness: one rooted not in idealized form, but in lived disruption, shared vulnerability and embodied resistance.

We do not conform to chrononormative rhythms or architectural expectations. We pause, tremble, stim and breathe at different speeds. In worship, in leadership, in liturgy, our presence reveals a deeper truth long obscured: that much of what the Church considers normative is actually exclusionary. When we enter a space, we bring with us not deficiency, but divine critique.

Scripture confirms that the prophetic call often begins not with strength but with hesitation, not with polish but with interruption. Whether in Mary's Magnificat, Hannah's weeping, or the paralytic man's friends dismantling a roof, divine revelation is constantly breaking through expectation and decorum. The prophet is rarely clean, calm or welcome. The prophet reveals the fault lines in what the faithful have taken for granted.

So too today. Disabled Christians are not merely challenging ecclesiology from without: we are embodying it anew. Our liturgies include pauses for breath, our theology emerges from bodies in pain, our churches are shaped by ramps, captioning and a slower sacred rhythm. These are not signs of concession. They are signs of conversion.

To follow the disabled prophet is not to be led backward into nostalgia or pity, but forward into truth. Truth that confronts the idol of perfection. Truth that exposes the limitations of symmetry. Truth that testifies, with every scar and every silence, that the resurrection does not erase the wound – it honours it.

Disabled prophets do not come to shame the Church. We come to save it – from its illusions, from its exclusions, from a holiness too brittle to bear grace.

We are not its problem. We are its pattern.

Polyphonic prophecy: living the contradiction

Disabled prophets bring a unique gift to the Church, not by simplifying, but by deepening. Our lives, prayers and witness refuse reduction. We inhabit contradiction. We do not collapse suffering and joy, protest and praise, silence and speech into binaries: we dwell in their tension. This is not an intellectual exercise but a lived, theological reality, inscribed in our flesh and carried into worship, protest, theology and daily survival.

Too often, the Church prefers single, manageable narratives, whether it may be the triumphant survivor or the tragic figure, the inspirational token or the silent recipient of care. But complexity threatens neat systems of inclusion. The disabled prophet says no. No more flattening. No more performance. No more digestible sainthood.

Instead, we offer a theology of unvarnished reality: lives marked by pain and delight, awkwardness and wonder, exhaustion and grace. We refuse resolution because we live what the tradition has too often forgotten, faith that pulses through paradox.

Scripture itself teaches this form of witness. Julian of Norwich, herself marked by chronic illness, proclaimed 'All shall be well' in the same breath as beholding the bleeding Christ.[4] Dietrich Bonhoeffer, imprisoned and dying under Nazism, insisted that faith must enter the world's suffering.[5] Sojourner Truth, a formerly enslaved woman who lived with disability, dared to speak into the sanctified spaces of white patriarchy, asking, 'Ain't I a woman?'[6] Her theology was her body, her memory, her protest.

We need to reorientate our understanding of contradiction, for theology often attempts to smooth tension, to resolve paradox, yet the Incarnation itself resists such resolution. *The Word made flesh* is not an abstraction but an embodied collision of divinity and vulnerability. Resurrection, too, refuses simplicity. Christ's body does not emerge perfected but *marked*, carrying its history into glory.

This challenges deep-seated assumptions about disabled embodiment. If Jesus' scars are not remnants to be erased but signs of divine presence, then disability does not stand in opposition to holiness – it reveals it. The limping, the stimming, the silent, the scarred: all are not obstacles to divine love but expressions of it. This is not a theology of repair but of recognition, an affirmation that glory is not found in the absence of wounds but in their transfigured presence. Holiness is not measured by conformity to an idealized body but by the persistence of love within bodies shaped by struggle, endurance and difference.

So disabled prophets stand as theological witnesses to the Church's temptation toward resolution. We offer a different path: the path of tension held in love. Our liturgies allow for disruption. Our prayers hold lament beside thanksgiving. Our bodies testify to a gospel that was never tidy.

This has radical consequences for heritage. It reveals heritage not as curated consensus, but as living memory. It insists that contradiction is not weakness but truth. That wounds are not errors but sacraments.

The scars of Christ are not decorative. They are didactic. They teach us how to carry memory: not polished, but broken and beloved.

Prophets as memory-bearers: lament, justice and counter-heritage

While prophets are often imagined as heralds of the future, their task is also to carry the past, not the triumphant, curated version, but the raw and often unspoken truth. The prophet is a keeper of buried memory.

Disabled lament is not a cry from the margins but a reckoning within the body itself. It is the insistence that exclusion does not silence presence – that remembrance is not destruction but restoration. Churches have long curated their histories to preserve authority rather than accountability, smoothing over the wounds of institutional violence, erasure and theological distortions. But disabled prophets perform sacred memory-work, ensuring that these histories are neither lost nor dismissed as unfortunate inevitabilities.

The framing of lament as covenantal protest amplifies this truth. To grieve is not to abandon faith but to hold it to its highest calling, to demand that the Church confront the realities it has denied, to insist that absence is not a breach of relationship but a site of radical engagement. Disabled prophets do not mourn as outsiders: they mourn as those whose very bodies bear witness to the failings and possibilities of ecclesial life.

This lament is profoundly theological, profoundly ecclesial. It resists the impulse to sanitize suffering, refusing easy reconciliation in favour of truth-telling. To cry out is not to fracture the Church; it is to insist that it sees, that it hears, that it reckons with what it has forgotten. And in that remembrance, healing begins.

This work also draws attention to the heritage industry's triumphalism. Too often, ecclesial heritage is curated to show continuity, elegance and sanctity, but hides exclusion, trauma and fracture. Memory becomes monument rather than ministry.

Disabled prophets reject that sanitized archive. We do not erase wounds – we name them. We declare sacred the spaces where suffering and grace collide. We re-member the broken body of the Church, not to shame it, but to redeem it.

This is deeply eucharistic. We do not deny Christ's breaking. We proclaim it. We bless it. The risen body is not broken, as though still needing repair, but is breaking, being shared, becoming presence for all.

This is the prophetic task embodied: not a theology neatly resolved, but one continually unfolding, sharpened by remembrance, shaped by justice. Memory here is sacramental, not merely historical but transformative. Lament is not a rupture but a liturgical act, a cry that carries the weight of belonging rather than abandonment. Heritage is not passive preservation but the active work of justice: what the Church chooses to recall, to reckon with, to carry forward.

This vocation refuses ornamental theology. It does not settle for the pristine but presses into the raw places where grace emerges, not in polished perfection but in the jagged edge of reckoning, where wounds are seen, held and transfigured. If the Church is to be the body of Christ, it must not erase its scars but bear them fully, rising not despite them but *with* them.

This is not theology for mere reflection; it is theology *lived*. It is an insistence that resurrection, justice and faith are not static doctrines but storied, embodied realities, unfolding in the midst of struggle, sustained in the act of remembering, carried forward in the radical persistence of hope.

Prophecy embodied: disability, activism and ecclesial transformation

Biblical prophecy is never disembodied. It is not merely voiced, it is lived. Prophets do not only speak disruption – they become it. They stand where they are not supposed to stand, act when silence is expected and move in ways that unsettle sacred and social order alike. The prophets of Scripture didn't ask politely to be heard: they bore witness with their lives, often at great cost. In the same spirit, disabled prophets today bear truth not only in speech or scholarship but in action, presence and protest.

This prophetic embodiment is not an accessory to theological life – it is its pulse. It forces the Church to confront how the exclusion of disabled people is not just pastoral failure but ecclesial contradiction. It asks the Church to reckon with its body talk: when the body of Christ is proclaimed but certain bodies are consistently excluded, theology becomes incoherent. Disabled prophets are not merely seeking access: they are re-forming what the body of Christ means by inhabiting and transforming the spaces and liturgies that once rejected them.

From protests outside inaccessible church buildings to the reclamation of pulpits, altars and leadership roles, these acts are not simply demands for equity. They are liturgical interventions – concrete declarations that exclusion is a theological error, not a logistical glitch. Each ramp constructed, each sensory-adapted service offered, is not charity. It is ecclesial repentance made visible.

Disability Equality Training (DET), now being implemented across a growing number of churches and theological colleges, exemplifies this shift. Led by disabled facilitators, these are not just workshops on awareness – they are confessions of ecclesial sin and invitations to conversion. They expose where doctrine, design and discipline have failed, and they offer a gospel-centred vision of wholeness rooted in justice, interdependence and grace.

Likewise, the expansion of disability theology into the heart of academic and ministerial formation is a prophetic act. Figures like Emily Richardson, Naomi Lawson Jacobs, John Swinton and Amy Kenny are not offering optional perspectives: they are articulating a theological imperative. Their work insists that ecclesiology without disability is incomplete. Not because disabled people are missing from it, but because Christ's wounded, risen body is.

Worship, too, is being transformed, not as accommodation, but as liturgical renewal. Movements like Inclusive Church,[7] Godly Play for All[8] and Dementia Friendly Church are not simply about making space. They reshape the very grammar of worship: the rhythms, postures, aesthetics and timelines that have long privileged certain forms of expression. They expose how often worship has been constructed around the bodies and expectations of the non-disabled, and they invite the Church into a deeper sacramentality, one rooted in mutuality, vulnerability and the Incarnation.

These liturgies are rehearsals of the kingdom. They are not niche alternatives: they are anticipations of the eschatological banquet where no one is marginalized, no one is rushed, and no one is forgotten. They offer a counter-narrative to ecclesial nostalgia, not erasing tradition but reforming it in the image of the wounded Christ.

In these acts, disabled prophets are not only critiquing exclusion – they are consecrating what could be. Their embodied presence and persistent truth-telling expose the idols of normativity, control and aesthetic perfection that have long shaped the Church's architecture and identity. And in doing so, they recall the Christ who healed through interruption, who dined with the excluded, who entered locked rooms bearing scars.

This is not protest for its own sake. It is theological disruption in the service of fidelity. It is the Church learning again how to become what it proclaims: a communion of broken, beloved bodies, where justice is not a footnote, but the shape of grace.

This is not rebellion. This is resurrection.

The prophet in conflict: the cost of truth-telling

Prophets have long been unwelcomed when their truths challenge the comfort of the community. Disabled prophets today experience this rejection not due to a lack of faith or love for the Church, but because we insist on being seen and heard as whole and indispensable to the body of Christ. Our presence exposes theological assumptions that marginalize and diminish.

Our 'transgression' lies in refusing to make our wounds invisible and in speaking hard truths about sacred matters, ecclesial complacency, theological idolatries masquerading as tradition and the subtle violence of 'niceness' that protects systems while silencing suffering. Like prophets before us, we suffer for this.

Put simply, the rhetoric of welcome is empty if it does not translate into real presence, participation and power, for anything less constitutes ecclesial violence, a quiet denial of full humanity.

Just as Jeremiah was cast into a cistern for refusing to preach only 'good news' (Jer. 38.6), and Jesus was crucified for disrupting religious norms (John 19.6), disabled prophets today often face ritual abandonment instead of repentance.

It is not lost on me that prophetic voice most often arises where truth and injustice collide and when this does occur it rarely goes unpunished. Today, disabled prophets are often silenced not with overt violence but through endless meetings, postponed promises and polite deferrals. We are told to wait for the next leadership review, the next budget cycle, the next 'more convenient time'.

This waiting is not neutral: it is a form of injustice masked as pastoral process, where welcome is perpetually deferred, and justice remains out of reach.

Such systemic silencing whispers to disabled individuals: 'you may attend but not lead; smile but not challenge; inspire but not reimagine'. It offers the appearance of inclusion while withholding actual presence, participation and power.

This is not merely a pastoral failure: it is a Christological one. It ignores the pattern of the God we claim to follow, a God misunderstood, rejected, wounded and executed by religious authorities. Jesus was silenced not for impoliteness but for speaking truths institutions could not bear. The cost of prophecy, then as now, is borne in the body.

Yet disabled prophets persist. Our courage lies not only in critique but in our continued presence. We remain within structures that have hurt us, pray with communities resistant to change and show up repeatedly – not because the Church has earned our loyalty, but because Christ calls us to a faithfulness deeper than institutional failures. This is cruciform fidelity, the willingness to carry the cross even when the sanctuary feels like a tomb.

The cross is where divine truth meets human resistance, where love is crucified by systems designed to protect holiness. Yet, mysteriously, it is also where life begins anew. Our hope is not grounded in institutional reform or optimism but in the Paschal mystery, the conviction that resurrection is possible, even here, even now, among dry bones and broken pews.

We linger, listen and wait, not passively, but with stubborn, sacramental hope. Our very presence is a theological protest; our refusal to vanish is an act of resurrection faith. We remain not because the institution deserves it, but because Christ has not abandoned his wounded Body, and neither will we.

Our faith is not naïve or romantic; it is rooted not in the goodness of systems but in the scarred hands of the God who still walks with the wounded, breathes peace into fearful rooms and bears the marks of crucifixion in his risen flesh, saying, 'Do not be afraid.'

Lingering in the aftermath of trauma is not a failure of faith but the practice of deep, wounded fidelity. This stubborn presence is itself prophetic, declaring: 'I will not be erased. I will not let you forget. I will not leave. Not because you deserve me, but because Christ calls me to remain'.

It is sacramental. It is costly. It is holy.

Prophets of the not-yet: eschatology, imagination and the re-membered Church

Prophecy has never been solely the task of critique. Its deeper vocation is to envision, to call a wounded world toward healing, not by erasing its scars, but by transfiguring them. True prophets do not merely name what is broken: they dare to imagine what could be. They hold open a future that is not yet but already drawing near.

Today, disabled prophets are doing just this. We are not only bearing witness to access denied and voices ignored, we are also articulating visions of ecclesial life shaped by justice, joy and radical welcome. We are helping the Church glimpse the kingdom of God not as abstract ideal, but as embodied transformation.

Throughout Scripture, the prophetic task includes summoning the people of God beyond the seduction of nostalgia and the rigidity of preservation. The book of Revelation offers not a return to Eden, but a vision of renewed creation: a city with open gates, flowing water and no temple dividing God from God's people (Rev. 21.22, 25; 22.1–2). This eschatological hope is not centred in purity or perfection, but in presence, justice and healing.

Crucially, the city John sees is not built on exclusion. It is not guarded by thresholds, staircases or elite access. It is accessible. It is relational. Its gates never close.

This is crip eschatology: the belief that the coming kingdom is not shaped by idealized norms, but by wounded presence, shared space and the erasure of no one. It is a vision where every scar is remembered, not erased, and where access is not concession, but covenant.

Disabled prophets proclaim that this future begins now. Access is not a legal formality – it is discipleship. Architecture is not incidental – it is theological. Disabled joy is not optimism – it is eschatological defiance.

Through liturgy, community and creative witness, disabled people are not reforming the Church from the edges. We are midwifing something altogether new, an ecclesiology of disruption and delight. We declare that holiness does not reside in a polished sanctuary but in the cracked spaces where grace gets in.

This reimagining must begin with how the Church remembers. Heritage has too often been imagined as static, stone, symmetry, unchanging rites. But true ecclesial memory is not conservation. It is eucharistic anamnesis: the remembering of Christ's broken body into new life.

This kind of memory refuses to flatten or sanitize the past. It acknowledges wounds. It names exclusions. And in doing so, it becomes prophetic. Not an archive, but a call. Disabled prophets insist that the Church is not a museum for the morally upright. It is a workshop of grace. Not a fortress of order, but a dwelling place for mutual transformation. The goal is not to preserve purity, but to embody the radical, inclusive love of God made flesh.

Our bodies do not need fixing to be included in this vision. They are not impediments to worship – they are its sacraments.

To say Christ reigns in glory is to affirm that the scars of crucifixion remain visible. This is not a theological concession. It is the cornerstone of hope. Divine perfection is not the absence of injury, but the resurrection of the breaking body into glory.

And so, disabled prophets are not calling for polite reform. We are calling for ecclesial rebirth. We are not footnotes to theology. We are its authors. Not guests in the house of God – we are co-builders of a church whose foundations are scarred and sacred.

This is not the 'inclusion' of the world's imagination. It is not an accessible pew at the back of the church. It is the transformation of the altar itself. It is the widening of the table and the breaking of the bread as revolutionary act.

Prophetic imagination, then, is not optional. It is the lifeblood of the Church. And disabled prophets are its pulse. We offer not a polished future, but a faithful one – shaped by lament, joy, justice and resurrection.

And the Church, if it is open to truth, will be changed by it.

The prophetic witness of disability: the poison of ableism

Disabled prophetic witness is not a footnote to theology. It is a recalibration of the ecclesial imagination. The presence and proclamation of disabled people within the Church is not merely an ethical concern or a pastoral responsibility – it is a theological revolution. It speaks to the core of who God is, how Christ is known and what the body of Christ is becoming.

Ableism, as encountered in the Church, is not just a social injustice. It is a theological distortion. It bends Christian vision away from the gospel of grace and toward a false ideal of sanctified normalcy. It replaces the scarred body of Christ with an airbrushed abstraction. It quietly redefines holiness as able-bodiedness, and treats fragility, need and interdependence as moral failings rather than essential features of redeemed humanity.

The danger of ableism is not only what it excludes, but what it forgets. It forgets the Incarnation's particularity and contingency. It forgets the open wounds of the Risen Christ. It forgets the holy disruptions of those who, throughout Scripture, speak truth not in power's voice but from the edge, from lips that stammer, hands that tremble and bodies that do not perform.

To confront ableism is to confront a heresy: a misrepresentation of God and a dismembering of the body of Christ.

The disabled prophet interrupts this. Not gently. Not apologetically. But necessarily.

Disabled prophecy is not symbolic. It is embodied. It is not rhetorical performance. It is lived resistance. Through physical presence, through theological insistence, through liturgical protest, disabled people are reorienting the imagination of the Church away from perfectionism and toward faithfulness.

We do not speak abstractly about inclusion. We speak sacramentally. Our lives, our scars, our joys, our exhaustion, are part of the liturgy of God's self-revealing. We name the hidden idolatries, the theology of independence, the aesthetics of symmetry, the ecclesiology of exclusion. And we do so not to destroy the Church, but to remind it of what it is called to be.

This witness is not about access as hospitality. It is about dismantling the architecture of holiness that has presumed able-bodied control. The disabled Christ stands at the heart of this confrontation. Not the sanitized Christ of sentimental piety, but the wounded, risen one who remains touchable in his scars. His is not the beauty of absence-of-damage, but the glory of transfigured pain. In him, impairment is not erased – it is made luminous. This Christ does not fit into the ecclesial logic of exclusion. He breaks it open.

To speak of disabled prophets is not to romanticize suffering, nor to reduce theology to experience. It is to declare, without apology, that God has always revealed divine truth in the margins, through the disqualified, the broken, the overlooked. We do not offer alternative perspectives. We offer ecclesial truth.

When we testify to the poison of ableism, we do so not as victims but as theologians. Not as projects of pastoral care, but as initiators of ecclesial reformation. We are not asking to be fitted in. We are calling the Church to be remade.

The gospel we proclaim is not polite. It is cruciform. It is not glossy. It is glorious in its wounds and a Church that listens will be changed, not because we bring novelty, but because we bring it back to the heart of its confession: that Christ is risen, wounded and with us still.

Notes

1 Naomi Lawson Jacobs and Emily Richardson, *At the Gates: Disability, Justice and the Church* (London: Darton, Longman & Todd, 2022), pp. 131–58.

2 Amy Kenny, *My Body Is Not a Prayer Request: Disability Justice in the Church* (Grand Rapids, MI: Brazos Press, 2022), pp. 1–19.

3 See Disability Conference archives, St Martin-in-the-Fields, https://www.stmartin-in-the-fields.org/whatson-tag/disability-conference, accessed 15.08.2025.

4 https://en.wikisource.org/wiki/Revelations_of_Divine_Love/Chapter_27?utm_source, accessed 15.08.2025.

5 Dietrich Bonhoeffer, *Letters and Papers from Prison*, ed. Eberhard Bethge (New York: Touchstone, 1997), pp. 131–7.

6 Sojourner Truth, "Ain't I a Woman?" speech, delivered at the Women's Rights Convention, Akron, Ohio, 1851.

7 St Martin-in-the-Fields and Inclusive Church, 'Something Worth Sharing' (2018), https://www.inclusive-church.org/wp-content/uploads/2020/05/Something-Worth-Sharing-WEB.pdf, accessed 03.11.2025.

8 Fiona MacMillan, 'Dementia-Friendly Church: Liturgy and Community', *Disability and Church Conference*, St Martin-in-the-Fields, 2023.

15

Toward a Crip Ecclesiology and Heritage Practice

So, what would the Church look like if its foundation were not the idealized, unblemished body, but the risen body of Christ, wounded, glorified and forever marked by trauma? Surely such a Church would not be built around conformity to cultural norms of strength, beauty or independence, but around shared vulnerability, mutual care and embodied truth. The scars of Christ would not be hidden; they would be honoured, even central, reminding the community that resurrection does not erase suffering but transfigures it. In this Church, access would not be an afterthought but a sacrament; disabled people would not be welcomed in despite their differences but recognized as essential to the body's wholeness. Leadership would arise not only from eloquence or efficiency, but from the deep wisdom of those who know what it means to live with limits and grace. This is not a Church that pities disability or erases it through false healing, but one that proclaims: here, in these bodies, Christ is risen.

For ecclesiology is not merely the study of what the Church says about itself. It is the way the Church is built, lived, embodied. It is manifest in pulpits and pews, sacristies and sermon outlines, leadership rosters and liturgical rhythms. It is incarnate in who speaks, who is seen, who can enter and who feels at home enough to stay.

What we call 'church' is already a theological claim made through brick and stone, ritual and rhythm, memory and muscle. And for too long, these claims have been shaped by ableist assumptions. Disability, when acknowledged, has typically been treated as a deficit to accommodate, a problem to be managed or a metaphor to be spiritualized. Rarely has it been embraced as a source of theological revelation.

But what if disabled lives were not marginal to the Church's self-understanding? What if they were central?

The vision of a crip ecclesiology begins there, not with the imagined wholeness of the able body, but with the truth of the wounded body, the stimming body, the slowed body, the non-verbal body, the body in pain, the body in praise. This ecclesiology does not retrofit the old structure to be slightly more inclusive. It reimagines the very blueprint.

As we have seen throughout this book, the legacy of ecclesial and heritage design has favoured symmetry, elevation and permanence, ideals often rooted not in gospel proclamation but in Graeco-Roman aesthetics and Enlightenment rationalism. The result: heritage practices that celebrate endurance but obscure access, that valorize order over welcome.

But memory, like theology, is not neutral. What we preserve reflects what we believe. And if we preserve spaces that exclude disabled people, we are preserving a lie.

The invitation, then, is not to ask, 'How can disabled people be included in what we already do?' The invitation is to ask, 'What would the Church become if we started with disability as the theological foundation?'

This is not about hospitality. It is about co-creation. Not about pity. About prophetic reordering. Not about adding ramps to a fortress. About building sanctuaries where no fortress is needed.

Toward a crip ecclesiology

The term 'crip', reclaimed from its history of insult, becomes in this context a theological tool of resistance. Crip ecclesiology challenges assumptions. It blesses interruption. It values silence, stimming, shared care and spacious time. It listens to bodies that have long been called disordered and names them icons of divine presence.

A crip ecclesiology embraces access as a sacramental principle. Interdependence is not a burden: it is the very mode of Christian belonging. Memory is not triumphalist: it is truthful. Beauty is not symmetry: it is radiance through rupture. Worship does not presume fluency: it attends to presence.

And its eschatology? It is not about perfection restored. It is about the glorified Body that still bears wounds, an open future where wheelchairs, sign language, rest breaks and relational time are not erased but redeemed.

A risen-body-centred theology

The risen Christ still bears scars. This is not incidental. It is central.

The glorified body of Jesus is not returned to Edenic symmetry but transformed through crucified love. That is the theological centre from which the Church must live.

To be the body of Christ is not to mirror perfection. It is to manifest resurrection through breaking held in love. This changes how we build churches: slowly, accessibly, attentively. It changes how we pray: with silence, movement, hesitations. It changes how we lead: through interdependence, vulnerability, creativity.

To imagine a Church shaped by the risen, wounded Christ is to imagine a community no longer obsessed with preserving control but committed to sharing grace.

This is not a utopia. It is a call. A call to repent of architectural idolatries and ecclesial exclusions. A call to remember that the gospel begins not with triumph but with incarnation, not with strength but with flesh.

It is a call to re-member the body of Christ, not as theological metaphor alone, but as an architectural, liturgical, ecclesial revolution.

Not the polished church. The living one. Not the flawless memory. The truthful one. Not the able body. The risen one.

Crip sacred space: building homes for resurrection

If the Church were to take seriously the claim that the risen Christ bears wounds not erased but glorified, then sacred space itself would look radically different. It would not be built to echo ideals of classical beauty, where symmetry and elevation project an abstract holiness. Instead, our sanctuaries would emerge from a theology grounded not in idealized form but in incarnational realism, in the textures, limitations and glory of embodied life.

A Church shaped by the risen Christ would never reduce sacredness to architectural ascension or liturgical precision. It would understand that grace does not move in straight lines or at uniform speed. It circulates through the space between, between pews, between silences, between bodies often left unseen. Such space would reflect not a logic of hierarchy, but a liturgy of hospitality.

In this vision, space is not an inert backdrop to worship. It is active theology. Aisles would be spacious not out of legal compliance, but because grace expands toward encounter. Platforms would not separate clergy from congregation but welcome participation from every single body. Altars would not be raised to create distance but lowered to abolish it, to declare that sacredness is not a summit but a table shared.

This kind of sanctuary would be intentionally crafted with slowness and quiet in mind. Not as afterthoughts, but as the sacred infrastructure of access. Texture, light, sound and movement would all be held in theological attention. Spaces for silence would be celebrated, not tucked away. Neurodivergent prayer – prayer that rocks, flaps, repeats or rests – would not disrupt worship: it would *be* worship.

Access, in this ecclesial architecture, is not a retrofit. It is a foundational proclamation of who God is: the One who comes close, who kneels to wash feet, who blesses the overlooked. In such space, ramps are not compromises: they are icons. Rest areas are not deviations: they are sanctuaries within the sanctuary. Every accommodation would become a sacrament of belonging.

'Come to me, all you that are weary,' Christ says (Matt. 11.28), and crip sacred space would answer that call not with lofty claims but with low thresholds, wide turns, soft places to land.

Such space does not pretend to erase difference. It dwells within it. It honours fragility not as deficiency but as revelation. It proclaims that holiness does not require uniformity of body or performance. It requires presence, participation and shared breath.

A crip sanctuary would not be a museum of perfection, but a home for those too long exiled by stairs, assumptions and silence. It would breathe with those who stim, pause with those who tire and hold vigil with those whose very being is a liturgy of survival.

This is not an architectural fantasy. It is a theological imperative. For the Church is called not to replicate the powers of this world, but to incarnate the coming kingdom, a kingdom already breaking in through the margins, already stirring in the wheelchair-accessible nave, the sensory-friendly chapel, the sign language hymn.

And no, it will not be perfect. But it will be holy. It will be spacious enough for truth, tender enough for grief, flexible enough for joy and real enough for resurrection.

Crip liturgy: worship in the time of resurrection

If our sacred spaces were truly transformed to honour woundedness and grace, then our worship would naturally reflect this transformation. Crip liturgy invites us into a rhythm shaped by resurrection time, a time that flows, moves and breathes differently.

This form of worship challenges longstanding assumptions that liturgy must be silent, linear, speedy, cerebral and predictable. Instead, it embraces the diverse rhythms of disabled lives, recognizing them as already living into resurrection.

In a risen-body-centred church, liturgy would be designed not for uniformity but for diversity. Words would slow down, allowing space for them to resonate. Pauses would become sacred rests, where silence is prayer. Visuals would come alive. Tactile symbols would be handled, touched and moved. Sounds would be varied and gentle, offered in multiple ways. Sermons could be delivered in short bursts, accessible through voice, text, images and movement, ensuring everyone can receive the Word.

Movement within worship would be reimagined. People who stim would do so freely, flapping, rocking, tapping, pacing, as sacred forms of prayer. Congregants would be invited to stretch, move around, sit, stand, or recline as needed, without shame. Liturgical choreography would encourage personal expressions of presence, where blinking assent or humming a response are vital forms of participation.

This worship would feel different. It would be a place where missing a beat does not exclude one from the rhythm of grace; where fidgeting, sighs, tapping, laughter, non-verbal vocalizing and communication devices are integral to the sacred soundscape. Presence, just as one is, would be the essence of liturgy.

In crip liturgy, relationship takes precedence over polish, performance or aesthetic control. Worship becomes about joining, making space for one another and encountering God in the collective gathering of diverse bodies.

Imagine a Pentecost where tongues of fire manifest as wheelchair wheels spinning, hands signing prayers, AAC devices proclaiming 'Alleluia!' and non-verbal humming filling the sanctuary with uncontainable sound. Worship becomes a meadow where everyone moves at their own pace, and every pace is prayer.

Crip liturgy is not an accommodation: it is a revelation. It reveals that God is worshipped not through perfection but through the authentic presence of those who bring their whole selves, limping, laughing, late, lost, longing, to the feast of presence.

This is the liturgy of the risen Christ. This is the worship of the wounded and the wonderful. This is the future of the Church.

A crip theology of Eucharist: brokenness shared, resurrection embodied

The Eucharist stands at the heart of Christian life, where memory, presence and hope converge. Yet it has often been confined by polished rituals and perfected performances. A crip theology invites us to reimagine the Eucharist through the lens of the risen body of Jesus Christ, a body that is wounded yet glorified.

Jesus said, 'This is my body[, broken] for you' (1 Cor. 11.24), emphasizing the sacredness of breaking. However, over time, the eucharistic table has come to resemble a display of performance-ready bodies, rather than a gathering of the wounded seeking grace.

In a community shaped by crip theology, the eucharistic table becomes a space where:

- bread is broken openly, honouring its fracture as sacred
- wine is offered with joyful, inclusive grace
- accommodations like gluten-free wafers, non-alcoholic wine and AAC-enabled affirmations are recognized as essential, not optional
- the altar table is accessible to all, welcoming the tired, the grieving, the neurodivergent, and all who embody the real body of Christ

The Eucharist, in this vision, is not about choreographed perfection but about presence: wounded, glorious, persistent presence.

In a crip Eucharist, we remember that brokenness is not a barrier to communion: it is communion. Bodies marked by scars, silence and slowness are not distractions from holiness: they are expressions of holiness. The feast of Christ is not for the flawless, but for the fragile.

Gathered around this table, the Church may not look efficient or tidy. It will look like resurrection.

Crip memory: telling the whole story

If the Church had truly embraced the risen, wounded body of Christ as its model, its approach to memory and heritage would reflect the fullness of its history. Rather than preserving only polished triumphs, it would acknowledge the scars that have shaped its journey.

Historically, the Church's heritage practices, its archives, art and curricula, have often reflected an ableist imagination:

- celebrating saints depicted as strong and serene
- highlighting architectural grandeur that remains inaccessible to many
- emphasizing victories while overlooking the struggles for inclusion and access

This selective remembrance has presented a narrative of perfection, sidelining the experiences and contributions of disabled individuals.

A 'crip memory' approach calls for a more truthful and inclusive recollection:

- acknowledging the efforts and delays in making sacred spaces accessible
- honouring disabled saints whose holiness was evident in their dependence, resilience and solidarity
- incorporating stories of both struggle and success into the Church's narrative

Such memory is not about nostalgia but about eucharistic remembrance, breaking open the past to reveal truth and grace. When we say, 'Do this in remembrance of me' (Luke 22.19), we recall a body marked by suffering and transformed by love.

Embracing this form of memory means:

- recognizing and honouring the Church's wounds
- telling stories of exclusion and resilience to bear witness
- celebrating disabled theologians, activists and artists as integral to the faith's ongoing development

Our sacred spaces and educational materials would reflect this inclusivity, depicting saints with diverse embodiments and teaching about the full spectrum of the Church's history. 'Crip memory' ensures that the Church's past is not a curated exhibit of perfection but a living testament to its journey, a body continually transformed by the Spirit. By embracing its scars, the Church can more authentically proclaim the message of resurrection.

Crip leadership: a Church led by the wounded

Leadership in the Church has too often been imagined in the image of worldly strength, smooth, commanding, uninterrupted. It has leaned into ideals of charisma, fluency and certainty, subtly reinforcing ableist assumptions about authority. But if the Church truly took the risen, wounded body of Christ as its source and model, our understanding of leadership would be fundamentally transformed.

The Christ who leads the Church is not pristine. He is not triumphant in spite of his wounds, but through them. He is the one who reigns with scarred hands, who calls disciples not with booming command but by washing feet, weeping at tombs and sharing bread from a place of vulnerability. His authority flows not from dominance, but from faithful presence in suffering.

A Church shaped by this Christ would never reserve leadership for the most agile or articulate. It would recognize that the Spirit speaks just as powerfully through bodies that move slowly, through speech that stammers or sings in unconventional rhythms, through silence that holds more than words can say.

In such a Church, leadership would be marked by attentiveness, by the ability to honour interruption, to notice what is easily missed and to allow the Spirit to emerge in unpredictability. It would welcome leaders who require rest breaks, who think in circles rather than lines, who pray with humming or blinking or assistive devices.

Leadership would no longer mean standing at the front with all the answers. It would mean making space, waiting well, witnessing pain without needing to fix it. It would mean trusting that the Spirit is present in the places the world too quickly dismisses as unqualified.

Crip leadership reshapes authority from within. It does not seek pity or permission; it practises witness. It invites the Church to stop measuring leadership by pace or polish and start measuring it by faithfulness, courage and interdependence. It refuses the false binary between strength and vulnerability. Instead, it insists that holy leadership is often fragile, often weary, often tender and always shared.

In this vision, a wheelchair at the altar would not be a sign of 'inclusion achieved'. It would be unremarkable. Neurodivergent preachers whose sermons spiral and shimmer would be understood not as 'inspirational' but as theologians with a different kind of clarity. A non-verbal priest using AAC would be received as someone revealing the Word in a new idiom of grace.

The Church has nothing to fear from disabled leadership. It has everything to learn. Because when we are led by those who know in their bodies what it means to be overlooked, to adapt, to hope in pain, to stay when it would be easier to leave, we are led more closely to Christ.

This is not about accommodation. It is about reformation. It is about the Church finally looking like the gospel it proclaims.

Final movement: a risen body Church

The vision of a risen body Church calls for a radical reimagining of ecclesial life, one that centres disabled wisdom, honours woundedness and embodies the inclusive love of Christ. This Church does not merely accommodate disabled individuals: it recognizes them as integral to its very foundation.

In such a Church, leadership is redefined. Authority is not measured by eloquence or physical prowess but by the capacity to listen deeply, to hold space for silence and stimming, and to embrace the Spirit's movement in unexpected ways. Leaders are those who, like Christ, bear their scars openly, leading not from a place of perfection but from shared vulnerability.

Worship in this community is transformed. Liturgy accommodates varied expressions, spoken, signed, gestured or silent. The Eucharist becomes a celebration of brokenness and shared grace, where all forms of participation are valued equally. The table is accessible, the rituals adaptable and the atmosphere one of genuine inclusion.

Memory within this Church is honest and holistic. It acknowledges past exclusions and celebrates the resilience of disabled individuals who have long contributed to the faith community. Stories of struggle and triumph are preserved, ensuring that the Church's history reflects the full spectrum of its members' experiences.

Ultimately, this risen body Church is a testament to the transformative power of embracing our collective woundedness. It stands as a beacon of hope, demonstrating that through shared vulnerability and inclusive love, the body of Christ can truly reflect the diversity and beauty of all its members.

Crip eschatology: the Church to come

If the Eucharist has been our shared meal, bread breaking in trembling hands, wine spilled in joyful clumsiness, bodies gathered in scarred hope, then what of the feast to come?

Too often, Christian visions of the afterlife have been shaped by cultural ideals of bodily perfection, envisioning a realm where every limp is gone, every stammer smoothed, every scar erased. But this is not the promise of the gospel. The risen Christ still bears his scars, and the Lamb who reigns at the centre of the New Jerusalem is wounded yet victorious (Rev. 5.6).

In Revelation, John envisions a city, not a sanitized garden, bustling and layered with human history and divine hope. Its gates are perpetually open (Rev. 21.25), and while tears are wiped away (Rev. 21.4), the histories that caused them are not forgotten. This future does not flatten difference but glorifies beloved diversity; it does not erase fragility but transfigures it.

A crip eschatology imagines a future where wheelchairs roll gracefully down golden streets, not discarded but glorified as instruments of perseverance. Signing hands are raised in the heavenly choir, making music through motion and rhythm. Neurodivergent minds, alive with dazzling visions, expand the worship of God into symphonies of perception and wonder. Bodies marked by old pains dance freely, not because their histories are erased, but because every wound is saturated with divine love.

On that day, difference will be delight, not deviance. It will be the very fabric of communion, the way the body sings its endless hallelujah. Resurrection will not erase what made us fragile: it will make that fragility shine with the unbearable brightness of mercy. Our scars will not be erased: they will be glorified.

Just as the wounded Christ invites Thomas to touch and see (John 20.27), so too will the wounded and risen Body of the Church say to the world: 'See what love can do.' Disabled prophets are not merely lamenters of what has been lost: they are heralds of what is coming. They call the body of Christ forward, pointing with stimming hands, signing hands, shaking hands, speaking hands toward the New Jerusalem already beginning to break in among us.

We insist that the Spirit is already at work, not building a Church that polishes its surfaces to hide its cracks but resurrecting a Church whose cracks become its testimony. A *kintsugi* Church. A Church whose beauty is not in seamless perfection, but in the grace and light of the risen Christ flowing through every fracture. A Church not obsessed with restoring itself to some imagined ideal, but daring to live, scarred, beloved, defiant, as a foretaste of the resurrection.

This is a Church not of the ideal, but of the risen. A Church whose gates will never be shut. A Church whose altars are wide and low enough for every single body. A Church whose songs require only love. A Church that finally knows, deep in its bones, that the Lamb who reigns still bears the marks of suffering. And that we, bearing our marks too, are not only welcome, we are witnesses, we are heirs, we are home.

Building what we have not yet seen: a kingdom not yet on earth as it is in heaven

The task before us is not to adjust the existing structures of the Church with superficial modifications, but to envision and construct a Church that embodies the fullness of Christ's resurrection – a community where woundedness is not hidden but embraced as sacred.

Imagine:

- a Church where disabled individuals are central, their experiences and insights shaping theology, worship, and community life
- a Church where accessibility is foundational, influencing every aspect from architecture to liturgy, reflecting a commitment to inclusivity
- a Church that remembers its history with honesty, acknowledging past exclusions and celebrating the resilience of those who have been marginalized
- a Church where worship is attuned to the rhythms of all participants, allowing space for silence, movement and varied expressions of faith
- a Church where leadership arises from diverse bodies and minds, valuing presence and faithfulness over performance
- a Church where the Eucharist is a shared meal that honours the vulnerability and beauty of all participants, reflecting the communal nature of Christ's body
- a Church where the resurrection is lived daily through acts of love, justice and inclusion, embodying the hope of new life in the midst of brokenness

This envisioned Church does not cling to an idealized past but moves forward, guided by the Spirit, toward a future where all are welcomed, valued and empowered.

As Revelation proclaims, 'See, I am making all things new' (Rev. 21.5). This renewal comes through embracing our collective wounds and allowing them to be transformed into sources of strength and unity.

In building this Church, we participate in the ongoing work of resurrection, creating a community that reflects the inclusive and redemptive love of Christ.

16

Re-membering the Body

The body breaks – not as symbol, but as truth. The heritage lies in fragments, scattered across time and memory. The story is ruptured, the remembering interrupted. This is no figure of speech – it is the deep wound of theology.

Throughout this book, we have journeyed through the ways ableism has wounded the body of Christ, not merely as a social injustice but as a theological distortion. Ableism reshapes the soul of the Church, dictating whose presence is expected, whose absence is excused, and whose voice is archived into memory. It transforms who the Church dares to become.

In *The Disabled God*, Nancy Eiesland argues that when the body of Christ is imagined only through norms of strength and independence, it no longer mirrors the wounded-and-risen Christ we proclaim but instead reflects a sanitized ideal rooted in worldly power rather than resurrection hope.[1]

The consequences are evident:

- cathedrals built with inaccessible steps and unreachable altars, where disabled pilgrims are visitors at best
- artistic depictions of saints as young, athletic and serene, aestheticizing suffering without acknowledging the realities of disability
- liturgies demanding perfect speech and constant standing, excluding many faithful worshippers
- archives where disabled prophets are overlooked or patronized, their contributions buried in footnotes

Ableism has not only excluded disabled people; it has diminished the body of Christ itself.

Yet the story does not end in fragmentation. Across history, and vividly in our own day, disabled people have refused to disappear. They have remade the centre:

- crafting new forms of worship where silence, movement and sacred rest are honoured
- offering rich theological reimaginings of God, humanity and holiness
- protesting inaccessible churches and demanding that access be seen as a sacrament
- creating art that reflects disabled bodies bearing divine light
- proclaiming that belovedness does not require fixing
- insisting that the Church can be more than it has been

Disabled people have not offered the Church a critique as outsiders but a call to conversion, a summons to become what it claims to be:

- a body breaking and shared, not flawless and preserved
- a sanctuary shaped by justice, not defended by tradition
- a memory healed by truth, not curated by nostalgia
- a future set free for joy, not chained to the idol of normalcy

The Church is not meant to be a gathering of perfected individuals but a community learning to live with its own and others' fragility in love and justice. Disabled prophets do not exist at the edges of ecclesial life: they reshape its very foundation, challenging assumptions about belonging and reorienting the Church's vision of wholeness.

Our witness is not about merely making space at the table: it is about rebuilding the table itself. Our presence is not an accommodation or concession: it is an embodiment of the risen Christ, still bearing scars, still naming wounds as holy, still speaking peace into rooms locked by fear.

If we have listened well to the journey of this book, through space and memory, worship and architecture, leadership and lament, then we now stand at the threshold not of minor reform but of deep reformation.

The breaking body is not beyond hope. The fragmented heritage is not beyond healing. The incomplete memory is not beyond redemption.

The Spirit is already at work, gathering the scattered, stitching the torn, lifting the hidden, re-membering the body. Our task is not to invent this movement but to join it, to be converted by it, to bear witness to it with all the faith, tenderness, courage and joy that resurrection requires.

Because the body is breaking and still it is blessed and still it is rising.

Re-membering the Church, redeeming the body

This book began with a question: what does it mean to be made in the image of God when one's body has been marked, marginalized and misunderstood by the very faith that proclaims that image? Over these chapters, I have traced the contours of that question through Scripture, theology, heritage, liturgy, architecture, memory and embodied witness. What has emerged is a theologically rigorous and deeply personal reclamation: of disabled lives, disabled bodies and disabled voices as indispensable to the life, identity and future of the Church, for we are each *fearfully and wonderfully made*, at every juncture of life.

At the heart of this work is a challenge to the idol of the idealized norm, the imperial body of Rome, for the legacy of ableism in Christian tradition is not peripheral, it is utterly foundational. It is built into the way we have interpreted Scripture, constructed cathedrals, canonized saints and curated memory. It is inscribed in who is remembered and who is forgotten, who is welcomed into the sanctuary and who is left at the threshold. But ableism, as I have repeatedly argued, is not merely a sociocultural failure: it is a theological heresy, a distortion of the image of God and a betrayal of the crucified and risen body of Christ.

Yet this book does not stop at critique. At every turn, I have sought to offer theological, architectural, liturgical and prophetic alternatives. I have reclaimed the disabled body not as problem, symbol or metaphor, but as sacred heritage, a living archive of God's presence, and in the process asserted that disability theology is not an addendum to ecclesiology – it is its reformation. That sacred space must no longer be shaped around abstract ideals but around the real, textured, storied presence of the whole body of Christ, scars and all.

In doing this I am so grateful for, and have sought to share, the profound and significant contributions of a wide range of theologians including Nancy Eiesland, Sharon V. Betcher, Amos Yong, Deborah Creamer, John Swinton and so many others, all of whom have further underlined the reality that disability is not a deficit to be healed or pitied, but a locus of profound divine revelation. The disabled Christ, risen and yet still wounded, is the theological centre from which a new vision of the Church must be imagined. And it is disabled people – prophets, pastors, scholars, artists, activists – who are offering the most urgent, creative and faithful visions of what that Church could become.

Throughout, I have insisted that heritage is never neutral. Whether in sacred architecture, historical narratives or liturgical practices, heritage performs theology. Heritage informs us not only who we have been, but who we think we are, and who we are potentially becoming, both good and bad. When our buildings exclude, our stories erase and our liturgies sanitize, we are not simply failing to be inclusive; we are proclaiming a distorted gospel. But when we begin to design, curate and worship from the reality of the risen, wounded Christ, we proclaim a Church that is not afraid of the action of breaking, because it has already been transfigured by grace.

In the final chapters, I have purposely offered examples of how this theology can and already does take flesh, as a source of inspiration, encouragement and hope. Through architectural examples that embody what I call *risen body design* – spaces where fracture is not hidden, where scars are not smoothed, but where grace shines through layers of memory – we are already being offered a glimpse of what the Church might look like when it is built not on the fantasy of perfection, but on the truth of resurrection. These places echo the lives of disabled people themselves: unfinished, beautiful and profoundly faithful.

To reclaim disabled bodies as sacred heritage is to re-member the Church. It is to gather again what has been dismembered by exclusion, to tell the stories that have been silenced and to celebrate a theological anthropology that reflects the God who came not in strength, but in vulnerability. It is to see in disabled lives not merely accommodation, but incarnation.

This work ends, then, where it began: with the witness of a disabled priest, and the cry of a wounded-yet-risen Church; with the theological conviction that disabled people are not guests in God's house, we are its builders, architects, theologians, prophets and priests of the new creation.

So let the stones cry out. Let the scarred bodies rise. Let the Church be re-membered, for this re-membered body, diverse in its expressions – be it through wheelchairs, AAC devices or trembling hands – will not conform to old ideals. It will reflect the risen body of Christ, bearing the wounds of love and offering them as the means of salvation.

In the remnants of old structures, in the inaccessible thresholds and in the persistent hope of those once excluded, the Holy Spirit breathes anew. And the Church will rise. Not by forgetting its woundedness, but by carrying it forward in sacred communion. Not by striving for perfection, but by being transfigured in divine love. Not by building taller walls, but by opening wide its embrace.

This transformation is not merely possible: it is already unfolding wherever disabled individuals lead, create and envision anew.

This is the heritage of hope: recognizing that disabled bodies are not the Church's challenge but its salvation. We signify that resurrection is not distant but already among us. In the breaking of bread. In the breaking of stone. In the breaking open of hearts. Until all are gathered, and all are remembered, and all are risen.

For the Word became flesh – not the Word became idealized marble; not the Word became stones and mortar, but the Word became flesh, human flesh, wounded flesh, disabled flesh, *kintsugi* flesh, risen and ascended flesh – and the Word dwelt among us, and we have seen his glory, the glory as of a father's only son, full of grace and truth.[2]

Notes

1 Nancy L. Eiesland, *The Disabled God: Toward a Liberatory Theology of Disability* (Nashville, TN: Abingdon Press, 1994).

2 John 1.14.

Postscript

Other Wounds, Same Body: Gender, Sexuality, Race, Identity and Class in the Shadow of Ideal Flesh

The principal lens of this book has been the protected characteristic of disability, through which the Church's assimilation to the idealized norm has been critically interrogated. This focus is not to suggest that other characteristics are unaffected by the same theological and cultural pressures. On the contrary, each of the protected characteristics, namely gender, sexuality, race, identity and socio-economic status, has also been profoundly shaped and constrained by the Church's allegiance to a Graeco-Roman anthropology. Ableism through our allegiance to the idealized norm has not only excluded disabled bodies but has also perpetuated marginalization across a wide range of embodied experiences.

Each of the dimensions explored in this chapter – gender, sexuality, race, identity and socio-economic status – is deserving of its own theological volume (and there are others who have written or are writing these). Each embodies a distinct set of challenges and inheritances caused by institutional ableism that require careful examination in their own right. What follows is not an exhaustive account, but a theological gesture, a passing on of the baton so to speak, a tracing of how Graeco-Roman anthropology has distorted Christian responses to these identities, and how a risen body theology can offer an alternative imagination. These are not merely sociological categories or contemporary concerns. They are theological flashpoints, points at which the body of Christ is wounded, and points through which the Church might be healed.

Theologically, each of these protected characteristics confronts the Church with a profound question of anthropology: what does it mean to be human in light of the Incarnation, crucifixion and resurrection? And yet, throughout the Church's history, there has been an unacknowledged elephant in the room: the idealized body norm of the Graeco-Roman worldview. This norm, shaped by ideals of symmetry, control, masculinity, rationality and social hierarchy, has become the implicit measuring rod against which all others are judged. Its presence is rarely if ever named and almost never questioned, yet it pervades ecclesial structures, liturgical aesthetics and theological assumptions. Whether in conversations about women's ordination, same-sex relationships, racial justice, trans inclusion, or poverty, the idealized norm has functioned as the default body, until now, unmarked, unquestioned and sacralized.

A risen body theology challenges this normative idolatry by placing at the centre of Christian anthropology a body that is wounded, relational, transformed – but not perfected. Christ does not return from the tomb as an abstracted ideal, but as a recognizably scarred human being. This theology subverts the static vision of humanity inherited from Graeco-Roman categories and reorients Christian thought toward the storied, interdependent and wounded body as sacred.

Each of these protected characteristics is not only a site of theological contestation but also a bearer of sacred heritage. Gendered lives, queer loves, racialized communities, trans journeys, and working-class struggles are not marginal to the Church's memory; they are its living archive. To ignore these bodies is to curate a distorted heritage, one that forgets the wounds through which grace often speaks. A heritage shaped by the risen Christ must be capacious enough to remember not only bishops and monarchs, but weeping women, rejected lovers, enslaved saints, transitioning prophets and the labouring poor. These are not additions to the Church's story: they *are* the Church's story.

Theologians across traditions, those working in liberation, queer, Black, feminist, trans and economic theologies, have each contributed to this reimagining. They remind the Church that God's image is not confined to symmetry, control or male authority. Rather, it is encountered in disruption, in the bodies that do not fit, in the lives that resist categorization. These theologians, in their various ways, offer a prophetic witness: that the Church's failure to affirm the full humanity of all its members is not merely unjust, but heretical.[1]

The sacredness of gender, the dignity of queer love, the *imago Dei* in Black and Brown bodies, the divine mystery expressed in gender transition, and the beatitudes spoken over the poor, all of these testify to a Church not yet fully realized. They are not new additions to the tradition but vital parts of its deep heritage. Through them, the risen Christ speaks again, not from imperial balconies but from scarred hands and broken bread.

What follows is an attempt to trace, in each of these dimensions, the fault lines left by classical anthropology, and to offer glimpses of what the Church might become when it honours the wounds of all its members and embraces the sacred heritage embedded in every excluded body.

Gender: the sacred beyond the binary

The idealized norm has long sacralized a binary, hierarchical understanding of gender, a construct inherited from Graeco-Roman anthropology and baptized into ecclesial tradition through centuries of theological reiteration. Masculinity has been canonized as the archetype of rationality, authority and transcendence, while femininity has been associated with emotionality, immanence and subordination. The Church, particularly in its hierarchical and liturgical forms, has mirrored this arrangement: robes, roles and rituals have consistently encoded a gendered imagination that privileges the male body as the bearer of divine function.

Womanhood, when acknowledged, has historically been constructed as derivative: a theological echo rather than an ontological origin. This derivative positioning stems from early patristic interpretations of Genesis, often read through the lens of classical philosophy that sees form as superior to matter, mind superior to flesh, and male superior to female.[2] This legacy has resulted not only in the exclusion of women from priestly roles but also in the aesthetic and architectural design of churches, where the centrality of the altar corresponds with the symbolic authority of the male celebrant.[3] These spatial and symbolic orders have silenced or marginalized not only women, but any gendered expression that resists the tidy binaries of ideal flesh.

A risen body theology, by contrast, resists this static essentialism. It does not view gender as a fixed metaphysical category, but as a dynamic, relational and storied expression of the *imago Dei*. The resurrected Christ does not reappear as a perfect embodiment of Graeco-Roman masculinity. He returns wounded, transformed and uncontained by the logic of binary expectation. His body bears the marks of vulnerability and solidarity, not of domination or detachment. This body – scarred, glorified and relational – becomes the new template for theological anthropology.

Theologians in feminist and womanist traditions have long insisted that gendered embodiment is not a deficiency but a revelatory mode of divine presence. They challenge the Church to see God not solely through the lens of patriarchal language but through the multiplicity of human experience – including that which has been feminized, queered or denigrated. A risen body theology resonates with this insistence, affirming that gender difference is not a deviation from divine order but a site of theological richness. The resurrection does not erase difference: it transfigures it.

The implication is profound: all gendered bodies – not only male, not only cisgender – are called to the centre of liturgy, leadership and theological imagination. The scars of Christ sanctify bodies that bleed, that transition, that resist containment. The risen Christ, who meets Mary Magdalene with tenderness and Thomas with wounds, upends the script of male control and binary power. In this reimagined anthropology, gender is not a liability to be managed but a sacrament of grace.[4]

Sexuality: love unshackled from normativity

The Church's sexual ethics have long been shaped not merely by scriptural exegesis, but by a deep inheritance from Graeco-Roman philosophical and social frameworks, which privileged order, lineage and symmetry. Within this framework, sexuality was constrained to procreative ends, and its value determined by its capacity to maintain civic structure and familial hierarchy. The idealized norm, then, was not simply male and heterosexual but reproductive, hierarchical and monogamous in a way that affirmed patriarchal continuity.[5]

Within this framework, same-sex love, queer desire and non-normative sexualities were not only viewed as morally suspect but ontologically disordered, each of them violations of cosmic and ecclesial harmony. The problem, as constructed by the Church's classical anthropology, was not simply behaviour but being: queer lives were rendered illegible in the theological imagination, as if their very embodiment disrupted the ideal of divine order.

But the risen body of Christ invites an entirely different anthropology. The resurrection does not restore Christ to a past ideal of bodily perfection or familial function. He is not raised into biological continuity; he sires no children, perpetuates no dynasty and blesses no model family. He returns instead into community, into relationship, into communion shaped not by bloodline but by grace. This reality reveals that the resurrection is not reproductive but redemptive. It is not about continuation, but transformation.

In the light of this risen body theology, queer love is not anomalous:

it is sacramental. It bears witness to the expansive, surprising and non-instrumental love of God. Queer theologies have long argued that it is precisely in the refusal to conform to imposed norms that queer desire reveals something divine: a refusal to reduce love to function, a commitment to presence over production and an embodiment of grace that flows outside the borders of inheritance and utility.[6]

The relationality of the risen Christ, who appears first to women, who shares food with friends, who invites touch and doubt, resists the control of normative frameworks. His body becomes the site not of returning to sexual 'order' but of inaugurating a new creation, where intimacy, desire and vulnerability are not circumscribed by reproduction or hierarchy.

Theologically, this calls for a shift from reading queer lives as exceptions to reading them as revelations. Same-sex partnerships, non-binary sexualities and diverse gender expressions are not merely tolerated variations; they are living testaments to the Spirit's refusal to be domesticated. They are gifts to the Church, sacraments of belonging, thresholds of grace.

A risen body theology therefore invites the Church to unshackle sexuality from its Graeco-Roman captivity. It invites us to see queer love not as deviation but as participation in the divine life, bearing witness to the God whose love is ever more abundant, ever more unexpected and ever more embodied than the idealized norm could ever contain.

Race: unmasking the unnamed norm

The racialized body has often been excluded not only from ecclesial leadership but from the very theological imagination of sanctity. This exclusion was rarely overtly doctrinal; rather it operated through aesthetic, spatial and symbolic norms that went unexamined. Whiteness became invisible by design, enthroned as the assumed default in sacred art, liturgy, ecclesial architecture and theological pedagogy. The classical ideal, shaped by Graeco-Roman notions of symmetry, serenity and noble bearing, was fused with early Christian understandings of purity, order and spiritual illumination. Whiteness, therefore, came to signify both theological authority and divine proximity, while Black and Brown bodies were marked as derivative, disruptive, or in need of redemption.[7]

This normativity was, and remains, a form of theological violence. By encoding whiteness into the Church's aesthetics of sanctity and the authority of its symbols, the Church established an anthropological hierarchy that disfigures the gospel. Liturgical colour, iconographic representation and ecclesiastical art continue to reflect this inheritance: light-skinned Christs, white-clad saints, pale angels in symmetrical procession, an entire symbolic world in which racialized bodies are absent or peripheral.

A risen body theology confronts and dismantles this legacy. It refuses to sacralize aesthetic ideals that erase historical suffering and bodily difference. The risen Christ is not a white, idealized figure, untouched by empire: he is a wounded, colonized body, scarred by the state, rejected by religious authority and resurrected not to empire but to communion. In this vision, the scars borne by the enslaved, the colonized and the displaced are no longer treated as historical burdens but as theological sites, marks of divine solidarity.

Black, Brown and Indigenous theologians have insisted that God's preferential option for the marginalized must be understood in historical and bodily terms.[8] Theologies arising from the African diaspora, Latin American base communities and Indigenous epistemologies name racism not simply as social sin, but as a deformation of theological vision. The silencing of non-white voices in theological heritage is not an oversight – it is a curated amnesia that rewrites history in the image of whiteness, cloaking dominance in piety and empire in purity.

But the witness of the risen Christ breaks open this narrative. His resurrection is not a return to an unmarked ideal – it is the vindication of a story that includes betrayal, state-sanctioned violence and public shame. His body becomes the sacred archive of collective suffering and divine presence. In this light, race is not a sociological inconvenience but a site of theological revelation. The experiences, resistance and joy of racialized communities are not marginal: they become sacramental. They expand the Church's understanding of the body of Christ and challenge its liturgies, symbols and spaces to reflect a fuller truth.

To be a Church of the risen Christ is to be a Church that remembers the crucified peoples of history. It is to unmask whiteness as a theologically constructed ideal and to centre the sacred memory of those whose flesh bore the wounds of colonialism, slavery, apartheid and systemic erasure. Only when these bodies are re-centred in our theology, our liturgy and our memory can the Church begin to reflect the full image of the resurrected one.

POSTSCRIPT

Trans identity: embodiment as becoming

Among all challenges to classical theological anthropology, trans identity most directly unsettles the assumptions embedded in the idealized norm. That norm, shaped by Graeco-Roman binaries, Christian scholastic essentialism, and later Enlightenment biologism, assumes embodiment to be fixed, static and immediately coherent. Gender is assigned, not discerned, in this worldview. The body is treated not as narrative or mystery, but as fact. Within this framework, to transition is to deviate from creation's design, a disruption of God-given order rather than a journey toward wholeness.[9]

Ecclesial life, formed in the image of this static, unyielding anthropology, has long struggled to see trans people not as theological dilemmas to be solved but as theological witnesses to be received. Spaces of worship, leadership and sacrament have been policed by binaries and norms that marginalize those whose bodies do not fit within inherited logics of male and female. Trans bodies, especially those that do not 'pass', disrupt the visual economy of ecclesial belonging. Their visibility exposes how tightly the Church has tethered holiness to legibility.[10]

Yet risen body theology offers a radically different vision of embodiment, one grounded not in fixity but in faithful becoming. The post-resurrection Christ is both continuous and discontinuous with the body that died. He is not unrecognizably other, but neither is he the same. He bears the marks of trauma and death, yet these are not signs of failure; they are the very icons of divine glory. The resurrected Christ enters rooms uninvited, appears in unfamiliar form and redefines presence through wounds that remain. He no longer conforms to expectation but calls others into recognition through relational encounter.

This Christology offers a profound theological home for trans experience. The process of transition, whether social, medical or spiritual, becomes not a denial of embodiment but a deepening of it. It is a form of truth-telling in flesh, an eschatological anticipation of the body made whole, not by conformity to inherited form but by alignment with inner truth and communal affirmation. Transition, in this light, is not a rebellion against God's image but a journey of vocation into its fullness.

The scars borne by trans people – whether they be surgical, emotional or social – are not signs of deviation, nor marks of self-harm, but traces of endurance and faithfulness. These wounds, often inflicted by systems, surgeries and society, mirror Christ's own: not erased in resurrection, but made integral to divine identity. Trans lives thus become sacramental sites where the Church's theology is reformed, not from above, but from within. The ecclesiology that emerges from risen body theology must therefore include, not marginalize, trans voices. These voices reveal the limits of traditional anthropology and invite the Church into deeper truth.[11]

Indeed, the theological transformation required is not only ethical or pastoral – it is doctrinal. It calls into question the Church's understandings of creation, incarnation and sanctification. It asks whether we believe in a God who deals in static categories, or in one who calls us into metamorphosis. It asks whether we worship the unchanging order of empire, or the transforming storied body of the risen Christ.

In this way, trans lives are not theological threats; they are theological renewals. They invite the Church to die to its rigid frameworks and rise into a more faithful, scarred and glorious anthropology. An anthropology where becoming is holy, and where every journey toward embodied truth bears witness to resurrection.

Class and poverty: the margins as memory

Socio-economic exclusion within the Church has too often been sanctified through the language of meritocracy, providential favour and moral discipline. Inherited from Graeco-Roman philosophical systems and reinforced by centuries of Christendom, wealth was frequently interpreted as a sign of divine blessing, while poverty became linked to failure, laziness or even sin. The theological imagination, shaped by this economic anthropology, produced ecclesial systems in which class became spatially inscribed: pew rents, robed hierarchies, elevated pulpits and restricted access to architectural and liturgical space.

The Church, in doing so, mirrored rather than resisted the logics of empire. Its cathedrals, vestments and ceremonial hierarchies too often spoke the language of wealth, not of solidarity. While charity was encouraged, systemic inequality went unchallenged. The poor were recipients, not leaders; objects of pity, not agents of grace. This aesthetic and liturgical stratification communicated a gospel of spiritualized abundance disconnected from the material realities of exclusion.

But the risen Christ offers a radically different economic vision. His post-resurrection appearances are not to Caesars or religious elites but to those on the edge: grieving women, frightened disciples and doubting friends. He shares meals not with the wealthy but with those who had fled, were denied or despaired. His glorified body is not clothed in gold but still bears the marks of imperial violence. In this, risen body theology dismantles the notion that divine glory is bound to economic or social status. It proclaims that sanctity resides in wounds, not wealth.

Liberation theologians have long insisted that God's preferential option for the poor is not a sentimental add-on but a theological imperative.[12] The economy of the gospel is not built on merit but on mercy; not on productivity but on presence. The Eucharist – Christ's body given for all – confounds the logic of scarcity and calls the Church to become what it receives: a breaking, shared and radically inclusive body.

Those who are working-class, precariously employed, homeless or structurally excluded from access to ecclesial power are not spiritual anomalies: they are central to the Church's theological identity. Their stories, labours and resistances are part of the Church's sacred memory.[13] To ignore them is not simply a moral failing – it is a eucharistic contradiction.

In this light, the Church must not only include the economically marginalized: it must be shaped by them. Sacred architecture must become hospitable; leadership must be representative; theology must be accountable. The glory of God is found not in cathedrals that echo imperial grandeur, but in communities where bread is broken in common and power is shared in trust.

The gospel does not ascend to the throne rooms of power: it is incarnated in the hunger of the crowd, the labour of the worker and the cry of the landless. To be Church is to remember this and to remember is to act.

Re-membering the whole body

Each of the identities explored – gender, sexuality, race, trans embodiment and class – has been shaped by the gravitational pull of the idealized norm. This norm has so profoundly shaped Christian heritage that it often passes as neutral theology. But it is not neutral. It is selective, exclusionary and distorting. And it has rendered entire segments of human experience, entire bodies, into theological anomalies or liabilities.

The Church has, for too long, treated these embodied realities as threats to orthodoxy, distractions from purity or compromises to liturgical decorum. But when viewed through the lens of risen body theology, they emerge not as deviations from divine order but as revelations of divine grace. They are not dissonant: they are prophetic. They speak of God's love for what is scarred, what is unexpected, what is still becoming.

This is not merely a gesture of inclusion, it is an act of theological repentance and reorientation. For to centre the risen Christ is not to centre an abstract perfection, but a wounded, transformed body; it is to declare that holiness is inseparable from history, that every scar has theological significance, and that nothing wounded is discarded in the economy of grace.

In this light, the Church's heritage is not what it has preserved in stone, but what it has learned to remember in flesh. Each act of exclusion, each unacknowledged body, each forgotten saint, each silenced voice, is not only a social injustice but a liturgical fracture. To re-member the body is to restore what has been dismembered by tradition, aesthetics and fear.

A risen body theology compels the Church to see these characteristics – gender, sexuality, race, identity, class – not as footnotes to the Christian story, but as chapters of the Gospel itself. They are sites of Christ's presence, icons of the Spirit's creativity and archives of God's faithfulness. They are sacred heritage, not because they conform to the past, but because they disrupt it in the name of resurrection.

To reclaim the Church's future, we must reclaim these stories. Not out of political expediency, but as an act of theological integrity. For the Church is not whole until the whole body is honoured. And the gospel is not proclaimed until every story is blessed.

This chapter has only begun to gesture toward the deeper work required. Each protected characteristic touched upon in this chapter deserves a full and rigorous theological excavation of how ableism and the idealized norm have co-opted the Church's heritage. Others must take up this baton: to expand, to challenge and to reimagine. For what is at stake is not simply inclusion, but the very nature of the gospel we proclaim. The risen Christ calls us to remember every wound, to honour every scar and to reconstruct our sacred memory in flesh and truth.

Notes

1 For the Graeco-Roman influence on Christian anthropology, see Caroline Walker Bynum, *The Resurrection of the Body in Western Christianity, 200–1336* (New York: Columbia University Press, 1995); and Robert A. Markus, *The End of Ancient Christianity* (Cambridge: Cambridge University Press, 1990). For contributions from liberation and identity theologies, see James Cone, *The Cross and the Lynching Tree* (Maryknoll, NY: Orbis Books, 2011); Marcella Althaus-Reid, *Indecent Theology* (London: Routledge, 2000); Musa W. Dube, *Postcolonial Feminist Interpretation of the Bible* (St Louis, MO: Chalice Press, 2000). For critiques of theological normativity, see Pui-lan Kwok, *Introducing Asian Feminist Theology* (Sheffield: Sheffield Academic Press, 2000); and Patrick

S. Cheng, *Radical Love: An Introduction to Queer Theology* (New York: Seabury Books, 2011). For theological reflections on memory and woundedness in Christ, see Jürgen Moltmann, *The Crucified God* (London: SCM Press, 1974); and Shelly Rambo, *Spirit and Trauma: A Theology of Remaining* (Louisville, KY: Westminster John Knox, 2010).

2 See Elizabeth A. Clark, *Women in the Early Church* (Collegeville, MN: Liturgical Press, 1990), for an overview of how early Christian theology absorbed Graeco-Roman philosophical hierarchies into its view of gender.

3 For a liturgical and spatial analysis of gender in sacred architecture, see Teresa Berger, *Gender Differences and the Making of Liturgical History* (Farnham: Ashgate, 2011).

4 For the theological implications of Christ's wounded resurrection body, see Moltmann, *The Crucified God*, and Rambo, *Spirit and Trauma*. For theological frameworks that decentralize patriarchal and binary constructions of gender, see works by Kwok, *Introducing Asian Feminist Theology*; Delores S. Williams, *Sisters in the Wilderness: The Challenge of Womanist God-Talk* (Maryknoll, NY: Orbis Books, 1993); and Althaus-Reid, *Indecent Theology*.

5 See Sarah Coakley, *God, Sexuality, and the Self: An Essay 'On the Trinity'* (Cambridge: Cambridge University Press, 2013), for a detailed theological engagement with how classical and patristic thought shaped Christian sexual anthropology.

6 For historical treatments of sexuality in early Christian theology and its Graeco-Roman context, see Mark D. Jordan, *The Invention of Sodomy in Christian Theology* (Chicago, IL: University of Chicago Press, 1997), and Dale B. Martin, *Sex and the Single Savior* (Louisville, KY: Westminster John Knox, 2006).

7 For historical theological constructions of whiteness as purity and spiritual superiority, see M. Shawn Copeland, *Enfleshing Freedom: Body, Race, and Being* (Minneapolis, MN: Fortress Press, 2009).

8 Cone's *The Cross and the Lynching Tree* is foundational for understanding the theological significance of Black suffering in relation to the crucified Christ.

9 For analysis of fixed binary anthropology in Christian tradition, see Susannah Cornwall, *Sex and Uncertainty in the Body of Christ* (London: Routledge, 2010).

10 Linn Marie Tonstad critiques the visual logic of ecclesial belonging in *Queer Theology: Beyond Apologetics* (Eugene, OR: Cascade Books, 2018), calling attention to how visibility is policed theologically.

11 Cheng's *Radical Love* articulates how queer and trans experiences of suffering and transformation reflect core Christological themes.

12 Leonardo Boff, *Cry of the Earth, Cry of the Poor* (Maryknoll, NY: Orbis Books, 1997) emphasizes that God's presence is found in the suffering and resistance of the economically excluded.

13 Mary C. Grey's *The Outrageous Pursuit of Hope* (London: Darton, Longman & Todd, 2000) affirms memory as theological method, especially in contexts of poverty and marginalization.

A Final Blessing: For Those who Would Re-member the Body

Blessed are you who have seen the breaking –
and did not turn away.

Blessed are you who have listened to the wounded –
and heard the voice of Christ.

Blessed are you who have lingered at the torn veil,
who have wept at the inaccessible altar,
who have stayed with the silenced story.

Blessed are you who have not sought a perfect church,
but a faithful one.
A risen one.
A breaking-and-blessed one.

Now go –
Go in the name of the Disabled Christ,
whose hands bear scars that are now thrones of mercy.
Go in the name of the Spirit who stirs in every interruption, every
    tremor, every sacred pause.
Go in the name of the God who makes all things new –
not by erasing our wounds, but by filling them with glory.

Build spaces wide enough for wheelchairs and wonder.
Shape liturgies slow enough for trembling hands and hesitant prayers.
Tell stories that are messy, marvellous and true.
Break bread that tastes of lament and laughter.
Lift voices – stammering, silent, singing – into one great hallelujah.

A FINAL BLESSING

Remember:
The body is breaking.
And still it is blessed.
Still it is rising.

You are not alone in this work.
You are surrounded by a great cloud of disabled saints – seen and
    unseen –
cheering you on, calling you forward,
teaching you the dance of the not-yet and the already.

Go.
Build the Church you have not yet seen.

It will not be perfect.

It will be better.

It will be holy.

It will be home.

Amen.

Index of Bible References

OLD TESTAMENT

Genesis
1.3	41
2.7	44, 144, 146
3.8	38, 40
6.6	42
8.21	42, 43
19.11	26

Exodus
4.10	191
4.11	26–7
6.6	41
31.18	41

Leviticus
21.16–23	27

Deuteronomy
4.34	41
28.29	27

2 Samuel
4.4	25, 28
9	28
9.13	29

1 Kings
19.12	44

2 Chronicles
7.15	40–1

Psalms
6.6	148
34.15	40–1
38.3–5	27
38.8	148
115.6	25
139.14	1, 3
150.6	148

Isaiah
6.1	41
6.5–7	193
6.9–10	30
35	34
35.5–6	31
42.6–7	31
52.13—53.12	32
53	44
53.2	32
53.3	32
56.10	24

Jeremiah
1.6–9	191, 193
5.21	30–1
38.6	201

Ezekiel
3.26	191
4.8	191
37	152, 168
37.9	149
37.11	168

Daniel
7	168

Hosea
11.8	42, 43

Amos
7.14	193

NEW TESTAMENT

Matthew
4.5–6	129
5.48	26
11.5	127
11.28	210
17.14–18	25
17.15	25
23.24	24

Mark
1.40–45	192
2	34
2.1–12	124–5, 194
5	138, 160
5.25–34	188, 194
7	34
9.14–29	25
9.17–18	25
10.46–52	194

Luke
4.18–19	31
9.37–43	25
13.10–17	192
14.13	125
14.21	157
19.3	138
22.19	213
23.26	146
24.30–31	157
24.39–40	171

John
1.14	122, 222
9	34, 125, 160
9.3	125
19.6	201
19.30	146–7, 151
20.20	182
20.22	144, 146, 147, 151
20.27	123, 141, 165, 191, 216

Acts
8	154
16	154–5

Romans
8.22–26	148
8.26	152, 179

1 Corinthians
6.19	142
10.17	155
11	159
11.24	212
11.26	160
12	133
12.7–9	191
12.22	17
15	166
15.43	166

2 Corinthians
12.7–9	191, 194

Revelation
5.6	167, 215
5.9	167
21.1–4	168
21.4	216
21.5	217
21.22	203
21.25	203, 216
22.1–2	203

Index of Names and Subjects

ableism 5, 8, 20, 23–4, 48–9
  as heresy 50–2, 204–5
  in liturgy 68, 93–119, 115
Accentuate (national programme) 181
access
  to church buildings 62, 64, 74–5, 209–10
  to God 43
accessibility improvements 7, 58, 64–5, 70, 74
African Independent Churches 12–14, 112–13
Alexandra Palace 86–7
All Saints (West Dulwich) 86
Alte Pinakothek (Munich) 87
anamnesis 55, 203
anointing 160
anthropomorphism, of God 37–45
assimilation 10–11, 18–21
Athanasius 32
Augustine (Saint) 18, 66, 127, 164
authority, in the Church 117

baptism 159
base communities 113–14
Basilika St Boniface (Munich) 87
Beethoven 179
Betcher, Sharon 48, 50, 54–5
Blackfriars Priory (Gloucester) 85–6
blindness 24, 51
Block, Jennie Weiss 121
body
  God's theology of 4
  as narrative 4
  normate 10, 61, 95–7
  normative 5–6
  perfection 4
  as sacred archive 122–4

  sacredness 8
body of Christ
  the Church as 19, 117–18, 133–5
  and the Eucharist 156, 160
Boff, Leonardo 18–19
breath 144–52
Bretherton, Luke 75
brokenness
  and sacredness 114
  as symbol of sin 10

cathedrals 78–9, 134
cathedrals *see also individual entries*
Chalcedon, Council of 19
China 14
Christ
  final breath 146–7
  glorified body 172–3
  as liberator 13
  and the prophets 194
  risen body 6, 116, 123, 132, 182
  transfiguration 108, 141
  wounds 10, 48, 50, 83–5, 108, 161, 169–70, 173, 207
Chrysostom 67
church buildings 57–9, 78–91
  access to 74–5, 209–10
  as catechisms 5
  see also cathedrals
Church of England, as established Church 93–100
civil religion 15–17
class 230–1
Clifton Cathedral 81
Cohen, Leonard 183
colonialism 13
Cone, James H. 55–6
Confucianism 14–15

Constantine 15
coronations 95–7, 116
Creamer, Deborah 33, 50–1
crip ecclesiology 207–17
crip interventions 176–89
crip memory 136–7, 177
crip theory 140
crip time 7, 123, 137–9

deafness 25, 179
dementia 69
Dementia Friendly Church movement 200
dependence 30, 110
digital platforms 185–8
disability
  as disruption of divine order 62
  as punishment and exclusion 26–8, 33
  as sin or deficit 21
  as source of theological revelation 55, 207
  as suffering 128
disability aesthetics 67
Disability Equality Training 200
Disability and Jesus (online ministry) 73
disability rights movement 186
disability theology 6–7, 191
disabled people
  marginalized 21, 67–9, 84, 110
  as prophets 176–89, 202–5, 218–19
  as witnesses 35, 45, 120, 191–205
  see also exclusion; inclusion
disabled saints 135–7
discrimination xiii
disruption 195–6
diversity 211

East Asia 14–15
Eastern Orthodoxy 106–8
Eden, garden of 37–8
Eiesland, Nancy 6, 24, 33, 47, 50, 52–3, 74, 123, 126, 147, 218
embodied memory 131–5
embodiment 172
empire 11–12, 17–19
  gospel as weapon of 12

epilepsy 25
Erickson, Scott 184
eschatology 25–6, 97–8, 111, 161, 163–75, 202–4, 215–16
Eucharist 132, 141, 155–60, 172, 212
exclusion 57, 61–91
  and doctrinal history 62
Ezekiel 149–50, 191

feminist liberation theologies 113–14
Francis (Pope) 101, 102
funeral liturgies 172–3

gender 225–6
Giles, Richard 85
Godly Play for All movement 200
Goldingay, John 38, 39–40
groaning 148–9
Gutiérrez, Gustavo 12, 48, 54, 113

Hauerwas, Stanley 26
healing
  and African churches 113
  by Jesus 34, 124–6, 129–30
  miraculous 34, 124–9
  praying for 131
  and wholeness 124–31
Hendren, Sara 67, 178–9
Hereditary Multiple Exostoses xi, 1
heritage 6–7, 49–50, 121, 203
  as act of curation 176
  and time 138
heritage studies 140, 169
Historic England 66
holiness 197
  and Eucharist 155–9
  and impairment 33
  and perfection 48
  and wholeness 6, 24, 76
Holiness Code 27
Holy Saturday 183
Holy Spirit 53, 105, 106, 109–10, 112, 142, 144–52
hope 31–2, 174
hospitality 30, 172, 179, 209
Hull, John 51, 64

iconography 181–2

image of God xi, xii, 3, 107, 115
  in sacred art 181-2
incarnation 20
inclusion
  or conversion 3
  is not benevolence 55
  and power 179
Inclusive Communion movement 200
inculturation 14
Indigenous people
  anthropologies 112-14
  resist Christianity 12-14
  theologies 114
interruption 188-9, 195
Irenaeus of Lyons 126

Japan 15
Jeremiah 191
Jesus *see* Christ
John Paul II (Pope) 101

Kafer, Alison 137-8, 140
Kaiser Wilhelm Memorial Church (Berlin) 87
kintsugi 183-5
Kolumba Museum (Cologne) 88
Korea 14-15

lameness 25
lament 198-9
Latin America 11-12
leadership, by disabled people 63, 71-3, 179, 207, 213-14
liberation theology 48, 54-6, 113-14, 140
listening 2, 215
liturgy, and disabled people 67-9, 211
Liverpool Metropolitan Cathedral 80-1
livestreamed services 185-6
Lo-Debar 29
Lourdes 127-9

McRuer, Robert 130, 138
Margaret of Castello (saint) 135
Mary (Virgin), image of 11
megachurches 16, 113
memory 139-42, 212-13

Mephibosheth 29
Meribbaal 28-30
metaphors, of God 37-45
minjung theology 14-15
mission 9
Moltmann, Jürgen 170-1
Moses 191

naming, in Hebrew 29
narrative prosthesis 49
national destiny 109-10
national liturgies 91-100, 113, 117-19
neurodivergence 158
New Jerusalem 169
Nicaea, 1st Council of 19
normative body 5-6

online communities 186-8
ordinations 116-17
Origen 18, 67

Pacific Islander theologies 114
papal conclaves 116, 104-6
papal infallibility 101
Paul (saint) 133, 191
Pentecost 144
  as disruption 110
Pentecostalism 108-12
perfection 23-36, 34-5
  in ecclesial ritual 115-16
  and resurrection 164-5
  and the Roman Catholic Church 101-6
pilgrimages 127-8
Pittman, Lauren Wright 182
Platonism 18
poverty, and sin 16, 230-1
power
  divine 51-2, 191
  ecclesial 115-17
  imperial 12-14, 19
  and liturgy 93-100
  spiritual 112-13
preaching 173
preferential option
  for the disabled 54-5
  for the poor 231

priesthood, in Christian traditions
    102–4, 116–17
prophets 192–205
    as memory-bearers 198
prosperity gospel 16
protected characteristics 223–31
purity, in Hebrew 27
purity codes 24

race 227–8
Rambo, Shelly 132, 183
re-membering the body 218–22
resurrection 164–7, 171
    is already here 222
Reynolds, Thomas 48, 53–4, 126, 133–4, 138–9
Ricci, Matteo 14
risen-body Church 215
risen-body theology 83, 115–19, 208–9
Roman Catholicism, and perfection 101–6
Roman Empire 17–19

sacraments 64, 153–61
    see also baptism; Eucharist
sacred space see church buildings
St Beuno's (Tremeirchion) 72
St John's Waterloo (London) 88–90
St Martin-in-the-Fields 72, 181, 195
Sanctified Art (organization) 182
sanctity 136
Scott, Judith 179
Servulus of Rome (saint) 135
sexuality 226–7
sin
    linked with disability 27, 33, 52, 67, 123, 124–5
    linked with poverty 16, 230–1
Sistine Chapel 104, 106
Smith, Laurajane 56, 62, 140, 169

Son of Man 168
South Korea 15
state funerals 97–9, 116
State Opening of Parliament 99–100
Stoicism 18
storied bodies 172
storied design 83
substitutionary atonement 32
suffering 132, 146–7, 156, 160, 188
    as failure 16, 27
    transfiguration of 165, 167–74, 196–8, 207
Suffering Servant 32–3, 44
Swinton, John 26, 48, 69, 167–9
syncretism 11–12

Taylor, Sunaura 182
Tertullian 164
Thomas Aquinas 26, 66, 164
Thomas, Hannah Rose 184
time 138, 140
tradition 189
trans people 229–30
trauma 131–5

Uganda 13
United States, civil religion in 15–17

Vatican Council (2nd, 1962–65) 78, 80, 81
Virgin of Guadalupe 11
vulnerability 50, 76, 120, 121

Walls, Andrew 9
wholeness, and healing 124–31
Worth Abbey 81

Yong, Amos 48, 53
York Minster 69–71

Zizioulas, John 107

www.ingramcontent.com/pod-product-compliance
Lightning Source LLC
Chambersburg PA
CBHW020611300426
44113CB00007B/596